DIVIDE AND CONQUER

GERMAN EFFORTS TO CONCLUDE
A SEPARATE PEACE, 1914-1918

L. L. FARRAR, JR.

EAST EUROPEAN QUARTERLY, BOULDER
DISTRIBUTED BY COLUMBIA UNIVERSITY PRESS
NEW YORK

1978

EAST EUROPEAN MONOGRAPHS, NO. XLV

940.312
F243

L. L. Farrar, Jr. is Lecturer on History at Trinity College

Copyright 1978 by East European Quarterly
Library of Congress Catalogue Card Number 78-050548
ISBN 0-914710-38-9

Printed in the United States of America

To my daughter Olivia
on the occasion of her graduation
from Milton Academy, June, 1978

"Dare To Be True"

ACKNOWLEDGEMENTS

A distinct aspect of the pleasure in seeing a manuscript published is the opportunity to acknowledge debts to those who have contributed to its realization. I would like to express special thanks to those who provided guidance and encouragement from the beginning, James Joll, A. J. P. Taylor, Alan Bullock and Agnes Headlam-Morley. A number of individuals offered suggestions on the finished manuscript: Richard Comfort, Gordon A. Craig, Robert F. Hopwood, Ernest R. May, John New, James Sheehan, and John L. Snell. Assistance in research and discussion of specific points were the contributions of Anne Abley, Dieter Ahlswede, Theobald Bethmann Hollweg (grandson), Georges Bonnin, Jean-Baptiste Duroselle, Klaus Epstein, Fritz Fischer, Imanuel Geiss, Martin Gilbert, Werner Hahlweg, Hans Herzfeld, George F. Kennan, Reinhold Lorenz, Wilhelm Michaelis, Wilhelm Mommsen, Rudolf Morsey, Agnes Peterson, Philip E. Rohrbough, David Savage, W. B. Scharlau, Klaus Schwabe, Harold Shukman, Paul R. Sweet, Anneliese Thimme, Richard H. Ullman, Eberhard Vietsch, John W. Wheeler-Bennett, Klaus Wilkens, Egmont Zechlin, and Z. A. B. Zeman. Finally I can acknowledge but never repay the debt to my wife, Marjorie, for her gentle criticism, wise counsel and constant company.

TABLE OF CONTENTS

INTRODUCTION

This study combines descriptive and analytical approaches. It re-
counts in detail German efforts to shatter the Entente by concluding
a separate peace with one of its members. An investigation is offered
of successive German civilian and military leaders' pursuit of this objective through a multitude of channels, with a variety of bribes and
threats, directed at a spectrum of elements in each of their opponent's
governments and societies. The study is thus in this sense frankly
monographic.

At the same time it involves an analytical aspect in suggesting a
reconsideration of the prevailing interpretation of German wartime
policy. This topic has been the focus of an extensive debate inspired
by Professor Fritz Fischer and involving a considerable number of
German historians and historians of Germany.[1] This debate focused
primarily on the role of German war aims: while disagreement emerged
over their extent and consistency, the centrality of war aims was
questioned by few participants. The present work argues that this
evaluation of German policy should be questioned. While an undeniably important indicator of what the German government might have
sought in the event of victory, war aims do not explain the actual
conduct of German wartime policy as satisfactorily as do the efforts
to divide the Entente.

An examination of this question necessarily impinges upon other
issues. Since the separate peace policy was advocated by and thus
identified with a number of German leaders, the role of personality
is implicated. Civil-military relations, frequently viewed as a dominant
theme in German policy-making, becomes involved in the formulation
and conduct of this policy. The relationship of policy-making with
domestic politics and public opinion must also be considered. German efforts to divide their opponents occurred in the context of
relations with their own allies, above all, Austria-Hungary. Thus the
issue links the major elements of German wartime policy-making.

In the process a number of broader problems are raised. German
leaders reveal their preconceptions about the state system and their
enemies. A comparison of what German leaders assumed about their
opponents with their enemies' actual views makes it possible to gauge
the validity of German perceptions. The efficacy of German policy can
be measured by comparing German aspirations and accomplishments.
Although unique in detail, the perceptions, objectives, methods,

difficulties, general failure and frustrations of German policy were symptomatic of wartime statecraft in general. A study of German policy consequently provides an insight into the nature of the First World War.

CHAPTER I

DIPLOMATIC CRISIS, SHORT WAR AND SEPARATE PEACE

The First World War was among many things a conflict between coalitions. Eventually central to the military and diplomatic evolution of the war, the significance of this element was comprehended only gradually by the leaders of the belligerent states.

The coalition problem had its roots in the prewar period. Though not always obvious, an important prewar diplomatic issue was whether the powers would regard their interests as better served by adherence to alliances or independent action. Behind the specifics of confrontations from the First Moroccan Crisis of 1905 to the Second Moroccan Crisis of 1911 and increasingly until the July Crisis of 1914, this was the operative question. In every instance each alliance held sufficiently to constitute a threat to its opponents but was not cohesive enough to satisfy all its adherents. The Germans in particular had sought to preserve their own alliance and to weaken if not dissolve the opposing coalition by isolating its members. A constant theme of their policy, it was pursued by a combination of threats during crises and bribes in between, as for instance their efforts to achieve a naval agreement with the British in 1912. Yet, despite its recurrence, the question remained open since it was not yet clear whether the powers would be willing to risk war in order to preserve their alliances.[1]

The question was answered during the July Crisis of 1914. Each of the powers sought to preserve its own alliance and to scuttle the opposite alliance. The Germans pursued these objectives by encouraging Austria-Hungary to threaten Serbian independence in the knowledge that Russia had committed itself to defend Serbia. When Russia in fact stood by Serbia, Germany warned that it would use force unless Russia renounced Serbia. Russia was accordingly obliged to test its alliance with France, which the Germans hoped would be deterred from fulfilling its commitments to Russia by the fear of war with Germany. Refusing to jettison its alliance with Russia, France accepted the risk of war with Germany, which now had to choose between losing its alliance with Austria-Hungary and fighting a war. Since German leaders assumed that war was both inevitable and would be conducted on two fronts, it was mandatory to preserve their alliance so that Austria-Hungary could deflect Russia until France had been defeated. A decision for war seemed their only choice.[2]

1

The prospect of war was rendered less onerous than it might have been by the prevailing assumption that it would be short. This view was particularly pervasive among German strategists, statesmen, politicians, businessmen and probably large portions of the population. It dominated the early months of the conflict and would prove to be the Great War's great illusion. The assumption was illusory because it contradicted the circumstances which had caused war. War had occurred because the allies had been willing to support each other militarily but would have been short only if they had been unwilling to do so. In short the decisions which had led to war made it unlikely to be short.[3]

The assumption of a short war was nonetheless fundamental to German strategy. The Schlieffen plan, the formula for success in a two-front war, was supposed to develop through two phases: after a rapid disposal of France, German forces would be redirected against Russia. In fact Schlieffen hoped that Russia's mobilization would proceed so slowly that it might be dissuaded from actually entering the conflict by the defeat of its western allies. German success depended on three imperatives: delay of Russian entry; rapid French defeat, surrender and conclusion of peace with German; and Anglo-Russian acceptance of German continental dominion. Rather than the recipe for winning a two-front war, the Schlieffen plan's success depended on what amounted to a one-front war against a France effectively unsupported by its allies. But such a war was highly unlikely since France would probably not have fought Germany unless assured of Anglo-Russian support. The Schlieffen plan was implemented only when France had immediate and significant Russian and British assistance. The Schlieffen plan was, however, unlikely to succeed under such circumstances. German strategy was consequently trapped in a vicious cycle from which there was probably no escape. The Schlieffen plan might have succeeded under conditions (namely, a divided Entente) which probably would have made it unnecessary but was necessary when it could probably not have succeeded (i.e., against a unified Entente). It failed therefore when Russia mobilized and attacked quickly. The implications of this event, however, were not clear to German leaders until their second attempt to win a decisive victory in the west failed in November and they realized that it would require concentration on one front.[4]

The assumption that the war would be brief also pervaded German diplomacy during the early months of the war. This expectation caused a corresponding de-emphasis of diplomacy to the status of handmaiden for strategy. German statesmen accordingly sought to preserve and ideally strengthen their own alliance, to avoid fortifying and ideally to weaken the enemy alliance, to deter neutral mediation for an unfavorable peace and to project war aims.[5]

The preservation of the German alliance depended in the first place on placating Austria-Hungary. In contrast with the relatively intense contact between Berlin and Vienna during the July crisis, the allies communicated little during the early months of the war, a fact probably best explained by German fascination with the prospect of victory in the west and corresponding de-emphasis of the east. Although German leaders sought to postpone or conceal rather than resolve differences with their ally, they had become concerned by September that Austria-Hungary might leave the war because of military setbacks and felt compelled to grant it sham concessions and greater military support. Their immediate purpose was to avoid distraction from the western front but their long range goal was to facilitate postwar subordination of Austria-Hungary to a German-controlled *Mitteleuropa*. This makeshift arrangement worked as long as the war was expected to be brief but maintenance of the alliance would loom as a more serious problem when the prospect of a short war disappeared at the end of 1914.[6]

The German alliance also hypothetically involved Italy but the Germans soon realized that Italian benevolent neutrality was probably the best they could expect. Events would demonstrate that German success with Italy as well as the Ottoman Empire, Rumania and Bulgaria would depend less on diplomacy than strategy; as long as these states felt the war would end quickly in a German victory, their neutrality was virtually assured; when this victory did not occur, the German task became considerably more awkward. German success in winning over Turkey at the end of October marked the transition from a supposedly short conflict determined exclusively by the great powers to a great power stalemate whose outcome seemed to depend on the entry of lesser states as new belligerents.[7]

The Germans meanwhile sought to weaken the Entente. In an effort to facilitate French capitulation after military defeat, they discouraged a popular war with a combination of reprisals for guerilla activities, rewards for surrender and a declaration designed to persuade the French people to conclude peace over the heads of their government. Some German leaders had meanwhile tried during the early weeks of the war to discourage or at least delay active British military and naval participation in the hope of inducing French willingness to capitulate after defeat and British acceptance of German continental domination. German public statements during this period were formulated so as to promote dissension among the Entente powers. Although such disagreement existed and would persist throughout the war, German military success caused the Entente powers to subordinate it to their common interest in preserving their alliance, as they indicated by their declaration at the beginning of September that they would not conclude a separate peace.[8]

A more real possibility during the early months of the war was neutral mediation which might prevent or limit a decisive German victory. A few days after the outbreak of war Italian Foreign Minister Antonio di San Giuliano suggested negotiations on the basis of *"ni vanqueurs, ni vaincus."* Such talks were regarded by German leaders as disadvantageous no matter how they developed: if used as a delaying tactic by the Entente, they might aid Russian mobilization; if genuinely pursued by the Entente, they might be exploited to save France from defeat; if accepted, some German leaders felt they would be rejected by the German people who were apparently determined to continue the war. Since they did not want to appear as the "disturber of the peace" by rejecting negotiations out of hand, the Germans discouraged the Italian move which was also reportedly refused by London—likewise on the grounds of its public opinion. When reports of German inclination to peace persisted, both the German Foreign Office and Admiralty made it known that "we have no intention of considering peace negotiations as long as [German military] successes continue in the west."[9] The most serious threat came from across the Atlantic. After having made a general, public mediatory offer at the beginning of the war, the Americans initiated more direct and discreet soundings in September. Again the Germans were confronted with an awkward choice: refusal might make Germany appear determined on a war *à outrance* but acceptance risked renunciation of territorial gains, a general peace conference at which the Central Powers would be in the minority, re-establishment of the balance of power and perpetuation of the Entente. With the support of Foreign Secretary Gottfried von Jagow, Under Foreign Secretary Arthur Zimmerman and Foreign Office expert on the United States Adolph von Montgelas, German Chancellor Theobald von Bethmann Hollweg sought therefore to discourage the Americans without alienating them. In rejecting precisely the general peace to which the Entente had just committed themselves publicly, the Germans effectively established the framework for the diplomatic contest which would persist until the end of the war.[10]

So long as it was assumed by German leaders that military means would be sufficient to defeat a united enemy alliance quickly and decisively, all of these diplomatic activities were logically regarded as secondary.

The assumption of such an eventuality, however, made essential one area of diplomacy, namely, the projection of war aims. German leaders had begun to explore the question of German objectives immediately after the outbreak of war and Bethmann accordingly requested suggestions from a variety of agencies and individuals.[11] In expectation of an imminent French collapse, Bethmann signed a statement on September 9 which argued that the overriding objective should be "the protection of the German Reich to the west and east for a foreseeable period." As a first step, "France must be so weakened that it cannot rise again as a great power," i.e., become a participant in an alliance against Germany; consequently strategic military, commercial, industrial and financial conditions should be demanded so as to weaken France, tie it to Germany, exclude English influence and thus insure that France would accede to a future German threat as it had not done during the July crisis. Then "Russia must be pushed back from the German border as much as possible and its dominion over the non-Russian vassal people broken." After Russian and English involvement in the European state system had thus been ended, the continent from France to Poland and possibly from Italy to Norway would be organized into a *Mitteleuropa* under German control.[12]

As they would throughout the war, German leaders disagreed in their perceptions of England. Bethmann and most of the Foreign Office apparently hoped until September that an accommodation might somehow be reached with the British, perhaps as a result of a severe defeat and rapid surrender of France. These hopes were dashed by the Anglo-French success at the Marne and the Entente's announced determination to conclude peace together. By contrast, Zimmermann, along with most military and naval leaders, felt that a final "settling of accounts" was necessary not only with Russia but also England, which they perceived as Germany's most tenacious enemy.[13]

When the prospects for a rapid separate peace with France receded in the latter half of September, war aims received less attention from top German leaders, although discussions continued among middle level bureaucrats and in unofficial circles. The revival of hopes for a French defeat in October caused new discussions of war aims but with an increased awareness among German leaders that the conditions of peace would depend less on their own plans than on battlefield events.[14]

* * * * *

As it turned out, events on the battlefield during October and November altered the context of German diplomacy. Erich von Falkenhayn, German Chief of General Staff after mid-September, tried to win the decisive victory in Flanders during October which

had eluded the Germans at the Marne in September. He failed, however, and, when the German attack was renewed in early November,
it was no longer in the hope of what Falkenhayn had described as a
"campaign decision in Flanders" but only a "visible success of arms
in the west" so as to avoid the impression of another setback. After
such an apparent success,Falkenhayn may have intended to assume
the defensive in the west and to transfer the main weight of German
forces eastward, where a "campaign decision" would be sought with
a rapid defeat of Russia. He hoped thereby to achieve the objective
which Schlieffen had anticipated from a quick victory in the west,
namely, Russian renunciation of France. Cause and effect would be
reversed: Russian defection which was supposed to result from Anglo-
French defeat had instead become the precondition for victory in
the west. Yet even such a minimal success in Flanders was not forthcoming and experience seemed to bear out Schlieffen's fundamental
assumption that Germany could achieve a decisive victory only if it
concentrated on one front.[15]

Falkenhayn consequently called upon diplomacy to escape his
dilemma. The tactic was suggested by Admiral Alfred von Tirpitz,
who claimed it was supported by Jagow and General Adjutant to the
Kaiser Hans Georg von Plessen. Germany should concentrate all its
forces in the west by arranging an "agreement" with Russia, which
was inclined to do so and could be persuaded that there was no reason
for Germany and Russia to bleed for England's gain. Despite certain
reservations, Falkenhayn accepted Tirpitz's suggestion and promptly
dropped the recourse of forcing Russia out of the war by a rapid defeat which he felt unlikely in any case as long as Germany fought on
two fronts. What had proven impractical by strategy would now be
sought by diplomacy.[16]

Falkenhayn immediately asked his civilian counterparts to create
the preconditions of military victory for him. Although they had realized operations in the west had not proceeded according to plan,
Bethmann, the Kaiser and most German leaders had persisted in the
first-west-then-east interpretation of the Schlieffen plan, i.e., the belief that Germany could win first on one front and then the other in
a two front war. Falkenhayn destroyed this illusion when he informed
Bethmann on November 18 that decisive victory was impossible as
long as the enemy coalition persisted. Berlin would have to detach
either Russia or France, of which the former seemed more likely to
Falkenhayn. If Russia could be won for a separate peace, Germany
might defeat the western powers decisively and dictate conditions.
The "psychological moment" for an approach to Russia would occur

when the Russians realized that they could undertake no further military operations until the spring. If it concluded a separate peace, Russia should have to grant only slight border rectifications. Although no overture should be made to France, "honorable" terms might be allowed if France requested a separate peace since congenial relations with France were necessary in order to deal with England, which would be starved into submission by a blockade based in Belgium as "the only lasting insurance against another war."

Bethmann's reaction was mixed. He accepted Falkenhayn's contention that the war had entered its "second period" in which a decisive German victory was unlikely as long as it fought a two front war. Just as he had favored the westward orientation of the Schlieffen plan, Bethmann agreed that the first priority was to defeat the Entente keystone, France, which could be achieved only "if we hurl our army, now engaged in the east, against France. Then, if desirable, we could even reject a possible peace offer from France and, if lucky, bring France militarily to its knees so that it would have to accept any peace terms we desire. At the same time, if the Navy does what it promises, we can compel England to bend to our will. At the price of leaving relations with Russia essentially as they were before the war, we could create suitable conditions in the west. With that, the Triple Entente would be finished." The major aims of the war as Bethmann envisaged them would thereby be achieved: the Entente would be destroyed, France incapable of allying against Germany, Russia isolated, and England both excluded from Europe and challenged on the sea. The best which could otherwise be hoped for would be general exhaustion—proof that the balance of power was destroyed but not yet replaced by German hegemony. Falkenhayn and Bethmann were consequently in broad agreement on ends.

They were, however, at odds on means. Falkenhayn expected that it would be a task of "slight value" to arrange a separate understanding with Russia once it had suffered a moderate setback in Poland. By contrast Bethmann found no indication of Russian inclination to peace and did not expect it even after a resounding defeat in Poland which was in any case unlikely according to Falkenhayn's own argument. Only if "the greater part of Poland" were conquered by either Germany or Austria-Hungary might such willingness be expected. This divergence of opinion would divide German military and civilian leaders into two groups. Falkenhayn was supported by the Kaiser and his close military advisers, as well as Tirpitz, the Navy and initially Jagow. Bethmann's argument was accepted by Zimmermann, Paul von Hindenburg, German commander on the eastern front, his subordinates, Erich Ludendorff and Max Hoffmann, and the Austro-Hungarian high command. These two factions would persist in general until mid-1916.[17]

The discussion was given immediacy when the possibility of Danish mediation was reported a few days later. Bethmann felt that negotiations would be premature until the results of the German offensive in Poland were clearer. Falkenhayn insisted, however, that an immediate and encouraging though general reply should be made so that no opportunity to achieve an understanding with Russia might be lost. He was supported by the Kaiser, who "desired a separate understanding with Russia as badly as Mr. *[sic]* Falkenhayn." Bethmann reluctantly submitted only after he had insured that Vienna would not be encouraged to leave Berlin in the lurch through fear of a Russo-German understanding. The Danish source was accordingly informed in early December that Berlin was not interested in a general peace or even a separate understanding with England but only a separate understanding with Russia.[18]

Despite his acquiescence, Bethmann remained unconvinced that an understanding should be sought before Russia had been made more amenable by force. His doubts were confirmed by Zimmermann, who—like Ludendorff, with whom he stood in close personal and political contact—tended to advocate force and will. While granting Bethmann's contention that it would be advisable to "drive a wedge between our opponents and make a separate peace with one or another of them as soon as possible," Zimmermann was essentially unaffected by Falkenhayn's analysis of the military situation. He remained confident that Germany could win a decisive victory on both fronts, should seek to fulfill its aims in both east and west, and therefore need not conclude a separate peace with any opponent. If a separate peace had to be sought, however, Zimmermann believed it should be with France, which was Germany's least dangerous enemy and might become responsive if English support slackened and the Russian "steam-roller" proved an illusion. England and Russia would continue to threaten Germany "as long as we do not succeed in energetically settling accounts with them." While Zimmermann felt it was generally accepted in official German circles that this would eventually have to be done with England, he claimed the suggestion was made "frequently" that a separate peace should be concluded with Russia before it had been defeated. He believed that this point of view disregarded the "most vital concerns of [German] self-preservation:" Russia had to be defeated in order to preserve Austria-Hungary and destroy Russian prestige among the Slavs.

Zimmermann therefore recommended that Germany assume the defensive in the west and transfer all available forces to the east. If such an alteration in military strategy was impossible, Germany should at least insure the defeat of Russia's protegé, Serbia, which would eradicate Russian prestige among the Slavs and make it willing to conclude a separate peace on the basis of the *status quo ante bellum* in the east and a moderate indemnity to Germany. Such an eventuality would have the advantages of releasing German troops for the western front, establishing German predominance in the Near East, and removing the threat of Italian and Rumanian entry into the war. Although Zimmermann differed fundamentally with Bethmann on military prospects and the long-range goals of German policy, he corroborated Bethmann's belief that Russia was still unwilling to conclude peace. He also gave Bethmann an argument for producing that willingness—transferral of German forces to the east.[19]

Bethmann immediately began to agitate for the change in military strategy which Zimmermann had suggested. The view that Russia would renounce its allies only if forced to do so was confirmed by Hindenburg and Ludendorff, who may in fact have inspired Zimmermann's statement in the first place. Bethmann decided at this time that not only Russian inclination to peace but also general military prospects would be improved if Falkenhayn were replaced by Hindenburg and Ludendorff. Because of this reassurance by the two generals in the east, Bethmann expected that Russia could soon be won for a separate understanding if the desired strategy were implemented. The ultimate objective of his policy remained the destruction of the Entente for the next fifty years which would be achieved by a combination of force and finesse. After it had been isolated from Russia, France would be "completely overpowered" and then won for a *rapprochement* with Germany. While Russia was thus to be neutralized and France forced into subservience, England was again paradoxically left out of consideration. Although it was repeatedly described as the perpetrator of the war and heart of the coalition against Germany, England was apparently expected to recognize the failure of its policy of encirclement and resign itself to German hegemony on the continent.[20]

Falkenhayn and the Kaiser had meanwhile remained unconvinced that Russia would soon make peace without a fundamental change in German military strategy. They impatiently sought to initiate the contact with Petrograd which had been suggested to Copenhagen but regarded by Bethmann as premature. In the expectation that peace could easily be won in this way, Falkenhayn adamantly refused to reinforce the eastern front and even hinted that troops might be transferred to the west. In his commitment to the western front, Falkenhayn discounted Russian determination to persevere and claimed its armies could easily be pushed out of Poland, after which it would sue for peace. While Bethmann's ultimate concern was also victory in the west, he had become convinced that the prerequisite was Russia's removal which could be achieved only by the re-orientation of Germany's main military effort toward the east. The two men had consequently committed themselves to two diametrically opposed views of what Germany's next step should be.[21]

When the belief that Falkenhayn was militarily incompetent became current among German leaders at the beginning of December, it coincided fortuitously for Bethmann with their disagreement on strategy. Bethmann supported Hindenburg as Falkenhayn's replacement for both political and military reasons. Due to his reputation as savior of the nation, Hindenburg was regarded by Bethmann as the only man who could persuade the German people to accept an unfavorable peace and provide the government with prestige which neither Chancellor nor Kaiser enjoyed. Bethmann had also become convinced that this change of command was the only way to remove Russia and defeat France. Hindenburg thus seemed both insurance against defeat and the key to victory. The Kaiser and his immediate military advisers bluntly refused, however; aware of the public adulation enjoyed by Hindenburg and alienated by Ludendorff, the Kaiser was chary of allowing them to supply the leadership he himself abdicated. By such negative decisions the Kaiser continued to exert an important influence throughout the war; while he instigated few policies or decisions, no large departure could be made without his approval. Bethmann accepted the Kaiser's decision but would intermittently renew his efforts until successful eighteen months later.[22]

Bethmann probably acquiesced for several reasons. He had been so impressed with the abilities and optimism of Hindenburg and Ludendorff that he hoped for further victories over Russia even without concentrating German military power in the east. Reports had already been received in Berlin of Russian internal difficulties and of the possibility of an understanding. Above all Bethmann demonstrated on this as on other occasions his fatalistic resignation in accepting an unfavorable decision. Despite his doubts, he proceeded to devote himself to the quest for an immediate separate understanding with one of Germany's enemies which would remain the major German diplomatic objective for the next two years.[23]

* * * * *

After having been largely displaced by strategy since August, diplomacy was thus reassigned a critical function in November. From the moment it was thus revitalized, war diplomacy came into conflict with war aims. As generally applied, war aims describe what is desired politically, economically and militarily at the conclusion of war and usually takes the form of territorial and financial acquisitions. As used in this study, war diplomacy refers to non-military efforts to create a situation in which military victory could be achieved and defeat avoided. The primary specific goal of German war diplomacy was the dissolution of the Entente through conclusion of separate understandings with its members. More simply, war aims were the end and war diplomacy the means.

The distinction is important. It emerged in discussions during the autumn and became central at the end of 1914 when diplomacy was called upon to aid military strategy. War aims would increasingly complicate the conduct of war diplomacy when subsequent conquests made acquisitions seem more feasible and diplomacy failed to shatter the Entente. War aims provide a useful insight into domestic politics in so far as they were either a reflection of or escape from domestic problems. They also indicate what German leaders and people would probably have demanded had Germany won a complete and rapid victory. War aims are therefore a significant problem.

It is, however, debatable whether "the question of war aims was the most important problem of German foreign and domestic policy during the First World War."[24] Although considerable evidence has been amassed to indicate that German leaders projected ambitious plans, it is not clear these plans actually affected the daily conduct of diplomacy. Generally war aims complicated the task of war diplomacy, and were less critical to the eventual successes and failures of German policy than factors beyond German control.[25]

The antithesis between war aims and war diplomacy reflected a struggle between two fundamentally different assumptions about German prospects in the war. For the sake of simplicity, they can be designated as two-front war and one-front war. Under the heading of two-front war fall those policies which assumed that Germany could win decisively in a war on two fronts, i.e., against a united Entente, and thus that no sacrifice of German aspirations was necessary. One-front war policies posited that Germany could not win against a united Entente but only if the enemy coalition were divided and the war conducted on one front; to arrange these circumstances, it might be necessary to forfeit some German aims. At times the proponents of a one-front policy implied that the dissolution of the Entente in itself might constitute victory, render continuation of the war unnecessary and make extensive war aims superfluous since Germany would in any case dominate the continent.

Most German leaders did not conclusively or permanently commit themselves to either of these policies. Although he sought to win separate understandings with Germany's enemies after the end of 1914, Bethmann for instance still entertained the possibility of annexations from both continental opponents; to the extent that he did so, Germany would have had to defeat a united Entente. In practice Bethmann, however, consciously postponed a final choice between these two contradictory policies in order to allow developments to dictate his eventual decision. He hoped that German public opinion would accept whatever peace was commensurate with the situation in which it was concluded; for this among other reasons, he advocated the appointment of Hindenburg, whose endorsement was expected to encourage public acquiescence. To retain his freedom of choice between the renunciation which war diplomacy might demand and the annexations which he regarded as desirable, he avoided as much as possible an official stand and discouraged public discussion of war aims; he and those members of the government in sympathy with his views therefore conferred as infrequently and superficially as possible with politicians, pressure groups and leaders of the Bundesstaaten. Since the government expected the shape of peace would ultimately depend on the extent of victory, war aims should be subordinated to strategy and diplomacy.[26]

The prevailing attitude toward war had altered radically during 1914. The Germans had sought unsuccessfully to divide the Entente on various occasions before the war and then during the July crisis. They opted for war in August not only because the alternative of diplomatic defeat was unacceptable but also because they expected to achieve the goal which had eluded them during the crisis, namely, dissolution of the enemy coalition. Their resort to war had been facilitated by the assumption that it would be short and successful; it would have been unattractive if not unacceptable had they assumed that the war would be long and unsuccessful. This view of war permeated German strategy, diplomacy and domestic policies during the early months of the war. It had proven fallacious, however, by early November because the Germans were unable to defeat any of their enemies as long as all continued to fight. Strategy now required statecraft to create conditions of success by dividing the enemy alliance, a significant departure indicating that the nigh total reliance on military means had been mistaken. Thereafter German leaders would rely exclusively neither on strategy nor policy but combine the two in their efforts to shatter the enemy alliance and thereby win a conclusive victory on one front.

Under pressure from the Kaiser and Falkenhayn, the civilian leaders began to explore the possibilities of a quick separate peace with Russia. The discussions during November and December which had caused open disagreement among the various components of German leadership had also revealed some less violent but nonetheless real differences among the civilians themselves. There accordingly developed three general views as to how and when peace with Russia should be sought. Jagow—not unlike Falkenhayn—at first believed Russia was inclined to conclude peace quickly and therefore needed only to be allowed the opportunity. Bethmann thought Russia would have to be induced to leave the war by military pressure. Although neither excluded the possibility or desirability of annexations in the east, a separate peace was foremost in their minds. By contrast, Zimmermann felt peace should be arranged with Russia only after it had been defeated. Consequently the views of Jagow and Bethmann would figure most importantly in the prerevolutionary efforts to win Russia for an understanding, while Zimmermann's arguments would receive wider currency thereafter. In effect, Bethmann and Jagow advocated a policy of one-front diplomacy, whereas Zimmermann was a proponent of two-front war and total victory on both fronts.

At the beginning of November (i.e., during the attacks on Ypres and before the Falkenhayn-Bethmann discussion) Jagow began to ascertain the feasibility of a separate peace with Russia. He explored "the idea of spinning threads to a Russian personality [unnamed but probably the Russian ex-Premier Sergei Witte] in order to rake up disagreements between the Tsar and/or his mother and Grand Duke Nicholas." He was told that direct approaches to Russia seemed unpromising but that Sweden and particularly Denmark were possible channels. Consequently the German representatives in Stockholm (Baron Hellmuth Lucius von Stoedten) and Copenhagen (Count Ulrich von Brockdorff-Rantzau) were alerted. On the day after Falkenhayn and Bethmann had agreed that a separate peace with one of Germany's enemies was desirable, Rantzau reported the fortuitous opportunity Jagow had been seeking. Rantzau had had a conversation with the Director of the (Danish) East Asian (shipping) Company and Privy Councillor to the Danish King, Hans Andersen, who had entrées

to both the Russian and English courts. Andersen had just returned
from a visit to England, where he claimed to have had conversations
with British leaders. As a result, he was anxious to work for the re-
establishment of peace on the basis of an Anglo-German understanding. Rantzau rejected this suggestion with the argument that England
did not genuinely desire peace. Several days later, Andersen expressed himself more openly to his old friend, Albert Ballin, head of the
German shipping line, HAPAG. Andersen asked Ballin what the
Kaiser's reaction might be if King Christian of Denmark were to suggest "completely on his own initiative" that the Kaiser, the King of
England and the Tsar consider negotiations. Ballin thought that the
Kaiser would find such a proposal attractive only after the Germans
had reached Calais and Germany's enemies had accepted the proposal
first. Nonetheless Ballin and Andersen were able to agree in the end
that "a far-reaching alliance between Germany and England" would
be desirable.[1]

This impulse gave a practical basis to the discussions among German leaders. Bethmann was sceptical and regarded an approach to
Russia as premature, whereas Falkenhayn and the Kaiser argued that
Andersen should be answered immediately and positively. The Chancellor finally agreed to inform Ballin that neither the Ango-German
understanding which Ballin and Andersen favored nor any kind of
general peace conference was desired by Berlin; instead Andersen
should be urged to arrange bi-lateral contact between Russia and
Germany. Ballin accordingly told Andersen at the beginning of December that the Kaiser believed "the continuation of the war . . .
necessary in the interests of the future peaceful development of Germany." Berlin would nonetheless consider Danish mediation for a
Russo-German *rapprochement* which seemed seemed "much less complicated" than an understanding with England since the Tsar was
weak and "would rather make peace today than tomorrow." The war
with England would have to be continued until the "guarantees of a
lasting peace" had been achieved, i.e., English recognition of German
continental dominion and an agreement over spheres of influence
throughout the world. Andersen's unenthusiastic reaction notwithstanding, German leaders chose to believe that King Christian would
immediately contact the Tsar.[2]

The Germans continued to hope that Andersen's influence in Petrograd could be used to "blow up the [enemy] coalition" even when it
had become evident that Andersen still desired an Anglo-German *rapprochement* and that there were disagreements in official Danish
circles on the desirability of a Russo-German understanding. When
no encouragement from Copenhagen was forthcoming by the end of

December, however, Bethmann concluded that the *démarche* had failed because of Russian disinclination to conclude peace at all or without consulting its allies. As he wrote Ballin, he "would be equally sorry in either case since for us everything depends on shattering the [enemy] coalition, i.e., on [concluding] a separate peace with one of our enemies—in the present military situation, with Russia." It turned out that the delay was in fact due not to Russian intransigence but the indecision of King Christian, who finally at the beginning of January dispatched to Petrograd a letter suggesting mediation among Russia, England and Germany. Bethmann remained sceptical: the Danish move could produce the "most desirable result" of a separate peace with Russia only if it avoided the impression of German weakness.[3]

Berlin simultaneously developed parallel channels to Petrograd, the most promising of which seemed to be the Russian ex-Premier and anti-war financier, Count Witte, with whom the Germans had unsuccessfully sought contact in late October. His influence appeared on the rise at the end of 1914 when he was reportedly mentioned as the next finance minister. Believing Witte was pro-German and thus regarding his re-emergence as "very advantageous," Bethmann suggested to Ballin that "a dove with a discreet olive branch" be sent Witte at the appropriate moment and urged Witte's German banker (Mendelssohn) to encourage Witte's working for a Russo-German understanding. Bethmann and Jagow consequently hoped that "Witte would build up an atmosphere for peace as a result of this hint."[4]

These efforts had been inspired largely by the contention of Falkenhayn and the Kaiser that Russia was already inclined to make peace either because of fatigue or disagreements with its allies: Germany need therefore only demonstrate its willingness to respond. The strategic corollary of this approach was continued concentration of German forces on the western front and accumulation of reserves for a new offensive against the British and French. During the first three weeks of January 1915, German strategy and policy were, however, abruptly changed. Along with the Austro-Hungarian commander, Baron Franz Conrad von Hötzendorf, Hindenburg and Ludendorff had rejected the decision against them and continued to bombard Falkenhayn with grand schemes for a joint Austro-German campaign in Poland to "annihilate" the Russian army. As he had in November and December, Falkenhayn dismissed these proposals as unrealistic, using Schlieffen's argument that the Russians could avoid annihilation by withdrawal. Pressed by Hindenburg and Ludendorff and probably frustrated by the disappointing results of his efforts to contact the Russians, Bethmann agreed to urge not only a change of strategy but also Falkenhayn's replacement by Ludendorff. When the Kaiser indignantly refused because of his distrust and probably fear of Ludendorff, Bethmann typically backed off and patched up a compromise leaving both Hindenburg and Falkenhayn in their posts but transferring Falkenhayn's reserves to the east for a new offensive. While Falkenhayn and the Kaiser continued to doubt that Russia could be seriously defeated and refused further reinforcements, Hindenburg asserted that German "diplomacy must hold off the wavering neutrals [above all, Italy] until the end of February, by which time we shall have achieved such obvious military successes [against the Russians] that the world will no longer be able to doubt our final victory in the east."[5] After Galicia and East Prussia had been cleared of Russian troops and Russian territory invaded, the campaign was discontinued in late February by the German government with the claim that it had been a resounding success. The military collapse of Russia predicted by Hindenburg, Ludendorff and Conrad had, however, not occurred.[6]

The reorientation of German strategy reinforced German policy toward Russia. The prospects for an understanding seemed favorable. Expectations that Witte might work for peace appeared to be fulfilled when he fumed against the war and English influence in Russia. The Russian internal situation augured well since "unfortunate conditions" were developing and allowed "the peace party which sought a separate peace with Germany to win great influence;" it was reported that "Russia could continue to fight for three months at most." Conflicts between the Tsar and Grand Duke Nicholas were supposedly jeopardizing internal unity and anger toward England because of insufficient support threatened the alliance. The atmosphere apparently had changed since the early months of the war as Germanophobia and Anglomania declined, while the "original enthusiasm" for war was replaced by depression, desperation and bitterness. The inclination of the court and aristocrats to end the war would become a general demand for a separate peace with Germany if Russia suffered another serious defeat. It was reported that the key to peace with Russia since the entry of Turkey on Germany's side at the end of October was the Dardanelles: Russians now realized that they "needed a motive for peace especially because they had none for war." These optimistic projections prompted the German Foreign Office to make further soundings on the possibility of Witte's taking office. Reassured that he was the appropriate negotiator, an approach was authorized at the beginning of February but Witte reportedly answered that nothing could be done *"for the present."*[7]

The Danish channel was meanwhile maintained. Ambassador Rantzau urged the Danes to work for a Russo-German peace even if the Anglo-German one desired by them did not materialize. Bethmann virtually guaranteed against an Anglo-German agreement by reiterating that "the only possibility is a separate peace with Russia." The Tsar's reply (of early February) to King Christian's letter (of early January) was, however, discouraging since it postponed Andersen's visit to Petrograd until the end of February. Bethmann reserved comment but Jagow interpreted this dilatory response as an indication that Russia was still disinclined to conclude peace and expected favorable developments such as Italian and Rumanian entry on the Entente's side. Andersen proceeded to execute one of his frequent *volte faces*, claiming that he would not work for a Russo-German separate peace even if the Tsar favored it. Andersen's reluctance notwithstanding, the Germans expected the end of February to be the "critical moment" for peace if recent military setbacks made the Tsar responsive.[8]

If the general military and diplomatic situation could reasonably be viewed as favorable by German leaders during January and February 1915, it could no longer in March and April. Victory not only escaped the Central Powers on the critical eastern front but the Russians also resumed the offensive which eventually forced a reluctant Falkenhayn to renounce his campaign in the west and divert all available reserves to rescue Austria-Hungary. The French and British meanwhile sought to prevent such transfers by maintaining pressure on the Germans and to prepare for a massive breakthrough in May. Apparently even more important for the general diplomatic and military situation, Balkan developments suddenly seemed to favor the Entente. The British attack on the Dardanelles at the beginning of March appeared promising and had immediate effects on the Balkan neutrals, particularly Greece and Italy, which moved toward joining the Entente. Berlin responded by pressing Vienna to make concessions which might postpone Italian entry, while Petrograd extracted from its allies a promise of eventual control over the Straits. The naval and commercial war intensified when the Germans increased their U-boat operations and the British retaliated by extending their blockade of Germany. A blow was dealt to German hopes for a separate peace with Russia by the death of Witte on March 13.[9]

German policy was again altered in response to these military and diplomatic events. When Bethmann visited eastern headquarters at the beginning of March, Hindenburg claimed that an offensive was impossible on either front and concluded that "there was no escape other than the immediate conclusion of peace—news which with one blow darkened the atmosphere of confidence in victory for the Berlin government." Bethmann apparently became "terrifically excited" and Zimmermann, who generally exhibited little emotion, was deeply disturbed, regarded the situation as extremely critical and believed a catastrophe was not impossible. German leaders consequently intensified their efforts to reach an agreement with Russia by using the carrot instead of the stick.[10]

The best prospective channel remained the Danes. Claiming that the situation in Petrograd was favorable because the Tsar wanted to conclude peace if the Germans made no excessive demands, Bethmann told Rantzau to have the Danes assure the Russians that Germany would seek "only small concessions in order to protect our eastern border, as well as financial and commercial treaties; we wish to live in permanent peace with Russia." Andersen had, however, returned in the interim from Petrograd with the conflicting report that the Tsar and his foreign minister, Sazonov, had unambiguously rejected a separate peace with Germany. The German response to this news provides an insight into their mind set. Despite Andersen's denials, Rantzau attributed the Russian reply less to the Tsar's own feelings than to his bellicose advisers and allies. Andersen's pessimism did not deter the Germans from enthusiastically accepting his suggestion of a visit to Berlin but their purposes remained totally opposite. While Jagow reiterated that Germany wanted "peace with Russia without England," King Christian claimed he could work "only for a general peace and must in consideration of [the interests of] my own country avoid offering myself for separate actions," a refusal which Andersen repeated. Undeterred, Bethmann suggested that the Kaiser tell Andersen that Germany was fighting a war of defense not conquest; Russia should initiate negotiations because Germany's military position was favorable; and Germany should receive compensation for the cost of war and security for the future. Bethmann urged the Kaiser to re-establish his personal relationship with the Tsar so as to sow dissension between the Tsar and his advisers and allies, while coddling the Danes into continuing their mediation with Russia but discontinuing the contact with England. Andersen would not renounce his planned visit to London but promised to arrange a meeting between Rantzau and a Russian representative which was "gratefully" accepted by the Kaiser. Although remaining reluctant about working for a Russo-German understanding, King Christian finally wrote the Tsar by the beginning of April and suggested that a Russian emissary be sent to Copenhagen. Meanwhile Danish Prince Waldemar reportedly urged the Tsar's mother to persuade her son to work for an understanding. Rantzau was uncertain about the prospects for success but felt that the soundings would at least provide Berlin with more accurate information on the sentiments of the Russian ruling circles and perhaps even encourage the Tsar to believe "that he was being misused by his allied and deceived by those around him."[11]

Berlin simultaneously explored alternative approaches to the Tsar. These too were based on family connections and the assumption that the Tsar could be won over if isolated from unscrupulous advisers and allies. The theme remained consistent: England was misusing the Tsar, who should return to the dynastic principle which linked him with the Kaiser and would be strengthened if peace were concluded by the two rulers. Contact was made at the end of February with Maria Wassilchikov, a naive former lady-in-waiting of the Tsarina who had been detained in Austria at the outbreak of war. She was persuaded to write the Tsar that the Central Powers would allow Russia free passage of the Dardanelles in return for an offer of peace which could include France and Japan but not England. In response to a purported reply that the Tsar "would not yet separate himself from his allies but the time would come," Jagow endorsed a second Wassilchikov letter which asserted German strength and Russian weakness, warned against England and Japan, reminded the Tsar that the Dardanelles could be obtained only from Germany, and asked him "entreatingly to conclude peace."[12]

On the suggestion of Wassilchikov, the German Foreign Office arranged an approach to the Tsar through his brother-in-law, Grand Duke Ernest of Hesse. As the rationale for such a move, Jagow reiterated that "no means should in my opinion remain untried since it must be our aim to split Russia [from its allies] if at all possible. Considering the character of the Tsar and the conflicting elements by which he is surrounded, . . . it is important to encourage pacific influences upon the Tsar from as many sides as possible in order to force him further into the frame of mind desired by us. His distrust of England apparently already exists. Now that Russia has lost a large part of Poland and meanwhile has conquered eastern Galicia, it should be easier for the Tsar to reconcile his sense of honor with a conclusion of peace with the Central Powers." The formula remained similar to the Wassilchikov letters: terrible Russian losses, lack of any possible Russian gains, tenacity of the Central Powers' positions in France, Poland and the Carpathians, and unlimited reserves of the Central Powers. With the concurrence of Bethmann and the Kaiser, Jagow had Ernest suggest a meeting in Stockholm in the expectation that it might combine with the Wassilchikov and Danish impulses to have a "good effect" on the Tsar.[13]

Berlin at the same time fostered the Danish and Wassilchikov feelers. When Andersen was discouraged by his visit to London about the prospects of peace with England, Rantzau encouraged him to work for a meeting between Rantzau and a Russian representative. Another Wassilchikov letter offered even more enticing terms to the Tsar. Behind both moves German policy assumptions remained what they had been since November: England was an unsuitable candidate for peace because it would insist on conditions unacceptable to Germany, i.e., the perpetuation of the Entente and the balance of power, whereas a separate peace with Russia might prove not only a military but also a diplomatic success since France might surrender without further struggle.[14]

The desired Russian response was, however, not forthcoming. At the beginning of June Andersen's suggestion of a meeting between Russian and German emissaries in Copenhagen was rejected and the letter of Danish Prince Waldemar to his sister, the Russian Queen Mother, remained unanswered. The best indicator was the Tsarina's reaction to her brother's letter: the representative sent by Ernest to Stockholm should not wait for a Russian envoy since "the moment had not yet arrived" for peace. An adjustment in German policy was apparently necessary to induce greater Russian responsiveness.[15]

* * * * *

The basis for such a reorientation was already emerging. A fundamental shift in the war's structure occurred during the spring of 1915 when the most important developments took place in the east and southeast rather than west, as many German, French and British leaders had expected. This change was produced by the actions of both sides. The French and British attempted to establish contact with Russia and to eliminate Turkey by first trying to run and then to take the Dardanelles. Italy entered the war and Serbia refused to leave it. Bulgaria and Rumania hawked their aid to both sides but joined neither. Russia and Austria-Hungary contributed more to the course of events by their weakness than strength. The Germans achieved the most impressive and lasting results without having planned them at all.

The adjustment in German diplomacy resulted from a reorientation of German strategy. The winter's dismal military situation began to improve at the moment of deepest desperation in April. After rigidly refusing to reinforce German eastern operations during the winter, Falkenhayn decided that a western offensive should be postponed temporarily in order to assist the hard-pressed Austro-Hungarians in Galicia. Contemplated as a relief operation, this decision produced at the beginning of May an unexpected Austro-German breakthrough which prompted the Austro-German commanders to conclude that their major offensive should be mounted on the eastern front.[16]

Developments elsewhere were not so favorable for the Central Powers. Because of their success in Galicia, the Germans and Austro-Hungarians postponed helping Turkey, which was threatened by the Anglo-French attack on Gallipoli, now reaching its crucial stage. Italian entry at the end of May made Bethmann fear for the defeat of the Central Powers if Rumania followed. Exorbitant Bulgarian demands caused its negotiations with Turkey to break down. German suggestions that Austria-Hungary bribe Serbia into concluding a separate peace failed despite what appears to have been a genuine effort. The "Lusitania's" sinking threatened to bring the United States into the war on the Entente's side and with it other neutrals. Most important of all, the Germans were not yet certain that they could hold against Anglo-French attacks on the western front.[17]

The general situation had thus improved but remained mixed and forced the Germans to choose among operations in the east, southeast and west. When the eastern campaign reached a cross-roads at the beginning of June, German leaders had to decide whether its objective was still merely the removal of Russian pressure on Austria-Hungary—which had been achieved—or the destruction of Russian offensive power. Regarding the Balkan situation as unpredictable and desiring to return to the western front, Falkenhayn argued for the more limited objective and another attempt to arrange an understanding with Russia, which might be more responsive because of its recent setbacks.[18] As he had done in November, Bethmann rejected Falkenhayn's suggestion and committed himself to the hard line now that the means seemed available. If Petrograd responded, it would probably offer only unacceptable conditions, i.e., a general peace or at least demand that German troops freed in the east not be transferred to other fronts; since Russia would certainly confer with its allies unless it became more desperate, the best Germany could expect would possibily be the *status quo* and probably the *status quo ante bellum*. Influenced by the failure of his recent soundings and Sazonov's recent rejection of separate peace before the Duma, Bethmann predicted that the Russians were more likely to reject an offer despite their military setbacks. A German peace suggestion might in fact encourage Bulgaria and Rumania to join the Entente immediately in the belief that the Central Powers were crumbling. Bethmann therefore counseled that Russia be made more amenable by further military and diplomatic defeats. Since the moment for concluding peace had not yet arrived, he advised against discussing annexations which were not only unrealistic but potentially dangerous since they might preclude a peace with Russia. If such aims became known in Petrograd, those already considering peace might be driven into the arms of the war party which was committed to a "war of desperation;" instead Germany should merely indicate that it intended to turn west after the Russian danger had been removed. In short war aims should be subordinated to war diplomacy.[19]

Disagreement between strategist and statesman over strategy had consequently been reduced by the reorientation of military operations to the east but the two men still interpreted the political situation quite differently. Whereas Falkenhayn saw Russia as sufficiently shaken to conclude a separate peace perhaps including extensive German annexations, Bethmann doubted Russia was desperate but might become responsive to a combination of further defeats and moderate German demands. Their conflict over policy and strategy was reinforced by personal and domestic political misunderstandings. Bethmann again felt Falkenhayn was shifting responsibility to civilian shoulders for a possible disintegration of the eastern situation, perhaps in an effort to replace Bethmann as chancellor. Bethmann parried this thrust by clearly separating military and political spheres: responsibility for military decisions and thus failures lay entirely with Falkenhayn, while political questions such as peace and annexations were his own. Met with this firmness, Falkenhayn agreed to continue operations against Russia and to shelve for the moment his idea of a separate peace.[20]

The general situation improved sharply for the Central Powers during June and July. Neither the anticipated Serbian attack on Austria nor Rumanian entry materialized and Italian entry proved less significant than expected. Relations with Bulgaria improved after negotiations for passage of German arms to Turkey were resumed in June and Turkish defense of the Dardanelles became more secure by July. Tension over the "Lusitania" died down and American entry became unlikely. The Germans decided by July that their defenses against Anglo-French attacks on the western front could hold without reinforcement from the east. Austro-German forces took back the Galician city of Lemburg at the end of June and Falkenhayn anticipated the complete defeat of Russia in July.[21]

Encouraged by these favorable prospects, German efforts to achieve a separate understanding with Russia reached their zenith in late June and July. Persisting in the belief that the Tsar was restrained by his uncle, the notoriously bellicose Grand Duke Nicholas, and Sazonov, the Germans tried to induce a response by the dual approach of urging peace and threatening defeat. Despite the Tsar's rebuff at the beginning of June and Andersen's repeated demand for Anglo-German talks, Bethmann urged Andersen to inform the Tsar that Germany was willing to conclude a peace mutually advantageous to both countries. Andersen finally agreed to approach the Tsar again but adamantly refused to suggest a Russo-German understanding. This refusal in fact corresponded with the Tsar's position: when he invited Andersen at the end of June, the Tsar reiterated his determination to conclude peace only in consultation with his allies. The Germans simultaneously renewed appeals to the Tsar through other members of his family and court. They optimistically anticipated that the combined effect of all these moves would remove the Tsar's scruples about abandoning his allies.[22]

Further policy discussions were meanwhile conducted among the Central Powers' leaders. Austro-Hungarian Chief of Staff Conrad provided the impulse and thereby indicated that the allies' eastern policy had come together by the summer of 1915. He asserted that a separate peace with Russia would be "so decisive and favorable ... that an attempt to achieve it should be made without fail." It would shatter the Entente, stabilize the Balkan situation, and free the Central Powers for other fronts. Imminent military successes such as the capture of Warsaw should accordingly be exploited diplomatically by constructing "golden bridges," i.e., renunciation by the Central Powers of demands for annexations, offer of Russian free passage through the Dardanelles, and an understanding with the Central Powers. Falkenhayn rejected the notion of "golden bridges" because he felt Russian weakness made it unnecessary but accepted Conrad's general objective and sense of immediacy, adding the threat that he would begin plans for returning to the west if a separate understanding had not been achieved by the time Warsaw fell.[23]

The response from German civilians was varied. Jagow agreed on the end but differed on means. He expected that a private approach would again be refused despite some auspicious signs. A German public offer would create awkward alternatives: Entente refusal could suggest German weakness and thereby strengthen the Entente; Entente acceptance and suggestion of a general peace conference could be refused by Germany, which would then bear the odium of continuing the war, or accepted with the disadvantages of being in a minority and accepting peace conditions which would "hardly correspond with our rightful desires," i.e., continental primacy. Although a general peace would have the appeal of demonstrating that the balance of power had been destroyed, it would force Germany to "renounce its world policy *[Weltpolitik]* for many years to come and to face very serious domestic financial difficulties." The choice apparently reduced to immediate destruction of the balance of power or eventual continental dominance. Jagow insured against responsibility for failing to remove Russia by asserting that the decision was "above all" military; a general, compromise peace would be sought if Falkenhayn deemed it a military necessity. Assuming it was not, Jagow preferred to continue the war in hope for a separate peace with Russia. The method should be inducements at the Straits rather than threats of defeat. Earlier in July Jagow had argued that the primary Russian war aim since Ottoman entry had been "domination of Constantinople. . . . As long as the Russian government does not achieve this goal or has not persuaded itself of its unachievability, peace will not be concluded;" the more defeats Russia suffered, the more it would cling to the hope. It would make peace only when its allies were demonstrably unable to force the Dardanelles and present Russia "the crown of Byzantium." Since this could be accomplished only by maintaining a firm link between the Central Powers and Turkey, conquest of Serbia was the precondition for an understanding with Russia. Jagow sought to test the proposition by informing the Russians that Germany alone could assure passage through the Straits and that their allies were not only incapable of doing so but also that England intended to encircle Russia by controlling the Straits. Falkenhayn, however, opposed any reorientation of military operations from Poland to Serbia in the belief that Russian defeat was imminent and the solution for all eastern problems; if it concluded a separate peace, Bulgaria and Rumania would remain neutral and render a Serbian campaign superfluous.[24]

Bethmann agreed with Falkenhayn, Conrad and Jagow on the desirability of a separate peace with Russia but envisaged yet another means of achieving it. Giving only passing consideration to a general peace and Serbian campaign, he believed the threat of defeat potentially effective and remained optimistic about the private soundings then in progress. He simultaneously rejected premature discussion of war aims with the assertion that "it is obvious any hope for such a separate peace would be as good as out of the question from the start if we had already disposed of large Russian territories on our own;" as he had agreed already to annexation of eleven thousand square miles of Russian land; his definition of "large" was distinctly relative.[25]

Zimmermann characteristically disagreed in espousing the views of Hindenburg and Ludendorff. Optimistic about general military prospects and regarding Russian defeat as Germany's first priority, he again rejected the notion of a separate understanding with Russia and advocated continuation rather than curtailment of operations.

Consequently he did not even discuss private approaches which might produce a separate peace and considered only the propaganda value of a public sounding, while completely discounting any possibility that peace might result. He supported Jagow's suggestion of a Serbian campaign not as a means for concluding peace with Russia but for excluding its influence permanently from the Balkans. It was eventually decided that operations should be continued on the eastern front.[26]

German hopes for Russian response were disappointed in late July and early August. Andersen found no admission of defeat or desire for a separate peace although Germanophobia had apparently lessened; as a result of press accounts of his visit, he renounced further efforts for a Russo-German understanding and returned to his original idea of an Anglo-German *rapprochement*. Other reports suggested that Russian public opinion had in fact become more anti-German and Russian rejection of an understanding was adequately confirmed by a series of official statements probably designed to squelch rumors of precisely such an understantding.[27]

This reaction precipitated yet another reappraisal of German policy. Since he now reckoned that the Russian menace had been effectively removed even without a separate understanding, Falkenhayn began to contemplate the transfer of military operations to the west and thus advocated construction of a "Chinese wall" in Poland to protect Germany's eastern flank.[28] While granting that French defeat was the ultimate goal, Bethmann contended that it could be achieved only by German concentration in the west and thus conclusion of operations in the east which required a separate peace with Russia. This goal was not only necessary but also possible if the appropriate means could be found. He now accepted Jagow's proposal of a Serbian campaign since Russia would make peace only when it had failed to win new Balkan allies and realized that free passage of the Dardanelles could be achieved from Germany alone.[29] Determined to discontinue large-scale eastern operations, Falkenhayn agreed to the Serbian campaign. His objectives were, however, more limited than those of Jagow and Bethmann: it seemed the only way to stabilize the Balkan flank, keep Turkey in the war and bring Bulgaria over to the Central Powers' side. German leaders accordingly agreed on means but not ends. Whereas Falkenhayn subordinated eastern considerations to the object of returning quickly to the west, Bethmann and Jagow still believed that a separate peace with Russia was both necessary and possible.[30]

German leaders made another attempt to conclude peace with Russia during the autumn. Despite his refusals during the summer, the Tsar was still assumed to desire peace and kept from acceding to his "good intentions" only by his oath to his allies, their threats, and the false advice of unscrupulous advisers. If he could be convinced Russia would gain nothing from the war and Germany desired peace, he might yet respond. Great hopes were therefore placed on the Serbian campaign which might show Russia that its allies could not give it the Straits, strengthen the Central Powers by securing Turkey, and shatter Russian prestige in the Balkans both by destroying its protegé, Serbia, and by winning over Bulgaria to the Central Powers. The contemporaneous German repulse of Anglo-French attacks on the western front would demonstrate Anglo-French impotency and German invincibility. The Tsar would hopefully conclude that the only way to rescue his position in southeastern Europe as well as in Poland was by coming to terms with the Central Powers.[31]

These presumed conditions of success were fulfilled by November 1915. Bulgaria had joined the Central Powers, Serbia had been defeated, Turkey saved and the Anglo-French attacks discontinued. The influence of Russian pro-peace statesmen was supposed to be on the rise, while that of bellicose leaders was reportedly on the wane. Family and court connections might persuade the Tsar to disregard his official advisers and reestablish friendly relations with Germany. Consequently the suggestions—made so frequently during the previous months—were repeated. The most audacious was through the Tsarina's former lady-in-waiting, Maria Wassilchikov, who conferred with Jagow in early December and was sent to Petrograd with letters; upon arrival she was, however, disregarded and her mission produced no result.[32]

German leaders finally recognized at the end of 1915 that the Tsar had not been won over to peace. All tactics—reminders of the Three Emperors' League and the dynastic principle, threats of defeat, loss of Poland, conquest of Serbia, offer of the Straits, entry of Bulgaria, Anglo-French failure—had proven ineffective. When efforts were renewed in the summer of 1916, they would consequently be directed more toward the Russian political parties than the dynasty.

*   *   *   *   *

The main objective of German policy during 1915 was a separate peace with Russia. Since it was sought above all with the established regime, primarily traditional means were applied: traditional channels (such as the royal family and prewar diplomatic connections whenever possible), traditional principles (e.g., dynasticism), traditional Russian concerns (Poland and the Dardanelles), and traditional friendship between the rulers. Although a separate peace with Russia would have had revolutionary implications for the war and international system, its specific objectives claimed by the Germans in their approaches to Russia were traditional: amicable relations and possibly an alliance with Russia. As Bethmann commented in November 1914, a Russo-German understanding would leave their relations more or less where they were before the war.[33]

Nonetheless the Germans meanwhile tested less traditional means to remove Russia from the war in seeking contacts with Russian dissidents. Their purposes in doing so were varied. The most important and immediate objective during the early months of the war was military, namely, to foster rebellions behind the Russian lines so as to complicate enemy mobilization and operations. Later German generals would advocate support of Russian sub-nationalities to encourage their recruitment as soldiers against Russia. With the decision of late 1914 to seek a separate peace with Russia, revolution in Russia took on the diplomatic purpose of putting pressure on the Russian government to leave the war. As it gradually became clearer that the Tsar and traditional elements in Russia would or could not conclude peace, the Germans explored the possibility of encouraging a takeover by elements who would; this would become their primary goal after the outbreak of revolution in 1917. Thus the main German concern in fostering revolution in Russia until the winter of 1918 was as an adjunct to military and diplomatic policy, i.e., as a means of war. They recognized, however, that the internal collapse of Russia would create conditions in eastern Europe conducive to the expansion of German influence, perhaps through small buffer states between Russia and Germany. Thus a revolution seemed desirable in terms of both war means and ends.[34]

The choice between traditional and revolutionary means was made on the basis of utility and notably unencumbered by ideology, sentiment or moral qualms. Presumably because it was obvious, this standard was generally unquestioned but occasionally justifications were offered. The basic impulse was necessity. Bethmann asserted to the Reichstag on August 4 in justifying the German violation of Belgian neutralitythat "necessity knows no law." Moltke reflected this sentiment in a memorandum of the same day in arguing for revolutionary means when he asserted that "the seriousness of the situation in which the Fatherland finds itself requires the application of all means which are likely to hurt the enemy." Rantzau, German minister in Copenhagen, claimed in December 1915 that "we have no alternative but to try this solution [of encouraging the Bolsheviks] because our existence as a Great Power is at stake—perhaps more than

that." In particular, Germany was threatened by the "Russian colos-
sus," the "nightmare," the "semi-Asiatic Muscovite Empire." The
German cause was regarded as good because Germany was fighting
a defensive war, whereas its enemies were bad because they had per-
fidiously conspired to surround and destroy Germany. Concern for
scruples was specifically condemned. Tschirschky, the German
ambassador in Vienna, criticized Berchtold's apparent reluctance to
encourage insurrection because of conservative principles. Rantzau
rejected legal or sentimental constraints. Jagow and Rantzau felt
that the Romanov dynasty had betrayed its friendship with the
Hohenzollerns and thereby disqualified itself for any special consideration. Some German leaders such as Rantzau recognized the risk
of fostering revolution but thought they could control it and in any
case believed it was worthwhile.[35]

The desirability of revolutionizing Russia was accepted by most
German leaders and ruling elements. The highest leaders—including
the Kaiser, Bethmann, Jagow and Zimmermann—were involved from
the start; later, Chancellors Michaelis and Hertling, and Foreign
Secretary Kühlmann perpetuated the policy. The efforts were supported by the generals from Moltke and Falkenhayn through Hindenburg and Ludendorff. Although operations were conducted primarily by the Foreign Office, the General Staff was deeply involved
through its Political Section in Berlin and the German Army invad-
ing Poland in August 1914 distributed leaflets advocating revolt
from "the Muscovite yoke." Activities were administered and indeed advocated by German envoys, most notably by Rantzau, Romberg in Bern, Wangenheim in Constantinople, Lucius in Stockholm,
Bussche-Haddenhausen in Bucharest, and in 1918 by Mirbach in
Petrograd. Bergen was specifically in charge of revolutionary policy
at the Foreign Office, supported by Oppenheim, who was in charge
of Near Eastern activities. Riezler, Bethmann's adviser, was involved
in contacts with the Bolsheviks from 1915 onward. The notion of
revolutionizing Russia was accepted by the political parties and
Bundesstaaten; some—such as the Socialists—were involved in the
Foreign Office's efforts. Although virtual unanimity existed on the
desirability of a revolution in Russia, there was some disagreement
on its likelihood. The most consistent and enthusiastic advocates
seem to have been Zimmermann, Bergen, Nadolny (head of the Political Section of the reserve General Staff in Berlin), and Rantzau.
After initial enthusiasm Bethmann became less hopeful and Romberg
more reserved. Jagow apparently became downright sceptical and
Finance Minister Helfferich resisted financial support of the Bolsheviks
before the revolution.[36]

While untraditional, a German revolutionary policy was by no means unprecedented. It accorded with the European heritage of *raison d'état* extending back at least to the Renaissance. Within the context of more recent German history, it had the example of Bismarck's investigating the possibility of encouraging insurrection as a threat to Austria in 1866. He and the elder Moltke had considered fostering revolution in Russia when war seemed imminent in 1871 and Waldersee, the elder Moltke's successor, had accepted the notion. These precedents and general support for the policy make its lack of coherence striking. There existed no general plan, organization, contacts or intelligence about dissident groups and prospects for revolution. German efforts were patched together as opportunities presented themselves or military operations developed. Cooperation with Austria-Hungary and Turkey proved difficult in part because prior consultation had been lacking. Thus German revolutionary policy was essentially pragmatic and developed in response to wartime conditions.[37]

Since virtually all conceivable means were explored, German activities are not easily categorized. They nonetheless fell into two types of national and social revolution. The Germans seem to have had greater hopes for the separatist aspirations of sub-nationalities under Russian rule—the Finns, Poles, Jews, Ukrainians, etc.—which were based on the so-called "orange theory" that the Russian Empire was an artificially constructed conglomerate which would collapse into its constituent parts under the pressure of war. The Germans simultaneously fostered social revolution in supporting the Russian left, above all, the Bolsheviks. No clear choice or distinction was made between these courses which were sometimes combined when nationalists were also radicals. The emphasis of German policy varied as prospects changed: in 1914 the Germans expected and fostered national agitation; the diminution of these prospects caused them to redirect their efforts toward less grandiose results during 1915 and to encourage social revolution; by late 1916 the prospects for social revolution apparently reduced but support for nationalist agitation persisted; efforts to assist the Bolsheviks were drastically stepped up after the March 1917 revolution; as the Bolsheviks seemed in trouble in the summer of 1918 and the Russian state on the verge of breaking apart, the Germans supported the sub-nationalities.[38]

With the outbreak of war the Germans immediately launched their efforts to foster nationalist revolts. Since the main purpose was to complicate Russian mobilization and operations so as to win the war quickly, their main focus was northern Russia. The German attempt to arouse the Poles failed for a number of reasons. They gave way before Austrian reluctance to ignite a Polish rebellion which might have the same effect on Galicia. The extensive demands of Polish nationalists in fact threatened not only Galicia but Prussian authority in Posen and West Prussia. The withdrawal of the German and Austro-Hungarian troops at the end of 1914 made their promises hollow and uncompetititve with the Russian government's offer of a unified Polish state including German and Austro-Hungarian territories and allowing considerable autonomy.[39] Meanwhile, encouraged by the Russian government's anti-Semitism and the exaggerated hopes of German Jews and Zionists, the German and Austro-Hungarian General Staffs issued a proclamation urging a rise of the Jews. But no rising occurred because of the Russian Jews' disunity, lack of support from world Zionists and American Jewry, Jewish dissatisfaction with German administration in occupied areas, the tendency of Russian Jewish Socialists to regard Germany with suspicion, and Jewish hopes for reform from the Russian government.[40]

Bethmann's simultaneous attempt "to encourage an eventual revolt against Russia" by the Finns likewise failed. The Germans could not land troops as the Finns demanded and a Finnish request for a promise of independence was avoided by the Germans at the end of 1914 because Berlin was pursuing a separate peace with Russia. Despite minimal prospects of a Finnish uprising, the Germans decided in spring 1915 to provide facilities for a Finnish legion for the eventuality of "the outbreak of a general, massive revolution in Russia" or Swedish entry and so as not to discourage other separatist activities in Russia. Few results accrued, however, and it was not until the Bolshevik revolution and the arrival of German troops in 1918 that the Finns rose.[41]

Jagow and Bethmann applauded efforts to ignite a Ukrainian rebellion which they expected would destroy Russia's great power status. They therefore funded extensive efforts during 1915 and 1916 run out of Bucharest, Constantinople and Bern. Again they were met with failure, in part because of Austro-Hungarian fears that a Ukrainian revolution would infect the Ruthenians in Galicia, but more importantly because the Ukrainians would not revolt without the actual military presence of the Central Powers which would not occur until 1918.[42] It was a similar story in the Caucasus and Central Asia. The Germans supported with funds attempts run from Constantinople to arouse the Georgians. But again they ran into opposition of an ally, this time the Turks, who had their own aspirations in the area. As elsewhere, a rebellion remained highly unlikely without an invasion by the Central Powers which had to await the

Bolshevik revolution. The Germans therefore reduced their expectations in 1915 from a general revolution to sabotage.[43]

Although each case involves specific explanations, all German efforts to arouse national separatist revolts foundered on the same basic facts. A combination of loyalty and the threat of governmental reprisal prevented any action until the social revolution caused the regime to collapse and the forces of the Central Powers invaded. The Germans were thus confronted with a dilemma: their military victory over Russia seemed to depend on national revolts but national revolts required a German victory.

The Germans meanwhile explored the possibility of fostering social revolution in Russia. Their objectives were the same as for national revolt: to hamper the Russian military effort and put pressure on the Russian government to conclude a separate peace. Furthermore a social revolution could cause the Russian state's collapse and allow a radical increase of German power in the east. Thus it could function as both a war means and war aim.

In contrast to nationalist revolts which they expected immediately, the German attempt to encourage social revolution began gradually. The first serious contact appeared in the person of Parvus Helphand, who persuaded the German government in January 1915 that destruction of the Russian state required coordination of social and national movements. In particular, he advocated fostering a reconciliation between the Mensheviks and Bolsheviks to produce a general strike, propaganda for which would require extensive financial support. The German government was sufficiently convinced to authorize considerable funds during 1915 and early 1916.[44] The Germans were simultaneously in touch with the Estonian Socialist Kesküla, who caused an important departure when he convinced the Germans to support only the Bolsheviks because the Mensheviks worked for a Russian victory by maintaining worker morale. To buttress his argument, Kesküla produced what he claimed was Lenin's peace program which included the point critical for the Germans that he would conclude a separate peace with Germany without regard for the Entente if the Germans renounced annexations and indemnities.[45] Despite the high hopes of Helphand, Kesküla and some Germans such as Rantzau, the revolution did not occur in 1916. Helphand claimed it was prevented by conservative, liberal and Menshevik counter-revolutionary activities and the inclination of court circles to conclude a separate peace with Germany. Even Lenin seemed sceptical about the prospects of revolution. The Germans continued to fund social revolutionary operations but at a declining rate during 1916 and placed their major hopes on separate under-standings with the existing Russian and French governments.[46]

The March 1917 revolution produced another departure in German policy toward social revolution. They tried to foster a Bolshevik takeover by expediting Lenin's return to Russia and radically increased funding for the operations of Helphand and Keskula. After the Bolshevik revolution in November 1917, the Germans sought to maintain Lenin by concluding peace and augmenting funds. This policy continued until the summer of 1918 when Bolshevik prospects for survival seemed in decline and the Germans decided to investigate more traditional elements such as the Liberals. Meanwhile the Germans encouraged dissolution of the Russian state by support for national separatist elements. Thus, while giving considerable financial support to efforts to precipitate social revolution, the bulk of aid was expended after the revolution had occurred.[47]

German expectations for social revolution in Russia varied according to individuals. Some—most notably Rantzau—had high hopes. An active and consistent supporter, Zimmermann was more moderate in his expectations and probably backed the Bolsheviks only as one of many dissidents who might produce results. The other top leaders were apparently even less sanguine, hoping at best for sabotage and minor incidents rather than a massive revolution. Despite his many contacts with revolutionaries, Romberg remained dubious, while Jagow was critical of Helphand, whose plans involved "a great deal of fantasy," according to Treasury Secretary Helfferich. Although they sought to encourage a Bolshevik takeover and retention of power after the revolution, most German leaders doubted Bolshevik chances for survival.[48]

These doubts notwithstanding, Berlin did seek to aid the Bolsheviks, primarily with funds. Difficult to ascertain precisely because of the secret nature of operations and the spotty records, the German government's financial aid designated for the Bolsheviks apparently amounted to around 40 million marks. In his disappointment, Rantzau therefore exaggerated when he complained to Zimmermann that Jagow had "totally ignored" Helphand's suggestions; in fact Helphand had been regularly funded, frequently with Jagow's authorization. Berlin could, however, have done more since the funds earmarked for the Bolsheviks constituted only about 10% of the total devoted to such purposes and less than those designated for Rumania or Persia. Thus German efforts to promote social revolution in Russia were considerable but not exceptional.[49]

It is even more difficult to ascertain what results German efforts achieved. It is tempting to perceive a causal relationship between

German actions and Russian events. The agents with whom the Germans worked generally claimed results: funds were supposed to have reached their desired destination and Helphand established an organization. Some German leaders—including Rantzau and Kühlmann—believed that German efforts had contributed importantly to the Bolshevik takeover. It is, however, virtually impossible to demonstrate the influence of German revolutionary policy. German efforts probably contributed little to the March revolution. Only a small part of the funds for the Bolsheviks were expended before 1917; in fact expenditures seem to have declined at the end of 1916. Helphand's organization was pitifully small—eight regular employees in Copenhagen and ten agents in Russia. The nature of such operations almost insures that much of the money sticks to the fingers of intermediaries or is wasted on pointless activities. Even if some did reach the Bolsheviks before 1917, the Bolshevik contribution to the March revolution is hard to prove. If funds reached the Bolsheviks before their takeover at the end of 1917, they probably had little influence on events. Bolshevik policy would have been much the same and their success was dependent less on their financial means than their political decisions. The crucial German contributions were likewise less financial than military and political: German operations during the early years of the war, the return of Lenin to Russia, and the conclusion of peace with the Bolsheviks in 1918. Thus the influence of German revolutionary activities was probably minimal at most.[50]

The lack of success of German revolutionary activities was probably due to a number of factors. Like their counterparts elsewhere, the Russian peasants and workers supported the war because of pervasive patriotism and nationalism, fear of Germany, hopes for reform, and fear of reprisal. The potential leaders of revolt, the Socialists, were divided between patriotic, reformist Mensheviks and anti-war, revolutionary Bolsheviks. As in the other belligerent states, the forces of the middle and right were pro-war and worked to prevent revolution. In contrast to national separatist movements, social revolution was at first discouraged by German invasion which allowed the government to unify the country by presenting itself as defender of the homeland. Revolution eventually erupted less because of the preparations by Russian groups or German agents than because of the stress of war and the development of conditions which few could comprehend and none could control. The Germans could exploit the revolution but they could not produce or direct it.

German revolutionary policy fit into general German objectives. National and social revolutions were expected to complicate Russian military operations and to put pressure on the regime to conclude a separate peace with Germany. Whenever they conflicted, revolutionary activities were subordinated to prospects of an understanding with the existing regime. Jagow advised at the end of 1914 that specific commitments to the Finns be avoided since "we cannot unduly overburden the program of our demands should the possibility of a separate peace with Russia now present itself."[51] This choice was not made because of ideological considerations but the calculation that a separate peace with Russia and thus the dissolution of the Entente were thereby more likely.

CHAPTER III

FRANCE 1915

During the early months of the war, Berlin had expected to reconstruct the European state system by conquering France, excluding Anglo-Russian influence, and organizing the continent into a German-dominated *Mitteleuropa*. When this proved unfeasible by November 1914, German leaders recognized that the old system had to be destroyed before a new one could be constructed. The only guarantee against the recurrence of an unfriendly coalition and the persistence of the balance of power appeared to be the defeat of France and destruction of its great power status. To this end, hopes for the expulsion of Russian influence from Europe had to be sacrificed and a separate understanding with Russia arranged. It was, however, realized in Berlin that an anti-German coalition could likewise be rendered impossible if France were won over for an alliance with Germany. Although it seemed a more difficult accomplishment and less certain solution, peace with France was a goal second in desirability only to an understanding with Russia.

The implications of such a separate arrangement with France were explored during the discussions among German leaders at the end of 1914. Tirpitz raised the eventuality in his conversation with Falkenhayn, who initially favored peace with France as an escape from the military stalemate but was persuaded by Tirpitz that Russia was more likely to respond. In the subsequent discussion with Bethmann, Falkenhayn argued that separate peace with Russia should be the primary objective but that a French request for peace should not be rejected out-of-hand. Despite what he perceived to be the French army's weariness, Falkenhayn regarded such a request as unlikely because the French government and people were still confident of victory and determined to continue the war. Although Bethmann accepted Falkenhayn's general analysis and advocacy of a separate peace with Russia, he apparently did not seriously consider an understanding with France at this juncture. On the contrary, he was inclined to reject any request for peace in order to defeat and dominate France. Bethmann nonetheless seems to have been more concerned than Falkenhayn about French tenacity which he hoped would give way to defeatism as a result of war weariness and antipathy toward

England. The opposite tack was taken by Zimmermann, who resisted separate peace in any form but regarded it as less onerous with France than Russia, which was the greater threat to Germany. Believing the war unpopular in France and continued only because of Anglo-Russian support, Zimmermann thought that the decline of allied assistance would prompt demands for peace from the French public and he concluded that reconciliation with France was consequently possible because the French had been sufficiently weakened to desire it.[1]

Bethmann may have reflected Zimmermann's influence in his statements on France during December 1914. Bethmann hardly mentioned France in his Reichstag speech of December 2 and placed responsibility for the war on Russia and particularly Britain; the majority of Frenchmen wanted to live in peace with Germany but had been misled by vengeful politicians. In a conversation with Gustav Stresemann, a member of the Reichstag, and Heinrich Roetger, a representative of heavy industry, Bethmann was more ambiguous. On the one hand, he argued that Franco-German relations were based on power: peace could be concluded only after France had been defeated; conditions would depend on German military success; borders would be determined by the General Staff; and France would pay for the war. On the other hand, he implied that relations should be governed by considerations of pity and pacification. It was a pity that France would have to bear the brunt of the war alone since it was Germany's least guilty, most respectable and chivalrous opponent, and the one he wanted to conciliate as much as possible; it would therefore be more appropriate to demand little and to compensate France with Belgian territory. Above all, he was anxious to pacify France in order to draw it away from the enemy alliance. Thus France was at once the most vulnerable but least vicious enemy and Bethmann advocated the contradictory policy of conquest and conciliation.[2]

These contradictory objectives confronted German leaders with an awkward choice in projecting war aims with regard to France. If conquest were pursued, Germany might make the practical gain of territorial acquisition at the political cost of perpetuating the Entente. But, if conciliation were pursued, Germany might make the political gain of destroying the Entente at the practical cost of renouncing territorial acquisitions. This incompatibility was pointed out by the banker Aruthur von Gwinner to Clemens von Delbrück, State Secretary of the Interior. "The eventual shape of peace conditions depends on whether the goal of [German] policy is to bleed France into exhaustion or to win it for reconciliation." Gwinner advocated compensating France for what Germany demanded but Delbrück realistically questioned whether France would respond. Although he seemed to agree with Gwinner, Bethmann characteristically prevaricated and prepared for all eventualities by instructing Delbrück to ascertain maximal and minimal conditions. Thus future developments rather than immediate decisions would determine German policy toward France. The explanation for this ambivalence, however, lay only partially in Bethmann's unwillingness to choose and more significantly in the situation. Both conquest and conciliation assumed that the Germans could end the military stalemate, whereas continued stalemate implied a compromise peace.[3]

Despite this fundamental ambivalence, certain themes ran through German efforts to arrange a separate peace with both France and Russia. The Germans assumed that the war was disadvantageous to both opponents and that peace with Germany was therefore desirable. While peace was favored by some political parties and opposed by others, the two domestic political equations were reversed: the Russian political right (particularly the Tsar) would favor peace, whereas the center and left would oppose it; the French right would oppose peace, whereas the center and left would favor it. These differing responses presumably reflected deeper antagonisms in French domestic politics which would ultimately dominate French foreign policy. Since French politics was believed to be hypersensitive to public opinion, the Germans expected propaganda to be particularly efficacious and therefore sought control over French papers. Their propaganda would stress the three themes of English duplicity, Russian impotency and German invincibility. French domestic considerations and the apparently greater likelihood of a separate peace with Russia made German leaders disinclined to offer France real inducements to conclude a separate peace. Thus, although they regarded an understanding with France as desirable, German leaders were unwilling to pay much for it.

Tentative feelers for a separate peace with France began to emanate from Berlin at the end of 1914. Zimmermann encouraged a French request for peace by bribing associates of Théophile Delcassé, the notoriously anti-German French Foreign Minister. An ostensible confidant of the French government was informed that France would receive more advantageous conditions if it sued for peace sooner rather than later. A campaign in the French press was considered but a suitable paper could not be located. The most publicized and in fact most serious German attempt to win over an influential French politician began when Berlin was informed that ex-Minister President Joseph Caillaux wanted to know whether or not Germany would conclude a separate peace with France. This controversial figure seemed to evidence all the required qualifications: antipathy toward England and the war, sympathy for a Franco-German *rapproche-ment*, deep personal enmity toward other French politicians, and extreme love of power. When Caillaux was persuaded by the French government to accept a mission to South America, a meeting became impractical but the Germans sought to maintain contact for the future. In place of Caillaux, the Germans were offered conversations with French politicians reputedly close to Caillaux—Ceccaldi, an intimate friend of Caillaux, and Gaston Doumergue, Minister of Colonies—but they also failed to appear. A channel to Joseph Noulens, a member of the Chamber of Deputies, was also tested without success. Thus all German efforts had proved unproductive by the end of 1914.[4]

When an understanding with Russia seemed unlikely at the beginning of January 1915, Bethmann favored one with France. He suggested contacting Paris via Rome to ex-Chancellor Prince Bernhard von Bülow, who had just arrived in Rome on a mission to discourage Italian entry on the Entente side. Bethmann claimed that Germany had "no interest in destroying France and could offer it an honorable peace in exchange for a war indemnity and colonial concessions." Such a peace with France would have the great advantages for Germany of "separating France [from its allies] which would enable us to finish the war against Russia and England with the certainty of victory. We would thereby achieve [the goals of] a relatively weak France, a dam against the Slavic danger, and a shock to English world hegemony." Although even the flamboyant Bülow rejected it as unrealistic, the suggestion revealed the central contradiction in German efforts. Despite his recognition that shattering the Entente was essential to German victory, Bethmann could not bring himself to renounce demands, much less offer concessions, to achieve it. Instead, he wanted the French to pay for the privilege.[5]

Vienna meanwhile sought contacts with the French. Assuming that Berlin was willing to consider a peace with France, Alexander Hoyos, an official in the Austro-Hungarian Foreign Ministry, asked Gagern, the Austro-Hungarian envoy in Bern, to seek an appropriate intermediary. Hoyos expected that the French would respond after German military successes in Flanders and Poland but Gagern had already ascertained that the French were interested only in a separate peace with Austria-Hungary which Vienna seems to have rejected. The incident indicated that such soundings could prove double-edged swords by opening up breaches in either alliance, tightening rather than loosening the Entente, or giving the impression of German weakness rather than strength.[6]

German success depended not only on German but also French policy. Indeed, since a French decision to accept a separate peace was the prerequisite, French policy was the critical element. Like all the belligerents, France was profoundly influenced by military prospects. As their counterparts elsewhere did, French leaders hoped for a quick victory and accepted the fact of stalemate only gradually and reluctantly. It had nonetheless become clear to them by the end of 1914 that neither victory nor defeat but deadlock and thus discouragement had become the great danger. This fact required the reconstruction of French policy and strategy. The German invasion facilitated the process by providing the obvious immediate objective of liberating the occupied areas. Yet mere liberation not only failed to satisfy desires for revenge and security but also paled by comparison with the more ambitious colonial aspirations of France's two major allies.[7] Liberation was likewise difficult to achieve: since the French had demonstrated the superiority of defense over offense during 1914, expelling the German invaders required reversing the relationship. Thus military prospects caused French policy to become at once more realistic but also more rigid than the other belligerents.

Circumstances also largely determined French politics. National danger precluded the luxury of open discussion and prescribed the politics of official unity. When the Chamber of Deputies was convoked briefly in December, the purpose was approbation rather than evaluation of policy or strategy; patriotism precluded politics, unity was eulogized, and public criticism was renounced by politicians and the press. Less public frictions nonetheless persisted among the soldiers and statesmen. Civil-military relations were governed by the fluctuating military situation. After the soldiers had tended to dominate during the German invasion, the civil-military balance was restored in December when the Germans had been stopped, the military situation stabilized, the government relocated from Bordeaux to Paris, and Commander in Chief Joseph Jacques Joffre had failed to expel the Germans from French territory. Consequently criticism of Joffre increased, dissension among generals emerged, strategic alternatives were suggested, and old political problems revived to complicate military decisions. Since France was no longer in extreme danger, French leaders could afford the luxury of limited disagreement. This dissension was, however, only on means and unanimity persisted on the aim of victory. France had avoided defeat but its leaders had not yet discovered the formula for victory.

French victory depended on preservation of the Entente, just as German victory required dissolution of the coalition. Like most alliances, the Entente was preserved by a common threat, namely, German power which forced its members to subordinate—though not solve—their problems. To insure the continued adherence of Russia, the British granted Russian aspirations at the Dardanelles in exchange for Russian recognition of British demands in Persia and the Mediterranean. Since the French were notably peripheral to these discussions, they were understandably alienated. They demanded recognition of their interests in Syria and Morocco in exchange for acceptance of British gains but were reluctant to confirm Russian aspirations at the Straits, criticized Russian activities in the Balkans, and were concerned about the apparent British inclination to consider withdrawing troops from the continent. The French realized, however, that self-defense required preservation of the alliance and consequently responded to Russian requests in December for a diversionary offensive, discontinued their soundings for a separate understanding with Austria-Hungary, and dropped their opposition to Russian aspirations at Austro-Hungarian expense. The Entente had thus not only been preserved but also consolidated by the end of 1914.[8]

* * * * *

German policy and strategy were revised at the beiginning of 1915. It seemed in December 1914 that the Germans would continue to concentrate on the western front but it was decided in January 1915 that an offensive should be launched against Russia to make it conclude a separate peace. While the hopes for this offensive were high in February, German leaders seldom considered the possibility of a separate peace with France. Falkenhayn was an exception in remaining adamant that Germany should seek "to spring France loose from the Triple Entente."[9]

French strategy meanwhile was rigidly fixed on the western front. Pressures came from within the French government and army as well as from the British and Russians for the diversion of some French troops to the Balkans but they were rejected out-of-hand by Joffre. He insisted that victory could be won only on the western front where he now sought it by exploiting the German distraction to the eastern front with a massive offensive of his own. Despite the depletion of their forces, however, the Germans were prepared and repelled the attacks at great cost to the French. Parliamentary criticism of the government and particularly the army increased as a result. The government successfully parried this criticism and squelched the discussion of war aims. Even the socialists announced that they were committed to victory though not to a war of conquest. The socialists were nonetheless able to extract from the government a statement of aims: continue the war, maintain the Entente, reestablish Belgium, and reincorporate Alsace-Lorraine. Despite military failure, France remained committed to the war.

The general military and diplomatic situation which favored the Central Powers in January and February became threatening in March and April. Not only did victory escape them on the eastern front but the Russians resumed their offensive and forced Falkenhayn to renounce his plans for an offensive against France in order to assist Austria-Hungary. The French and British meanwhile prepared for a massive offensive on the western front at the beginning of May. Balkan developments suddenly favored the Entente because of the promising British attack on the Dardanelles which encouraged Greece and Italy to join the Entente. The naval and commercial war intensified when the Germans increased their U-boat operations and the British retaliated by extending their blockade of Germany.

These developments caused another alteration of German policy. Bethmann was informed by Hindenburg that an offensive was impossible on either front and thus "there was no escape other than the immediate conclusion of peace." The transfer of German troops to the eastern front not only made French defeat unlikely but rendered German military setbacks on the western front possible because of the impending Anglo-French offensive. Although depressed by this news, Bethmann and Zimmermann managed to convert it into a potential advantage by assuming that exaggerated Anglo-French expectations for their offensive would become deep discouragement when it failed. Thus disillusionment rather than defeat would be the key to peace with France.[10]

The Germans prepared for this eventuality by intensifying their efforts to make contact with France, Russia and Britain. The French case was somewhat special since the Germans sought contact with the opposition, whereas they tried to reach the Russian and British governments. This distinction reflected different objectives: the understandings envisaged with Petrograd and London were relatively moderate from the German—though not the Russian or British— point of view, whereas the peace with France was extreme because it assumed German domination of France. Because such an arrangement was unlikely with the existing French government, the Germans sought contact with the opposition. Peace with France therefore implied both diplomatic and domestic political revolution, while peace with Russian and Britain assumed only Russian and British diplomatic renunciation.

The Germans accordingly sought channels to the French opposition leaders and means to disseminate propaganda and to encourage revolutionary activities. Contacts were pursued above all with those leftist politicians—most importantly, Caillaux—who were thought to be opposed both to the war and the political system. The most consistent and comprehensive effort was made in the area of propaganda which emphasized the dual themes of defeatism and dissatisfaction with France's allies. It was hoped that both would occur as a result of the failure of the French spring offensive. When they were informed that many French politicians were dubious about France's ability to win a decisive victory and were thus prepared to conclude an "acceptable" peace (including small German concessions in Alsace-Lorraine and part of Belgium), Zimmermann and Jagow intensified their efforts to influence the French press. One of their intermediaries urged Jagow to expend ten million francs in founding a radical-socialist paper of the Caillaux-Briand type, purchasing shares in such papers as *Temps* and *Figaro*, influencing the provincial press, bribing influential politicians, creating a news service in Geneva, purchasing the Paris humorous journal *Cri de Paris*, and placing articles in the Swiss *Journal de Genève*. Jagow suggested that Vienna be included but Heinrich von Tschirschky, German ambassador in Vienna, disagreed since "France is our domain." Jagow agreed to fund the operation in the hope that the French press would gradually advocate peace and attack England and possibly Italy.[11]

The Germans also tried to make contact with the French through Turkish intermediaries. Djavid Bey, former Turkish Finance Minister, reportedly met Jean Dupuy, a former French minister and director of the *Petit Parisien*. According to Dupuy, the French people recognized that the Russian steamroller had failed and that Germany could not be defeated. Although he felt France would collapse if the war lasted until the autumn, Dupuy believed the chauvinistic French government and generals kept popular hopes aroused and made it impossible at the moment for any politician to advocate peace publicly. Furthermore France was apparently under English influence despite mutual antipathy. The Germans seem to have hoped initially that the French would respond. Hans von Wangenheim, the German envoy in Constantinople, asked: "Is France perhaps seeking an answer from us via Djavid?" Jagow apparently hoped so at first but later concluded—probably correctly—that the French were only seeking a separate peace with Turkey. Although without practical result, the incident revealed German preconceptions.[12]

The Germans meanwhile approached the French opposition. Tschirschky encouraged a move by Caillaux through the ex-Khedive of Egypt. Acting as an agent of the Khedive, a bizarre French novelist called Bolo Pasha produced a scheme dignified as the "Bolo Plan," which involved raising Caillaux's status and exploiting antipathies among French generals. [13]

None of these activities produced anything which could be regarded as a serious prospect. They were perpetuated primarily because they were regarded as investments for the future. Propaganda might put pressure on the government and contacts with the opposition might establish channels for subsequent negotiations. Gisbert von Romberg, German envoy in Bern, expressed the hope that "the idea of peace would make very acceptable progress in France within a few months" as a result of German propaganda, contacts with the opposition, and French disappointment.[14]

German success therefore still depended on French reactions. As the Germans assumed, the French had great expectations for their massive spring offensive. Despite these hopes, few statements on war aims were made by French leaders or politicians. President Raymond Poincaré had given the typical admonition to French troops on the eve of their February offensive but the government was more interested in preventing than promoting discussion of war aims. As a result of official prohibition, the press campaign of Maurice Barrès for a French border on the Rhine was discontinued and a demand in the Chamber for removal of these restraints was rejected by the government. Although parliamentary criticism of the conduct of the war was more difficult to deflect and critics began to congregate around dissident generals, Joffre was able to parry these threats and retain control of strategy. The essence of this criticism remained not whether but how the war should be conducted. Joffre's critics demanded "a vigorous, brutal action" to expel the Germans from France rather than Joffre's strategy of attrition. They included all political colorations including the left. The Germans were thus correct in assuming that exaggerated hopes were attached to the French spring offensive but wrong in believing that French politicians in general or even those on the left were disposed toward peace.

* * * * *

After favoring the Entente during March and April, prospects improved for the Central Powers during the summer. The Austro-German offensive against the Russians achieved a great breakthrough in May and completely reversed the situation on the eastern front by June. The Anglo-French attack on Gallipoli reached its critical point in May and essentially failed by July. Italian entry in May proved much less significant than German leaders had anticipated. After obstructing negotiations, Bulgaria allowed passage of German arms to Turkey. German fears of a Serbian and/or Rumanian attack against Austria-Hungary turned out to be groundless. German-American relations deteriorated because of the sinking of the "Lusitania" but the United States did not enter the war as some German leaders feared. Perhaps most important of all, Germans found that they could repulse the Anglo-French offensive with reduced forces. As a result, the pessimism of March gave way to optimism by July.

This change was reflected in German efforts to extract a separate peace from France and/or Russia. Considerable energy and funds were expended to influence the French press and dissident politicians. Although German leaders frequently expressed doubts, hope persisted that the French would respond. Romberg, the German envoy in Bern, advocated increasing expenditures. Falkenhayn urged Jagow to support a self-proclaimed contact with the French opposition and forwarded to Jagow and Bethmann a General Staff memorandum which concluded that the French government would soon have to choose between a separate peace and a hopeless war; a French decision for peace would probably cause Britain and Russia to make peace. Falkenhayn even considered launching a new offensive on the western front in order to encourage a French request for peace. Apparently sharing these views, Jagow advocated a propaganda campaign to exploit French disappointment with the failure of the Anglo-French offensives and to expose an assumed British threat to keep Calais if the French sued for peace. In short, German leaders let their predilections affect their perceptions.[15]

The great French hopes of March and April were in fact shattered in May and June. Indicative of the new situation was concern that a German counter-offensive might prove successful. Despite his subsequent denial, Joffre had apparently encouraged some ministers to expect a French victory by June. Consequently, criticism of Joffre by ministers, parliamentarians and many generals intensified and a campaign was launched to replace him with a popular leftist general. Although civil-military frictions increased, the government supported Joffre in order to avoid reinforcing the impression of military failure and he managed to maintain his post. The government meanwhile came in for its share of criticism particularly because of the munitions shortage which led to the edge of a ministerial crisis. Disappointment with Anglo-French, Russian and Italian military failures caused widespread pessimism which the government feared might turn into defeatism.

Rather than encouraging a quick peace, however, military failure seems to have convinced Frenchmen of the necessity to prepare for a long war. Financial measures were passed unanimously by the parliament, government spokesmen publicly reaffirmed France's determination to persevere until victory, and the socialists—on whom the Germans placed their greatest hopes—announced their continued support of a defensive war. Symptomatic of the left's commitment to the war were their efforts to replace Joffre with a general who was believed by the left to be better able to produce victory. The government meanwhile sought to discourage discussion of peace: German contacts with such agents as the ex-Khedive of Egypt, Bolo Pasha and Djavid were known but not seriously considered and the recourse of a separate understanding with Germany rejected. Although disappointed, the French were not sufficiently desperate to accept defeat.

* * * * *

The general situation increasingly favored the Germans during the autumn of 1915. While renewed Anglo-French attacks failed on the western front, at the Dardanelles and Salonika, and the Italians bogged down, the Central Powers advanced against Russia and defeated Serbia. The Germans therefore continued to pursue their goal of dissolving the enemy alliance. Although an understanding with Russia remained the primary German objective during the autumn of 1915, public rejection of peace by the Russian government in August made France seem a more viable alternative.

German leaders therefore redoubled their efforts to make contacts which could lead to negotiations. Jagow informed the Progressive Swabian Reichstag member Conrad Haussmann that the government desired an understanding and urged Haussmann to discuss it with a middleman reputedly in contact with Albert Thomas, the French Under-Secretary of Munitions. Jagow said the French should be told that, since German prospects were favorable and the war served only England, France should conclude peace with Germany, which did not wish to destroy France and would offer moderate conditions (though not concessions in Alsace-Lorraine). Claiming to represent not only Thomas but also the French Foreign Ministry, the middle-man proposed a meeting between French and German socialists when the Anglo-French Dardanelles expedition had failed and the Germans had renounced all aspirations to French territory. He predicted that French military failures might cause the pro-war Viviani ministry to be replaced by one more disposed toward peace. Following Jagow's prescription, Haussmann refused German concessions in Alsace-Lorraine and threatened that the cost would rise for France if it did not conclude peace soon. This formula seems to have been the official line. Matthias Erzberger, another member of the Reichstag who was active in the service of the German Foreign Ministry, told a different agent that Germany did not want to destroy France but warned that "France must hurry if it wants easy terms since offers from other sides [presumably Russia] are already at hand. He who makes peace first gets away easiest."[16]

Berlin meanwhile sought contacts with the French left and center which were assumed to favor peace. Jagow authorized considerable financial support (five million francs) of a group which reportedly might displace Viviani's ministry and conclude peace. The intermediary was Ernest Judet, editor of *L'Eclair*, which attacked England and such proponents of war as President Poincaré. The Germans were informed at the same time that Caillaux's presumed supporters, the Radical Socialists, feared a rightist reaction from either French victory or defeat and preferred to conclude a compromise peace with the German Social Democrats on the basis of small gains for France which would silence their ultra-reactionary and nationalist critics. To frighten these elements into advocating peace, Romberg, the German envoy in Bern, urged that Lenin's program for social revolution in Russia (and thus the possibility of Russian defection) be leaked to the French opposition but Jagow refused since the Russian government might be informed and squelch social revolutionaries. Romberg also began to support the defeatist propaganda of the *Bonnet Rouge*, whose editor Georges Duval was probably one of the better investments of this kind. The paper played upon French fears that the Germans could never be expelled from France and may thereby have contributed to the army mutinies of 1917. The later claims that Caillaux and Louis Malvy, subsequently Minister of War, also subsidized the paper are not substantiated by the German documents but it is possible since Duval seems to have been in contact with Caillaux.[17]

Entente failures during the late autumn on the western front, at the Dardanelles, and in Serbia made an understanding seem more likely to the Germans. They therefore authorized a meeting between the Bavarian socialist, Adolf Müller, and the French socialist Minister of Works, Marcel Sembat, who failed to appear. Judet encouraged the Germans' impression that Viviani's resignation in October was a blow for peace. Probably the most specific attempt to arrange negotiations occurred in November. When the Germans were informed that Caillaux was anxious to meet a high German official, preferably Jagow, the latter replied through Judet that "we would certainly be prepared to enter into contact with him." Caillaux was reportedly willing to receive communications from the Germans but not to meet a German agent *"for the moment."*[18]

The Germans simultaneously sought to encourage other opposition politicians. Romberg had been applying financial means since September and urged small concessions in Alsace-Lorraine but Jagow refused. In a discussion with Judet, Romberg gave what was probably a summary of the official German perception of relations with France at the end of 1915. He began from the premise that France should renounce further offensives and make peace because it had no chancce of military victory. Anxious to divide French people and government, he asserted that the French people were not anti-German but had been misled into the war by their vengeful politicians. Although the Central Powers' military successes might encourage groups within Germany to demand more extensive annexations, Romberg hoped that an understanding with France would still be possible if France responded quickly. Judet remained adamant, however, that minor German concessions to France in Alsace-Lorraine were necessary. He felt that the new French ministry under Aristide Briand was intransigent and, although it might be brought down quickly by another severe setback, it could be replaced by an even more rigid "ministry of desperation" under Georges Clemenceau, who would fight to the end. Judet distinguished between leading French politicians who were not unfavorably disposed toward peace—Paul Deschanel, President of the Chamber of Deputies, Briand, and Caillaux—and others who were—President Poincaré, Louis Malvy, Minister of the Interior, and Albert Thomas, Under-Secretary of War. The critical objective was to disabuse the French people of their illusions of victory through more intensive propaganda which Jagow authorized in the amount of two-three million francs.[19]

As the Germans assumed, the French actually were discouraged at the end of 1915. Despite the failure of their spring offensive, French hopes for the September campaign had revived, buoyed up by the promise of new British troops, the Italian offensive against Austria, and perhaps even by the Russian retreat which kept the Germans occupied in the east. Dashed by Anglo-French failure on the western front which was repeated virtually everywhere, exaggerated expectations again gave way to disappointment and frustration. Criticsm increased both for Joffre's strategy of attrition and the government's failure to produce sufficient means of war or to anticipate events in the Balkans. After avoiding a crisis during the summer in order not to reinforce the impression of failure, Viviani's ministry resigned. Though not caused specifically by failure, the change of ministry was symptomatic of the general situation. Discouragement, malaise, and even pessimism spread among French leaders.

Nevertheless they persevered. Briand's new cabinet frequently repeated its determination to win. French aims remained what they had been since the beginning of the war: restitution of Belgium, reunification of Alsace-Lorraine with France, and destruction of Prussian militarism. This program was supported by all parties, including the socialists, who restated their formula of a defensive war without annexations (Alsace-Lorraine not being considered an annexation). Strategic thinking shifted for the moment from offensives to plans for husbanding resources until France's allies were ready for combined operations in the spring of 1916. Measures preparatory to a longer war were extended in the areas of finance, food, fuel, munitions, blockade of Germany and tightened censorship. Since the government considered peace at best premature and at worst treasonous, public discussion of war aims and peace was discouraged. The French government continued to follow German attempts to contact dissident groups but dismissed them as either absurd or insincere. Despite their severe disappointment, the French were determined to fight on. There seemed nothing else to do.

German prospects at the end of 1915 were mixed. They had destroyed the balance of power in the sense of demonstrating that their alliance was equal to the Entente and had dominated the continent militarily. They could not insure, however, that this domination would persist unless they defeated their opponents and shattered their alliance. German efforts to do so had failed during 1915. The Their goals consequently remained the same in 1916 but new means had to be found.

German strategy and policy were again reoriented at the end of 1915. The demonstration of German military invincibility had failed to induce either France or Russia to sue for peace and some more effective method would have to be found. The Entente simultaneously assumed a different significance. Since German predominance on the continent had been virtually imposed, shattering the enemy coalition was necessary less to establish than to maintain it. Having proven itself militarily equal to France and Russia, Germany's primary concern was no longer its continental opponents. The real threat seemed to be the possible perpetuation of the enemy alliance. As long as England held it together, Germany's dominant position would never be guaranteed. The ultimate German aim during 1916 consequently became English renunciation of its allies and recognition of German continental hegemony.

Guidelines for this new policy were drawn at the close of 1915. Falkenhayn gave the impulse by asserting in a memorandum of late November to Bethmann that the war had become a struggle for German existence; peace could not be won by negotiation but only by force. Then as subsequently, Bethmann rejected this assumption. Precisely because force had proven inadequate to produce peace, he felt negotiation was the only recourse and still hoped that the feelers put out to Russia and France might yet produce understandings. When these hopes were disappointed during early December, Bethmann concluded that the two continental enemies now counted on the British strategy of exhausting Germany. Meanwhile Falkenhayn temporarily accepted Bethmann's contention that peace with France or Russia might be won through negotiation but continued to assume that force alone would make England conclude peace.[1]

Falkenhayn presented his new strategy based on these assumptions to his civilian and military colleagues at the end of December. He started from the premise that England was "the arch-enemy of this war" and would stop fighting only if forced to realize that the war was hopeless by being isolated from its continental "tools," France, Russia and Italy. The crucial question had accordingly become how to render these allies useless by concluding peace with them or neutral-

izing their military power. The means already tried had failed and
Germany could wait no longer since it might face exhaustion by the
end of 1916. England's allies must therefore be induced to conclude
peace quickly. A separate peace with France seemed most desirable
because it was at once England's "best sword" and yet most vulnerable, whereas Russia was momentarily weak and Italy always impotent. France need not be defeated but merely convinced that continuation of the war was pointless. He therefore advocated an attack
on Verdun whose objective was less to take the fortress than to force
the French to exhaust their reserves in defending it. When France
had thus been "bled white," Falkenhayn was convinced it would sue
for a separate peace.[2]

Bethmann had no alternative to suggest since neither negotiations
nor previous military operations had split the Entente. The situation
seemed propitious for Falkenhayn's strategy: security on the eastern
and southern fronts allowed Germany to concentrate against France
and possible German exhaustion argued for a quick peace. Bethmann's
acquiescence was not in itself a departure; he had always hoped England would recognize German continental hegemony once France
had been destroyed as a great power. English recognition had, however, been transformed into the ultimate objective rather than just
the byproduct of French defeat, whereas a separate peace with
France had become the means to this end rather than the end itself.[3]

This agreement between Bethmann and Falkenhayn was short-
lived. Falkenhayn had won Bethmann's support with the argument
that England would conclude peace if left in the lurch by its allies.
Falkenhayn was, however, persuaded by the Admiralty to revive his
idea of a "war of existence" which assumed that England would persevere alone and have to be threatened with starvation by unrestricted U-boat warfare. When Bethmann opposed the U-boat, Falkenhayn
insisted it was crucial: unless the U-boat paralyzed England, the
Verdun operation would not succeed. The separate peace with
France that was supposed to isolate England had now become condi-
tional on it. Bethmann reversed the equation by insisting that England
would conclude peace if isolated but persevere if threatened by the
U-boat and shore up its alliance with the probable assistance of the
United States and other neutrals; the U-boat should be utilized only
as a last resort if isolation failed to make England ask for peace.
When Falkenhayn and the Admiralty persisted, Bethmann considered a compromise peace which would be preferable to a protracted
struggle between the economically declining Central Powers and an
Entente strengthened by the United States. Bethmann, however,

persuaded the Kaiser at the beginning of March 1916 to reject intensified U-boat warfare and dropped the alternative of general peace.
Since U-boat warfare had been postponed rather than permanently
renounced, it became more necessary than ever for the civilian leaders
to conclude a separate peace with France.[4] Falkenhayn and Bethmann accordingly committed themselves to the same strategy for
different reasons. Falkenhayn won support from conservative and
annexationist elements of the German ruling class in part because
they believed the Verdun campaign would be accompanied by U-
boat warfare. In contrast Bethmann acceded precisely because he
hoped it would render the U-boat unnecessary. Having no alternative,
he and Jagow became more outspoken proponents of Falkenhayn's
strategy than Falkenhayn himself.[5]

In order not to miss an opportunity to conclude a separate peace
with France, Berlin maintained its channels to French dissidents.
The arguments remained much as they had been during 1915, with
the crucial addition of the Verdun operation. Disagreements between
England and France continued to be reported and assiduously encouraged by Berlin. The replacement of Premier Aristide Briand by
either a pacifist Socialist or a desperately belligerent ministry was
promoted in the belief that either would foster peace. Hoping to remove an obstacle for the French Socialists, Berlin considered mock
plebiscites in Alsace-Lorraine. By hinting in response to an ostensible
French sounding at the beginning of January 1916 that no French
territory would be demanded if conversations began immediately,
Jagow seemed momentarily aware that annexations would be superfluous if France were isolated from its allies and dominated by Germany. In the belief that Russia was Germany's main opponent,
Zimmermann encouraged an understanding with France by offering
Caillaux through an intermediary the alternatives of French defeat or
German evacuation of northern France after an understanding.
Jagow claimed at the beginning of February that the French people
would turn to politicians such as Caillaux if the Central Powers parried Anglo-French attacks in the Balkans and on the western front
while at the same time attacking Verdun.[6]

Launched at the end of February 1916, the Verdun operation reportedly caused the expected French desperation and German leaders
began to assume that peace was imminent. An opposition group supported by the German envoy in Bern, Romberg, was supposedly
about to replace Briand and was accordingly informed by Bethmann
and Jagow that their "program of an inexpensive peace" still existed.
Bethmann was so heartened by reports of French discouragement

and the Verdun campaign's progress at the end of March that he expected an immediate French collapse which might produce a Franco-
German *rapprochement* and even an English suggestion of peace. He
purposely omitted any mention of France from his Reichstag speeches
of April 5 and 6 in order to encourage a French appeal and Berlin
continued to express its desire for a French "request for an honorable
separate peace" during April. Yet German leaders could not bring
themselves to renounce demands commensurate with German military
success and thus refused prior conditions or concessions in Alsace-
Lorraine in order to foster negotiations. They seemed to forget that
the Verdun campaign's ultimate objective was a separate peace with
France to which all else had to be subordinated.[7]

When the Verdun attack had still failed to precipitate the desired
French request by the end of April, Bethmann again had to defend it
in discussions following the lines established in January. To Falkenhayn's complaint that neither France nor England would make peace
without intensified U-boat warfare, Bethmann replied that France
would soon make peace, whereas England would refuse to recognize
Germany's victory only if forced by the U-boat. As he had done in
previous disagreements, Bethmann regarded Falkenhayn's attempt to
make Verdun's success contingent upon the U-boat as a device to
shift responsibility for military failure. Bethmann sought both to
avoid this pitfall and to exclude Falkenhayn's encroachment upon
diplomatic policy by designating Verdun's prospects as a military
question but Anglo-French intentions as a political issue. Faced with
this renewed threat to their policy and authority, Bethmann and
Jagow again contemplated a compromise peace which seemed the
lesser of evils because of the momentarily unpromising economic
and military prospects as well as the possibility that the U-boat
might worsen things by bringing in the United States. When a decision on the U-boat was again postponed at the beginning of May,
Bethmann and Jagow were able to pursue the more desirable goal of
an understanding with France. Although their confidence in the
Verdun campaign had been somewhat shaken by Falkenhayn's pessimism, Bethmann and Jagow still hoped that France would have to
conclude peace by summer if not before.[8]

This expectation was inspired by the apparently improved prospects of peace with both France and Russia at the end of April and
beginning of May. Romberg believed that promising channels to
France might produce a request for peace if the English attacks in
Flanders failed and the Verdun operation continued. Assuming
these conditions could be fulfilled, Jagow authorized Reichstag

member Conrad Haussmann to renew French contacts. Jagow simultaneously investigated the possibility of using Italian mediation "to blow up the enemy coalition" but dropped the idea when Italian demands from Austria-Hungary proved exorbitant and Vienna initiated a promising military offensive. Berlin made renewed attempts during May to arouse the French left wing opposition and to smooth the way for talks between the Socialists of both countries. Bribes were combined with the threat that Berlin's "good disposition" to conclude an "inexpensive" peace might change unless peace was made quickly. But no response was forthcoming.[9]

These efforts reached their acme between late May and late June. When the Verdun operation progressed in late May, Romberg declared that "the question of a separate peace with France has hereby reached its decisive stage and we must definitely make up our minds." He felt that French popular support for "the conclusion of a separate peace and establishment of a lasting understanding between the two countries" was possible only if Germany guaranteed Caillaux and his supporters "sufficiently honorable peace conditions." These conditions would have to insure that "France not appear completely defeated and receive certain compensations for the service which it would do us by shattering the enemy coalition." Romberg recommended making these concessions as the only way to destroy the enemy alliance and to settle accounts with England.[10]

Romberg's insistence provided the impulse for intensive discussions at the end of May. The civilian leaders accepted Romberg's analysis because they had begun to doubt that peace would otherwise be feasible. His confidence revived by the events at Verdun, Falkenhayn regarded the moment as inopportune for a German initiative and therefore refused concessions. This obstinacy caused the civilians to reconsider advocating Falkenhayn's replacement by Hindenburg, who they believed both willing to concede and able to persuade the German people that concessions were mandatory. When Falkenhayn won his point and ambiguous instructions were sent, Romberg retorted that they would permanently preclude peace and concluded with a bitter indictment of Falkenhayn: "If Berlin assumed an intransigent attitude towards France because of military considerations, it would destroy the prospect of a reckoning with England . . . and thereby create the danger of a new Congress of Vienna and an indefinite prolongation of the war."[11]

The possibility that "every prospect of destroying the coalition would be lost forever" frightened Romberg's superiors into accepting his demands. Jagow agreed to allow France concessions in return for dissolution of the Entente by public French renunciation of England and formation of a "lasting understanding" with Germany. Otherwise Jagow would assume that France was secretly preserving its alliance with England and no concession could be granted, in which case "there would remain nothing for us to do but seek the fulfillment of our war aims in the complete defeat of France and indemnification at its expense." The contradiction in German thinking toward France was thereby exposed. If "the goal of shattering the [enemy] coalition through a separate peace with France" was the most important objective, all other considerations should have been sacrificed to its achievement. Prior commitment to a formal dissolution of the Entente or an anti-English alliance with Germany would be redundant. If France were isolated from England, it would be dominated by Germany in any case.[12]

The policy of Bethmann and Jagow toward England was even less clear. If French defection caused England to recognize German continental hegemony, a German alliance with France and continuation of the war against Engand would be unnecessary; if not, the Verdun campaign and a separate peace with France were pointless. The alternative of unrestricted U-boat warfare was rejected because they doubted it could "conquer" England before American help arrived. Unwilling to follow their assumptions to their ultimate conclusions, they seemed to prefer leaving the implications vague, perhaps in the hope that military events would resolve them. They never decided precisely what the Entente's dissolution was supposed to accomplish but sensed only that it would somehow be advantageous—which it doubtless would have been. Possibly their awareness of the Entente's tenacity made them curiously chary of risking all available means to shatter it.[13]

During the two weeks following these discussions the Germans intensified their pressure on France. They tried at the end of June to render French retention of Verdun impossible and thereby obliged the French to contemplate its abandonment. The situation was, however, reversed when German troops were required against the Russians and British. No French request was forthcoming before the British Somme offensive was launched at the beginning of July and Berlin realized that France could not be forced to surrender. Jagow decided that a negotiated peace might nonetheless be possible if Germany could survive the desperate military situation at the beginning of July. German perseverance had suddenly replaced puissance as the key. He consequently encouraged Romberg to augment his efforts even though Germany had been unable to make France conclude peace and the defense of Verdun had in fact revived French confidence. Romberg had meanwhile utilized Jagow's authorization of concessions to encourage negotiations and predicted at the beginning of July that Caillaux would soon make an attempt to oust Briand if France were threatened with defeat and if Berlin more clearly demonstrated its desire for peace.[14]

The general situation became increasingly unfavorable for an understanding with France. Soon after Jagow's renewed encouragement to Romberg, Falkenhayn was obliged to discontinue his attack of Verdun. Despite Romberg's reiteration that peace with France was the only recourse and that Caillaux was ready to move at the end of July, a bitter and protracted struggle among German leaders prevented their responding. As it turned out, revived French optimism and military setbacks for the Central Powers at the beginning of August caused Romberg to admit that the demands of his interlocutors had inflated and that the French were even trying to split the Central Powers by concluding a separate peace with Austria-Hungary. Prompted by desperation, Jagow made a final stab at peace by offering the most moderate conditions Berlin ever considered in order that "the thread not be broken." Romberg accordingly promised French agents definite border rectifications in Alsace but received no reply.[15]

Military and diplomatic failure produced a revision of German policy in August 1916. Apparently possible in June, a French collapse was no longer likely in August. Concluding that "the decision lies more than ever in the east," Bethmann recognized that the attempt to conclude a separate peace with France had been unsuccessful.[16]

* * * * *

Explanations for this failure can be sought on various levels. Most important, France was unlikely to conclude a separate peace. Although the French internal political crisis of May and June had been instigated by the left as the Germans had hoped, it was motivated by criticism of the war's conduct rather than of the war itself. The French parliament desired a more successful war, not a separate peace; Clemenceau and Barthou not Caillaux had been the names whispered in the Palais Bourbon's corridors. The implications of a separate peace which made it so desirable to Germany made it even more undesirable to France. Renunciation of its allies was tantamount to French abandonment of its great power status. A more subtle but nonetheless operative impulse for French refusal may have been their inability to conceive of Europe without the alliance system.[17]

The Germans may have been guaranteed failure by their own behavior. Lacking sufficient singleness of purpose and confidence in their own assumptions, they were unwilling to grant concessions which might have tempted the French and need have been temporary in any case. Although unlikely to respond Caillaux might have been induced to advocate peace by conditions more attractive than those France could expect from continuing the war. German leaders could not, however, bring themselves to grant more than token and grudging concessions. They shared with large portions of their public aspirations at French expense. Perhaps victims of their own propaganda, they believed that France needed peace and would therefore not have to be paid for concluding it. Unable to escape the spectre of a postwar Anglo-French alliance, retention of strategic points seemed necessary for a future war. Perhaps the Germans like the French could not destroy the alliance system because they too were incapable of envisaging Europe without it. Finally and not least important, German policy may have been affected by Germany's ambiguous position. The Germans had been unable to shatter the Entente, win a total military victory and guarantee their continued predominance on the continent; some German leaders were in fact concerned that Germany could not maintain what it had in a protracted war of exhaustion. Germany had, however, demonstrated its military superiority over its continental opponents and occupied considerable enemy territory. Germany was at once too successful but not successful enough—too successful to make concessions seem necessary but not successful enough to make them unnecessary.

CHAPTER V

RUSSIA AND FRANCE LATE 1916

The pursuit of a separate understanding with France during early 1916 had implicated German policy toward Russia. As long as the Verdun campaign promised to produce a French request for peace, Russia remained a secondary consideration. This order of priorities was based on several premises. It assumed that England was Germany's main enemy and would accept German continental hegemony only by the defection of its continental "tools" France, Russia, Italy, Belgium and Serbia. Believing France to be the most important to England and yet the most vulnerable whereas Russia was no longer a threat but could not be defeated, Falkenhayn had concentrated the bulk of his forces in the west. He had thereby differed sharply with not only the German commanders in the east, Hindenburg and Ludendorff, but also many other high ranking German officers and the Austro-Hungarians, who all contended that Russia was both threatening and susceptible to defeat. Although these so-called "easterners" granted that England was the ultimate enemy and that the defeat of France was desirable, they felt that victory in the west was impossible until Russia was defeated, the eastern situation stabilized, and *all* German power concentrated against France. Falkenhayn had, however, managed to win the support of the Kaiser, naval, conservative and chauvinistic groups by linking the Verdun campaign with intensified U-boat warfare and the easterners were forced to postpone their resistance until the campaign had failed and their estimate of Russian power had been vindicated at the beginning of June 1916.[1]

In contrast to both previous and subsequent debates over the relative importance of the eastern and western fronts, German civilian leaders played a somewhat passive role in the discussions at the end of 1915. Faced with the failure of their efforts to separate Russia in 1915, they consented to Falkenhayn's strategy in the hope of forcing France to conclude peace. When Falkenhayn tied his strategy to the U-boat, Bethmann and Jagow ostensibly became even more committed to the Verdun campaign than Falkenhayn himself since they hoped it would make intensification of U-boat warfare unnecessary. In reality they remained sceptical regarding Russian impotence, doubts which were the basis for their continued receptivity during the first half of 1916—particularly after the Verdun attack faltered—to the possibility of a separate understanding with Russia. Because Bethmann had been thus maneuvered into becoming an outspoken supporter of the Verdun campaign and to submerge his concern about the eastern front, his opposition to Falkenhayn became even more bitter when the campaign failed and Russian strength was demonstrated in June 1916.[2]

The decision to seek a separate peace with France during early 1916 caused Berlin not only to subordinate a peace with Russia but also to revise its war aims in the east. As long as a separate peace with Russia had been the main German objective during 1915, war aims at Russia's expense had remained relatively moderate and informal. When peace with France became the first priority at the end of 1915, German leaders considered more seriously the fulfillment of their eastern aspirations. This departure was immediately registered on the barometer of Russo-German relations, the Polish question. Having withstood both Austro-Hungarian and domestic pressure for a definitive decision on Poland, Bethmann indicated soon after his approval of the Verdun campaign in December 1915 that he was considering an anti-Russian Polish policy. By the beginning of February 1916 the civilian leaders renounced their temporizing over the possibility of Austrian control of Poland and began instead to advocate an autonomous Polish buffer state under German authority. This would remain their policy until a separate understanding with Russia again became their primary goal during the summer of 1916.[3]

Failure to achieve an understanding with Russia during 1915 likewise persuaded German leaders to revise their opinion on which Russian political element was most inclined to make peace with Germany. There had been signs during the autumn of 1915 that the Russian dynasty's power was being qualified both by an increase in parliamentary demands and by the Tsar's personal isolation which had previously been expected to permit an independent policy but now appeared instead to be subservience to pro-war elements (such as the British ambassador) or even political impotence. Berlin consequently made no effort after 1915 to arrange a separate understanding with the Tsar on the basis of dynastic interests but turned increasingly to different and slightly broader sections of the Russian political spectrum—first the right and then the middle.[4]

While the last preparations were being made for the Verdun campaign, Russian events seemed more encouraging to peace. Boris Stürmer, an arch-reactionary and bitter antagonist of the pro-war

Liberal (Cadet) Party, replaced J. L. Goremykin as prime minister at the beginning of February 1916. Although German intelligence sources initially differed as to its significance, this development seemed favorable, especially when it was suggested to the Germans two weeks later that Sazonov might consider peace if Russia were given the Dardanelles. Although Jagow replied that free passage but not control over the Straits would be granted, no Russian response was forthcoming.[5]

During the initial assaults on Verdun in February 1916 there began what seemed the most promising means of achieving peace with Russia. S. Ushida, the Japanese envoy in Stockholm, suggested discussions to the German envoy, Lucius. As seems to have been the case in sporadic discussions between representatives of the two countries during the previous year, the Japanese probably wanted to cover themselves in the event of a victory for the Central Powers. Assuming this to be Ushida's motive and anticipating that success at Verdun would render a separate peace with Russia unnecessary, Lucius refused the suggestion, even though Ushida remarked enticingly that "Japan possessed the key to a separate peace between Russia and Germany.[6] When operations at Verdun bogged down in mid-March, Jagow reprimanded Lucius for discouraging Ushida and ordered a resumption of talks although without definite commitments which might encourage the French. Seeking at once to expedite conversations but to insure that they could be disavowed if necessary, Jagow and Bethmann authorized the brash industrialist, Hugo Stinnes, to meet Ushida at the end of the month. In exchange for German recognition of Japanese aspirations in China, Ushida tantalized Stinnes with the prospect of a Russo-Japanese-German understanding enhanced by the possibility of replacing the Anglo-Japanese treaty of 1903 with a German-Japanese Entente to divert Russia toward India.[7] Increased tension with the United States over the U-boat made the Germans more amenable. Although he refused the general peace which Ushida now obstinately advocated, Lucius offered further concessions in Asia for Japanese mediation of a Russo-German understanding which Berlin believed Tokyo could produce. Such a Russo-German arrangement was envisaged by the Germans as quite different from the revived Three Emperors' League they had contemplated during 1915. Believing an actual alliance with Russia would "bring us into fundamental opposition to the West" and thus commit Germany to a policy of *"finis Britanniae à tout prix,"* Jagow instead advocated merely a separate peace with Russia which might persuade Britain to renounce further struggle and recognize German continental hegemony.[8] German hopes were, however, dashed when Ushida insisted on a general peace. The Kaiser summarized the German position with his sometime clarity and usual brusqueness: "As soon as it becomes obvious that no separate peace can be concluded, the whole swindle is of no importance; one can then accomplish more by thrashing." The episode ended when it became known that the Japanese had kept their allies informed of the negotiations, probably in order to extract larger concessions from the Russians.[9]

This failure and the apparent improvement in the prospects of peace with France made an understanding with Russia at once less feasible and less necessary during late May 1916. To another possibility of negotiations with Russia Berlin reacted with conspicuously less alacrity than it had to the Japanese. Russian Minister-President Stürmer reportedly requested German conditions for a separate understanding and offered territory in eastern Europe in exchange for concessions from Austria-Hungary and Turkey including free passage of the Dardanelles. Jagow and Bethmann replied that Germany would not be interested unless Russia demonstrated its willingness more positively and France refused to consider peace. The prospect disappeared abruptly when Russia launched an offensive at the beginning of June and thereby demonstrated that it had not been rendered militarily impotent.[10]

German civilian leaders thus sought a separate peace with Russia during the spring of 1916 but subordinated it to an understanding with France expected to result from the Verdun campaign. Since peace with France would have facilitated eastern annexations, they were discussed more seriously than theretofore but Bethmann and Jagow refused to commit themselves to any particular aims. Had a separate understanding with Russia seemed to depend on it, they might have renounced most annexations from Russia; in fact they believed that the Russians would grant extensive territorial concessions to achieve peace with Germany. The German civilian leaders thus continued to assume that peace conditions could not be firmly established until negotiations were actually in progress. Their primary goal remained what it had been since late 1914: *bona fide* conversations for a separate peace with Russia and/or France.[11]

* * * * *

At the beginning of June 1916 began a series of events which would culminate in the reorientation of German policy during August. Bethmann became increasingly convinced that Russia had to be removed from the war before France could be forced to conclude peace.

It would therefore be necessary to reestablish the priority of the eastern front. Because he refused to do so, Falkenhayn would have to be replaced by Hindenburg. Hindenburg's appointment likewise seemed mandatory on domestic political grounds: only he could persuade the German people to accept conditions moderate enough to allow a separate peace. Thus the eastern front's priority and Hindenburg's appointment seemed mutually dependent since the eastern front would be given priority only if Hindenburg were appointed and Hindenburg would be appointed only if the eastern front were given priority.

As long as the Verdun offensive promised to produce a French request for peace, Bethmann disregarded his differences of opinion with Falkenhayn since their policies had run parallel. When Falkenhayn seemed, however, to forget the original purpose of the offensive and refused at the end of May to make concessions in order to arrange a separate peace with France, Bethmann considered renewing his efforts to replace him with Hindenburg. The crucial point in their relationship occurred with the Russian attack on Austria-Hungary at the beginning of June. This revival of intensive two-front war destroyed the most important precondition for the Verdun operation's success, namely, German concentration in the west. Falkenhayn's failure to take Verdun at the end of June was even more awkward than his inability to win the war quickly at the end of 1914. Not only had he failed to defeat France but the facile recourse of offering Russia a separate peace had been removed by Russian refusals during 1915. Concentration against Russia was the only option but required renunciation of the Verdun campaign to which Falkenhayn had committed his reputation against his rivals, Hindenburg and Ludendorff. Falkenhayn consequently had to choose between Verdun and his office: he could either recognize Verdun's failure and assume the eastern command himself or continue the Verdun attack and risk augmentation of his rivals' power if the eastern front received higher priority. Unwilling to admit failure, he chose the alternative of intransigence in the hope that the eastern situation would somehow be stabilized sufficiently to allow the attack on Verdun to continue.[12]

Falkenhayn initially succeeded in preventing an eastern reorientation. The British Somme offensive in July at first provided him with the rationale against turning east since all available troops were required in the west; this argument proved, however, to be a double-edged sword when he was forced to discontinue the Verdun attack to avoid a British breakthrough. Bethmann and his supporters meanwhile tried to improve the eastern military situation and prepare for Falkenhayn's removal by urging Hindenburg's appointment as supreme commander of all Central Powers forces on the eastern front. Falkenhayn managed to parry this thrust temporarily with the assertion that the eastern situation did not require a major German effort and thus Central Powers forces need not be unified under Hindenburg's command.[13]

When the Austro-Hungarian military position became undeniably precarious at the end of July, Bethmann was able to make its rectification contingent upon Hindenburg's appointment as supreme commander in the east. In order to overcome the Kaiser's resistance, Bethmann reiterated the contention that the German people would accept a "disappointing peace with him but not without him" in command. In spite of Falkenhayn's threat to resign, the Kaiser reluctantly acquiesced at the end of July. Hindenburg's appointment did not, however, cause an immediate reorientation of German strategy. Continued British pressure at the Somme and a major Italian offensive insured that eastern considerations must remain secondary during the first half of August. Still lacking recognition of the primary necessity for an understanding with Russia, Bethmann was in fact obliged to discuss territorial aspirations in Poland with the Austro-Hungarians but managed to postpone any definite departure. Falkenhayn's removal was nonetheless made virtually inevitable since his judgment had been questioned and victory had now become inextricably connected with Hindenburg's personality.[14]

The case for turning east was reinforced by apparent developments in France and Russia. While the prospect of an understanding with the French diminished in July, Russian willingness seemed to increase. On the day Falkenhayn discontinued his attack on Verdun, Berlin was informed that certain Russian Conservative and Liberal parliamentarians were inclined to discuss an understanding with Germany. They reportedly recognized that "a continuation of the war with Germany was pointless" and expected to initiate serious discussions in the near future. Although the Russians took no further initiative, this episode seemed to have "great promise" and inspired "joy" at the German Foreign Office. It was also reported in Berlin that Stürmer had removed Saxonov for political reasons and had assumed the office of foreign minister himself—events interpreted by German leaders as "an indisputable sign of [Russian] desire to initiate peace negotiations." Jagow contemplated "renewed peace feelers" but decided that the unresolved military situation necessitated a temporary postponement of these contacts and concentrated instead on efforts to influence the Russian press toward a Russo-German understanding.[15]

Bethmann was finally able in mid-August to gain the Kaiser's acceptance of the eastern front's primacy. When the western and southern fronts appeared secure, the Kaiser came around to "the position long argued by Bethmann: that Russia should be militarily forced out of the [enemy] coalition—whereby France would probably be carried along with it and Germany would thus retain a free hand against England." To facilitate an understanding with Russia, the Kaiser ordered that no decision be made regarding Poland, that Russia be bribed with the prospect of dynastic solidarity and Austro-Hungarian territory, and that contacts with Petrograd be resumed immediately. With this encouragement, Bethmann again committed himself to the attainment of a separate understanding with Russia. He heartily applauded the Kaiser's suggestion that no decision in the Polish question should be made and asserted that there were definite signs of Russian willingness to initiate peace negotiations. If Germany brought sufficient military pressure to bear by assuming the defensive in the west and concentrating in the east, Bethmann believed that Germany could "blow up the Entente" and achieve "a final decision in this *Volkskrieg*," i.e., French surrender and British isolation.[16]

It was obvious to Bethmann and his colleagues that the military strategy necessary to achieve these results required Hindenburg's replacement of Falkenhayn. From the moment Hindenburg had been appointed to command in the east at the end of July, he and Falkenhayn had disagreed over reinforcements, i.e., the relative importance of the two fronts. When the Kaiser accepted Bethmann's argument that the defeat of Russia deserved priority, Falkenhayn sought a showdown. While agreeing in principle with Bethmann's strategy, Falkenhayn tried to render it unfeasible by committing all available troops to renewed operations at Verdun and unnecessary by arguing that Rumania would not attack and that Russia was already ripe for an understanding. After a final attempt to persuade Falkenhayn had failed, Bethmann informed the Kaiser that only Falkenhayn's replacement by Hindenburg could prevent Rumanian entry and produce Russian exit. But the Kaiser still refused. Only when Rumania in fact declared war against Austria-Hungary on August 27 did the Kaiser become so disillusioned with Falkenhayn that he immediately appointed Hindenburg. After months of agitation, Bethmann had finally succeeded in accommodating strategy and strategist to his policy.[17]

It soon became clear, however, that Bethmann's victory was both brief and pyrrhic. Rumanian entry which had produced Hindenburg's appointment had also lessened the likelihood of a rapid separate peace with Russia; indeed Bethmann was momentarily so shaken that he dismissed the possibility of an understanding with either Russia or France before winter.[18] More important, Bethmann proved mistaken in his estimate of Hindenburg and Ludendorff. He had sought their appointment "for reasons of war and peace" in the belief that they shared his views on strategy and policy. In particular he assumed that they recognized the necessity of isolating England through separate understandings with Russia and France which might in turn require Hindenburg's using his personal prestige to win the German people's acceptance of moderate war aims.[19] Hindenburg and Ludendorff immediately indicated their doubts that England would make peace if isolated from France and Russia; in fact they assumed instead that the continental powers could be defeated only if England were first forced to sue for peace by intensified U-boat warfare. Nor did they seek a separate peace with Russia through concentration in the east but merely stabilization of the eastern front in order to allow intensified U-boat warfare against England—as Falkenhayn had advocated a year before in preparation for his Verdun offensive. Far from being inclined to win popular acceptance of moderate war aims, they advocated extensive annexations as the reward of the victory they expected. Perhaps the supreme irony of the change in personnel was that the prospect of a separate understanding with Russia would revive during the autumn because of the successful German campaign against Rumania under Falkenhayn's command. So diligently sought by Bethmann, the change in strategists would complicate rather than facilitate policy.[20]

* * * * *

Bethmann's conduct during the autumn of 1916 was conditioned by the realization that his policy might be threatened if it were not successful in the near future. Unless England were forced to conclude peace, the war might continue until the exhaustion of one side which was likely to be Germany. After recovering from the shock of Rumanian entry, he consequently resumed his pursuit of separate understandings with Russia and France both more purposefully and desperately than ever before.

The possibility of intensified U-boat warfare and the momentary unlikelihood of a separate peace combined to cause Bethmann and Jagow to consider their usual recourse when Germany's position was in danger of worsening, namely, an American suggestion of general peace. Since Hindenburg and Ludendorff believed that U-boat warfare should be intensified once Germany's eastern flank was secure, improved prospects of a German victory over Rumania in September made intensified U-boat warfare more likely. Bethmann tried to avoid this eventuality by encouraging an American *démarche*. If it were refused by the Entente but accepted in principle by the Central Powers, the United States might conclude that the Entente was determined to extend the war unnecessarily and then refuse further aid. Such a public discussion might have the further advantage of improving the atmosphere for Bethmann's policy not only by encouraging French and Russian peace parties but also by gaining support within Germany. An American move seemed the best way of producing these results since it might preserve American neutrality and avoid the impression of German weakness.[21]

The Rumanian situation's improvement during September meanwhile encouraged hopes for a peace with Russia. Previous Russian refusals as well as the augmented demands of Hindenburg and Ludendorff for war aims from Russia caused the civilians to alter their approach. They had to resolve the basic dilemma that those Russian elements which were apparently inclined to peace (first the Tsar and then the Conservatives) were incapable of concluding it, whereas those which were capable (such as the Liberals) did not want it. Reportedly concerned primarily to preserve the dynasty and the old order, the Conservatives required certain territorial acquisitions (the Dardanelles, in particular) as alternatives to domestic reform. Since it was, however, dubious that the Conservatives were sufficiently powerful to conclude peace on their own, the Liberals would have to be enlisted either to support the Conservatives or to replace them. The Germans believed that the Liberals were mainly interested in reform which they assumed Germany would resist but were opposed to annexations which they regarded as a Conservative device to avoid reform. It accordingly seemed necessary first to destroy the Conservative case for annexations by a striking victory in Rumania and then to allay Liberal fears of German opposition to reform. Bethmann therefore announced in the Reichstag at the end of September that Germany was disinterested in Russian domestic affairs. The Germans in effect pursued the double policy of resuming contact with the Conservatives while trying to win over the Liberals.[22]

Hindenburg and Ludendorff meanwhile complicated this policy by demanding proclamation of Polish autonomy so as to encourage formation of a Polish army on the Central Powers' side. Since Jagow believed the Russian Conservatives already regarded Poland as lost whereas the Liberals desired to exclude all non-Russian territories, he thought Poland "immaterial" and doubted it would render an understanding either "impossible or considerably more difficult." Although Bethmann had sought to foster a Liberal initiative in his Reichstag speech, he had not yet become convinced that Poland was irrelevant and recommended against a declaration on Poland since it might "seriously endanger the possibility of a separate peace" with Russia. When prospects for such an understanding suddenly seemed to improve, Bethmann was able to defer a move on Poland.[23]

The negotiations with Russia which appeared imminent at the beginning of October would mark the last German attempt to reach an understanding with the pre-revolutionary regime. The enigmatic and unscrupulous Duma Vice-President, A. D. Protopopov, who had conducted secret talks with German agents during June, was appointed Minister of the Interior by Stürmer on October 1 and further domestic developments favorable to peace were expected by the Germans. When they were advised that the moment was opportune for an approach, Bethmann and Jagow authorized conversations with the Russian envoy in Stockholm, Anatole Nekliudov. Military operations in Rumania meanwhile progressed to the point where a separate peace with Rumania seemed possible. After it was reported that Nekliudov still regarded free passage of the Dardanelles as a *sine qua non*, Bethmann advocated extracting this concession from Turkey in order to achieve an understanding with Russia.[24]

The absence of a Russian response obliged Bethmann to alter his approach to an eastern understanding. Nekliudov's reported admission that Russia expected Poland to become independent in any case persuaded Bethmann that a German declaration of Polish autonomy might not necessarily constitute "an absolute barrier to an understanding with Russia;" he was, however, not sufficiently confident to advocate the declaration himself and left the decision to the Kaiser. This proved to be a tactical blunder since Bethmann thereby renounced an advantage he had won earlier in the month when the Kaiser had ruled that the Polish question was primarily political and thus Bethmann's domain. Hindenburg and Ludendorff immediately seized their opportunity: claiming diplomatic considerations were subordinate to military since only total victory was either possible or desirable, they demanded that "even the most definite prospects of a rapid understanding with Russia" had to give way to the need for Polish troops. Bethmann acceded but tried to minimize the decision's negative effects by asking that it not be announced when Bucharest fell, i.e., the moment expected to be most favorable for an understanding with Russia. His reluctant acquiescence was probably due in part to the recognition that a declaration had become unavoidable and in part to the belief that the Russian Conservatives were unable to conclude a separate peace while the Liberals were unconcerned about Poland.[25]

The Germans accordingly sought to prepare the way for an understanding with the Russian Liberals. In requesting the assistance of King Ferdinand of Bulgaria, Bethmann explained that it was necessary for the Central Powers to conclude a separate peace with one of their enemies, of which Russia seemed the most likely despite the repeated refusals of "this unfathomable sphinx." Although willing, the Russian Conservative government was unable to make peace because it lacked popular support and was paralyzed by the Tsar's indecision. Since only the Liberals were strong enough to conclude peace, they should be persuaded to take the initiative. As Jagow had argued a month before, Bethmann now contended that the Liberals were interested primarily in reform and continued the war only because they believed that defeat and revolution would make reform more likely and that Germany opposed it. The Central Powers therefore had the dual task of threatening Russia with defeat while indicating that they did not oppose reform. Since the Conservatives remained in power only by promising such "safety valves" against reform as the Dardanelles, the way would be opened for a Liberal government if Russia's prospects for possession of the Dardanelles were destroyed by Austro-German victory over Rumania. He had already sought to reassure the Liberals that Germany was disinterested in Russian domestic affairs. Bethmann concluded that the time was near for suggesting conversations to the Liberals.[26] King Ferdinand agreed that Russia seemed inclined to peace and that the Liberals should be encouraged but advised against completely writing off the Conservatives, for whom free passage of the Dardanelles remained a *sine qua non*. Not sufficiently sure of his own arguments to reject this advice, Jagow agreed to keep open the door to an understanding with the Conservatives on the basis of free passage. When Russia had been threatened with defeat, the Liberals would, however, become more likely candidates.[27]

The possibility of awaiting such favorable developments was threatened at the end of October by the report that the English were considering a public suggestion of general peace based on the *status quo ante bellum*. German leaders feared such a move since acceptance might imply German renunciation to continental hegemony and perpetuation of the Entente but refusal suggested that the German government wished to prolong the war. Bethmann and his supporters decided to avoid such a choice by anticipating the English move with a German suggestion of peace on the basis of the existing *status quo*. Because of the pacifism which they assumed was prevalent in all enemy countries, a German offer might be accepted and thereby confirm German continental hegemony. The more likely eventuality of the Entente governments' refusal might ignite a popular revolt among the French and Russian populations, encourage separate understandings, strengthen the German government's position at home, and discourage American entry despite intensified U-boat warfare. Bethmann consequently began preparations for a German statement.[28] The Kaiser unqualifiedly supported the idea but Hindenburg and Ludendorff—while expecting only favorable results—demanded that the offer be made at the moment of German military success and after the Polish proclamation so as to avoid giving the impression of German weakness. Bethmann agreed that the move should be coordinated with a German military success since it might encourage an initiative by the Russian Liberals but only reluctantly acceded on the Polish question which he had already conceded to military considerations. Although the offer was postponed, it would become integral to Bethmann's subsequent strategy and ultimately be regarded by him as the decisive impulse for achieving separate understandings with France and Russia.[29]

The offer's purpose changed by the beginning of November. Rather than primarily a countermove against a British suggestion which now seemed unlikely, it became a device to foster Russian and French pacificism. Since he had committed himself to making the Polish proclamation before the peace offer, Bethmann decided an understanding with Russia would be least jeopardized if the unfavorable effects of the proclamation were allowed to wear off before the offer was made and accordingly issued the proclamation on November 5. Meanwhile the offer's formulation was adjusted to conform with its new purpose. It was decided that the demand for the *status quo* which was to have replaced the British *status quo ante bellum* formula should not be mentioned since a separate peace might best be encouraged if no condition was indicated. Such a procedure was in fact more consistent with Bethmann's view throughout the war that his diplomatic freedom of action in negotiations should be preserved by avoiding prior discussions or commitments. Likewise pacifism in enemy countries might also be fostered if Germany concealed its intention to retain occupied territories. When Vienna demanded in mid-November that conditions be worked out *before* the offer was made, Berlin therefore refused but at the same time encouraged the Austro-Hungarian suggestion of a peace move so as to shore up its alliance. Bethmann meanwhile resumed his efforts to foster an American mediatory offer since it might be less complicated than one by the Central Powers. Berlin thus conducted "a policy of two irons in the fire:" while developing a Central Powers *démarche*, an American move was sought.[30]

In the interim prospects for a separate peace with Russia were altered by Russian domestic developments. The Polish proclamation provided the decisive impulse for a series of events which culminated in the fall of Stürmer's government in late November. The Germans had already become convinced in early November that Stürmer lacked the strength to conduct peace negotiations. Since only the Liberals were presumed powerful enough to take such an initiative, it would be necessary to bring them to power. From the moment they were induced by the Polish proclamation to attack Stürmer, the Liberals demonstrated, however, that their policy had been completely misinterpreted in Berlin: even more imperialistic than the Conservatives, they accused Stürmer not of trying to subvert reform with annexations but of subordinating Poland and other war aims to a separate peace with Germany. The Germans were forced to readjust their policy once again and decided that the Liberals like the Conservatives would conclude peace only when defeat threatened and their aims could be fulfilled only with German approval. Assuming any Russian setback would increase Liberal willingness to make peace, the fall of Bucharest was perceived by the Germans as the appropriate moment for a suggestion of negotiations. In the expectation that Liberal leader P. N. Miliukov would eventually be willing to make peace under these conditions, Jagow tried to arrange contact with him. Berlin had thus reverted to its original method of achieving peace with Russia but had altered the potential negotiator.[31]

The approach to a separate peace with France was simultaneously readjusted. The Germans had dismissed the possibility of an arrangement with the French for the two months following the failure of the Verdun campaign in August. Indeed the French were so heartened by their success that they expected a "breakthrough to the Rhine" because of their local victories around Verdun, the Anglo-French attacks at the Somme, and Rumanian entry. Even after the Somme attacks diminished in intensity in mid-October, Bethmann doubted that peace with France was likely "for the moment." The threat of a British peace offer at the end of October, however, induced the Germans to reconsider the possibility of peace with France. They decided that the prospect of an understanding with France as with Russia might be improved by a German public peace suggestion. Hoping that the defeat of Rumania and a Russo-German arrangement might cause the fall of Aristide Briand's government and a Franco-German *rapprochement*, Jagow sounded out the feasibility of mediation between France and Germany through King Alfonso of Spain.[32]

The French internal and external situation could in fact be interpreted as conducive to peace. It was frequently reported to the Germans that Rumanian defeat and French failure at Salonika would precipitate Briand's fall. In an effort to exploit sectional differences and the pacifist sentiment reported in southern France, Jagow informed ostensible French agents that "France could have had peace without noteworthy territorial sacrifices" for a long time. The undeniable lack of any striking Anglo-French military success on the western front was believed by the Germans to have fostered French defeatism. German leaders thus felt at the end of November that both French and Russian hopes for victory and fulfillment of war aims had been sufficiently shattered to produce willingness to consider peace.[33]

The confluence of military, diplomatic and domestic events persuaded Bethmann to make his desperate attempt to launch peace negotiations at the beginning of December. The imminent fall of Bucharest would produce the impression of German strength while promoting French and Russian pessimism. Since it appeared that an American mediatory suggestion would be postponed, a German initiative was mandatory both in order to exploit the favorable Rumanian situation and to encourage American neutrality in the event of intensified U-boat warfare which seemed increasingly likely. By demonstrating to the German people that their government did not wish to prolong the war unnecessarily, Bethmann hoped for sufficient popular support to overcome the resistance of Hindenburg and Ludendorff to peace talks. Bethmann's offer of December 12 to the Entente was consequently as convincing and pacific a statement of German willingness to discuss peace as the generals' increasing opposition seemed to allow.[34]

It was uncertain what reaction the *démarche* would produce but the Germans hoped for a number of favorable eventualities. If the Entente as a whole agreed to discuss a general peace, the Germans would demand recognition of the existing *status quo* and thus German continental hegemony. If the French and Russians responded but the British refused, dissension would be encouraged and separate understandings sought. A refusal by the Entente as a whole was most likely, in which case Berlin would support the efforts of French and Russian peace parties to force peace on their governments. An Entente refusal might also persuade the United States to remain neutral even in the event of intensified U-boat warfare.[35]

As long as a positive Entente response seemed possible, Berlin encouraged conversations and sought to avoid actions which might deter them. In order not to alienate the Russian Liberals, Zimmermann refused an ostensible approach from the Russian Conservatives. The German offer reportedly was met with great popular if not official French response and a reputed French suggestion of talks coincidentally arrived in Berlin on the eve of the German offer. Bethmann and Zimmermann meanwhile investigated again the possibility of mediation between Germany and France through King Alfonso of Spain. Although Zimmermann's hopes soon disappeared, Bethmann remained optimistic until the end. His hopes were bolstered by President Woodrow Wilson's mediatory offer since Bethmann assumed Wilson would not have acted without Entente, particularly English, approval. Yet the German offer was refused out of hand by all the Entente powers, who recognized it for what it was—an effort to employ peace as a means of winning the war. Even Bethmann admitted at the end of December that the tactic had failed either to shatter the Entente or insure American neutrality.[36]

CHAPTER VI
RUSSIA EARLY 1917

The undeniable failure of efforts to split the Entente caused a radical alteration in German strategy. At the beginning of January 1917 Bethmann reluctantly acquiesced in the decision to conduct unlimited U-boat warfare which had been demanded exactly a year before by Falkenhayn and had become virtually inevitable with the appointment of Hindenburg and Ludendorff. Bethmann, most civilian leaders and many military and naval men had opposed the decision in the expectation that it would bring the United States into the war against Germany and thereby insure German defeat. Their opposition to the U-boat was consistent with the view that the war was essentially a limited struggle between coalitions and would be won with military and diplomatic means. Hindenburg, Ludendorff and the Admiralty argued in favor of unlimited U-boat warfare which they felt would force Britain to sue for peace before it could be rescued by the United States. This position was consistent with their frontal approach to problems and the assumption that the war was essentially total, i.e., involved not merely diplomatic and military means but also economic, social and psychological aspects and ultimately required the exhaustion of one side.

The opponents of unlimited U-boat warfare had been successful before 1917 for several reasons. Falkenhayn and the other advocates had only minimal prestige and thus lacked the ultimate recourse of threatening to resign. Probably more important, the alternative diplomatic and military means of splitting the Entente and defeating its members separately still seemed feasible before the end of 1916. These factors changed by the end of 1916. Hindenburg's prestige was such that he was generally regarded—even by opponents of the U-boat like Bethmann—as the only personality who could persuade the German people either to continue the war or to accept an unattractive peace; Hindenburg therefore could employ the *ultima ratio* of threatening to resign as Falkenhayn and the other advocates of unrestricted U-boat warfare could not. Furthermore the alternative of dividing the Entente with diplomatic and military means had failed undeniably with Bethmann's unsuccessful peace offer at the end of 1916. The matter was accordingly decided in a conference at the beginning of January 1917 and unrestricted U-boat warfare announced at the end of the month. Hindenburg's prestige and Bethmann's failure combined to tip the scales.[1]

This decision was a turning point both in German policy and the war. The policy of splitting the Entente had not always dominated German actions theretofore but it had been the most consistent theme after November 1914; after January 1917 it would not disappear but would be applied under more severe restrictions. This change of policy affected German perceptions of their enemies. Efforts to split the Entente had been directed at England's continental "tools," France and Russia, on the assumption that England would resign itself to German continental domination if abandoned by its allies. Unrestricted U-boat warfare reversed the roles: if England were forced to sue for peace, its continental allies would hopefully follow and separate understandings with them consequently would become effect rather than cause. In a more general sense, diplomatic policy itself became less critical since the war's outcome seemed to depend on the U-boat's efficiency. The decision on U-boat warfare also marked a distinct step in the transition from relatively limited, coalition warfare toward total war. Control of policy-making simultaneously shifted from a relative balance between civilian and military leaders to the new High Command. Finally the U-boat decision was the first in a series of events breaking the logjam which had characterized the war since November 1914. The conflict might have remained stalemated without foreseeable end had it not been for American entry and the Russian revolution which combined to alter the subsequent course of the war and thereby the context of German policy.

* * * * *

Bethmann and his supporters did not renounce their policy despite its failure and the declaration of unlimited U-boat warfare. They even granted that the U-boat might make the Entente more amenable to peace but assumed that it would still be necessary to split their opponents at an eventual peace conference. The prospects for peace appeared dim, however, during the winter of 1917. The Germans felt that conversations—particularly with the French—would be pointless until the expected Anglo-French spring offensive had been repulsed and British collapse because of the U-boat had forced France to recognize that victory was impossible. Berlin therefore merely maintained contacts with prospective negotiators and encouraged pacificism in enemy countries whenever possible.[2]

Prospects of peace suddenly seemed to revive during late March 1917. At first an understanding with France appeared more likely than peace with Russia. Bethmann and Zimmermann were informed

in mid-March by the new Austro-Hungarian Foreign Minister, Ottokar Czernin, that France had requested conversations with Vienna.
This was a conscious misrepresentation on Czernin's part since the
impulse had originated with the new Habsburg Emperor, Carl. In
communicating it to the Germans, Czernin advocated accepting the
ostensible suggestion and requested a program of maximal and minimal German war aims. Bethmann was sceptical: although the U-boat
campaign against Britain and Russian domestic troubles could have
made the French somewhat more inclined to peace, he doubted that
they would negotiate until their spring offensive had failed. Yet he
did not wish to miss any opportunity for an understanding and consequently agreed to conversations but stipulated that no condition
be mentioned until genuine negotiations were underway. After
Czernin was informed that large German concessions in Alsace-
Lorraine were necessary, it became Vienna's objective to cajole,
bribe or frighten Berlin into making them. Bethmann not only refused but also made even the smallest border corrections in the provinces contingent upon German acquisition of French territory
around Briey-Longwy and extensive rights in Belgium. To avoid this
stumbling block, Bethmann reiterated his assumption that no precise
condition should be mentioned until the initiation of *bona fide* talks
since, once begun, they would not be discontinued. Zimmermann
was even more obstinate because he believed that the domestic disturbances inside Russia and the failure of the Anglo-French spring
offensive would make France accept a peace without any German concession. Faced with this intransigence, Vienna offered to make concessions to the Entente and even to Germany but warned that the
Habsburg Empire might disintegrate if peace were not concluded
quickly. Although he refused again, Bethmann sought to preserve
the French contact.[3]

Because of the unpromising conditions demanded by Vienna,
Berlin initiated its own approaches to the French. When the long-
anticipated fall of Briand's cabinet became known in Berlin, the Germans decided that the moment was propitious. Zimmermann consequently informed the French through a Swiss mediator that "Germany is inclined to allow France a favorable peace if it asks in time;"
despite unattractive conditions, Zimmermann and his mediator expected a positive response. Bethmann was somewhat less sanguine
and more inclined to offer concessions, however limited; in accord
with his consistent supposition that conversations would be precluded if conditions were mentioned beforehand, Bethmann conspicuously avoided any mention of France in his Reichstag speech at the end

of March. The possibility of a meeting between the President of the French Chamber, Paul Deschanel, and the German political adviser in Brussels, Oskar Lancken, was meanwhile reported in Berlin. It thus appeared at the beginning of April that "an understanding with France might be possible" in the near future.[4]

The prospect of peace with Russia had meanwhile improved to such an extent that it seemed even more, promising than an understanding with France. The Germans were informed in March that serious domestic disturbances had occurred in Russia and realized by the end of the month that revoluton had broken out. German leaders hoped for revolution in Russia, used it as a threat to induce Russian Conservatives to sue for peace, tried to remain informed about its likelihood, and sought to encourage it whenever possible. The event nonetheless came as a surprise because the Germans had never taken predictions of revolution very seriously—and—to the extent that they had anticipated it—had expected it only after Russia had been forced to conclude a disadvantageous peace (as in 1905) and as a result of national rather than social tensions. Events had disproven these expectations: revolution preceded peace and was precipitated by social discontent. Instead of peace causing revolution, revolution might facilitate peace.[5]

There reportedly existed three Russian currents of opinion regaring peace. The Conservatives apparently wanted an unfavorable peace (either immediately or after further defeats) in order to expedite a counter-revolution. Then in control of the Provisional Government, the Liberals desired an immediate, moderate peace in order to consolidate their position. The Social Democrats would resist peace until they could exploit it to gain power, at which time they would seek concessions similar to those desired by the Liberals. German Center Party Reichstag member Matthias Erzberger, who regarded rapid understandings with Russia and France as imperative, advocated peace with the Liberal Provisional Government as the quickest and surest means of removing Russia from the war; since they "desired genuine friendship with Germany" and had achieved their major war aim in the "abolition of autocracy," the Liberals would make peace if openly encouraged by Berlin. Erzberger's view seemed to be corroborated by a Bulgarian contact with Russian Liberal leader Paul Miliukov. Bethmann was convinced and consequently addressed to the Russian government an encouraging Reichstag speech along the lines prescribed by Erzberger. The Provisional Government's "Statement on War Aims" was interpreted by Bethmann as a veiled response.[6]

Other German elements were, however, less disposed toward peace with Russia. In order to respond publicly to the Russians, Bethmann had to win over the Kaiser, who was in an optimistic mood about the prospect of dictating peace to Russia and thus opposed negotiations in which Germany might have to renounce annexations. Bethmann nonetheless arranged for a press release which at least recognized the Russian statement and reiterated German willingness to discuss peace. Despite the Kaiser's refusal and the High Command's mounting opposition, Bethmann decided that the Provisional Government's reported desire for peace could not be encouraged by vague public pronouncements but required genuine negotiations. He therefore confidentially authorized Erzberger to follow up his ostensible contact with the Provisional Government in order to arrange an armistice on whatever terms were required to launch talks. It momentarily seemed that Bethmann might be able to present the generals and Kaiser with a *fait accompli* in the form of negotiations for a quick eastern understanding which they would then find difficult to refuse.[7]

The High Command had meanwhile been developing a quite different approach toward Russia. The generals perceived peace with Russia not merely as a means to win the war but also as a major objective of war—it was there that Ludendorff hoped to construct his personal empire. Feeling that a separate peace with Russia was not incompatible with extensive annexations, they viewed moderate conditions as both undesirable and unnecessary. As generals, they quite naturally interpreted the revolution in military terms, namely, as the result of German victories and an opportunity to produce complete Russian defeat which in turn would hopefully induce the western powers to sue for peace by the end of 1917. In contrast to Bethmann, the High Command wanted to precipitate the disintegration of the Russian state through all political and military means at their disposal.[8]

This divergence of approaches was immediately provided a practical basis. An apparently promising opportunity to paralyze Russia militarily occurred at the beginning of April when deputations of Russian soldiers asked the Germans to guarantee a moderate peace and non-intervention in Russian internal affairs. The High Command interpreted this as proof that a breach between the Russian army and government—if indeed not complete Russian military collapse—could be brought about by an encouraging reply. With the enthusiastic support of the Kaiser and Zimmermann, Hindenburg and Ludendorff suggested to Bethmann that definite conditions for peace with Russia should be decided upon. Since Bethmann wished to conclude peace quickly with the Provisional Government rather than to cause its collapse and desired to keep control over negotiations himself, he had sought to reassure the Russian government and thus opposed any attempt to separate it from the Russian army. This negative response disappointed the Kaiser and induced him to refuse Bethmann's request for public authorization of peace talks with Russia. When it was rumored at Headquarters that Bethmann had discussed peace with Russia on the basis of the *status quo ante bellum*, the Kaiser in fact demanded that Bethmann make a public disavowal of such negotiations.[9]

Bethmann realized that his policy was severely threatened. If he were to present the Kaiser and High Command with a *fait accompli*, he would have to avoid commitment to any conditions or public statements which would preclude a quick peace with Russia. He tried to accomplish this awkward feat by the tactic of asserting that German policy remained what it had "always" been, i.e., to shatter the Entente. The immediately unfavorable military situation and American entry made it more imperative than ever to conclude peace with one or both of Germany's continental opponents. In an effort to place the High Command on the defensive, Bethmann claimed that their disregard for diplomatic considerations had ruined a recent opportunity for peace with France; it was therefore mandatory that a chance to do so with Russia not suffer the same fate. Since Russia was not yet defeated as the generals themselves admitted, "golden bridges" should be built in the form of a moderate peace. Conditions should not, however, be established beforehand since they would depend entirely upon the situation in which peace was concluded. As was obvious in this particular instance, Bethmann used the argument as a device for controlling eventual negotiations. In an effort to satisfy the High Command and Admiralty with sham concessions, Bethmann mentioned but did not commit himself to the war aims programs which the two services had advocated at the end of 1916. He simultaneously resisted the Kaiser's demand for a public statement on war aims since he anticipated that the High Command would insist on conditions which would preclude peace with Russia. Despite the possible validity of his arguments, Bethmann realized that they could not prevail as long as they were resisted by Hindenburg, whom he now sought to win over. In effect, Bethmann was trying to eradicate the compromises he had made since the end of 1916 and to reestablish the priority of diplomacy over strategy.[10]

When Bethmann's move became clear to Ludendorff, he easily convinced the Kaiser and Hindenburg that Bethmann's policy was indecisive and insured its defeat by forcing the Kaiser to choose

between Bethmann and Hindenburg. The discovery that Bethmann
had confidentially authorized Erzberger to negotiate with the Provisional Government was exploited by Ludendorff to convince Hindenburg that the High Command should approve peace conditions.
A conference on war aims was therefore scheduled at headquarters
in Kreuznach on April 23. The central issue was less the details of
war aims than who should determine them and on what grounds.
Considering the preceding events, its location and indeed the fact
that it took place at all, the conference's outcome as a victory for
Ludendorff was virtually a foregone conclusion. Convinced that the
U-boat could subdue England, the High Command demanded that
conditions for peace with Russia should be considered solely in
terms of their advantages to Germany. Bethmann granted as always
that annexations in the east were desirable but reiterated that their
achievement depended upon German ability to dictate terms. Since
this seemed unlikely, a quick separate peace with Russia and therefore renunciation of most annexations were required. The Kreuznach conference adequately demonstrated that the High Command
retained the political power it had taken after the failure of Bethmann's policy at the end of 1916. This was made embarrassingly
clear on the day after the conference when the High Command discovered that Erzberger had actually discussed an armistice with an
ostensible representative of the Petrograd Government. The conditions of this armistice according to Ludendorff were "impossible and
atrocious" and designed to produce a result "quite the opposite" of
what the High Command sought. He was even able to persuade the
Kaiser that Bethmann's actions were an encroachment on the Kaiser's
authority and that peace negotiations should not be resumed without the Kaiser's approval. The generals thereby convinced the Kaiser
that his personal prestige depended upon the annexations they desired. The episode proved that the High Command would dominate
policy formulation as long as total victory seemed feasible.[12]

The struggle continued although at a greater disadvantage to Bethmann. The High Command immediately sought to consolidate its
victory by imposing the Kreuznach program on Germany's allies.
Bethmann meanwhile persisted in his belief that Germany could win
a favorable peace only by splitting the Entente. Still convinced that
the western powers might discontinue the war if their hopes for victory were shattered by a Russian defection, he intended to resume his
pursuit of peace when Russian developments again became propitious.[13]

This precondition occurred immediately. The impulse came from
Russian soldier deputations which had contacted the Germans at the

beginning of April. Ludendorff's attempt to split the Russian army and government had apparently failed by mid-April. Soon after the Kreuznach conference the Russians, however, renewed the contact by asking for more precise terms. Ludendorff interpreted the move as an admission of defeat and assumed the Russians would accept the Kreuznach program; since the request came from a military source and had ostensibly been caused by military defeat, he claimed peace should be arranged by the High Command on strictly military bases. The civilians insisted that a Foreign Office representative be present and tried to prevent the ruination of present and future peace prospects by "dressing up" the High Command's aims to appear less extreme. The civilians' demands might have been refused had similar conditions not been simultaneously stipulated by the Russians. In order to launch talks, Ludendorff finally acceded; Bethmann acquiesced in a set of unpromising although modified conditions, and they managed to agree only that "the question of a general peace should not be discussed." Ludendorff remained determined to treat negotiations in completely military terms under his own control, whereas Bethmann hoped to win control of negotiations through his representative.[14]

Contemporary developments in Petrograd suggested the possibility of another route to peace talks. While Bethman had been secretly pursuing negotiations with the Russian Liberals during April, Zimmermann and several German agents had regarded the Russian Socialists as more promising because they might either accept extreme conditions or promote such internal chaos that Germany could defeat Russia and dictate terms. Zimmermann had consequently arranged Lenin's return to Russia, authorized conversations between all hues of German and Russian Socialists, and financially supported the Russian Socialists' peace campaign. These efforts seemed to have borne fruit by late April when the Socialists began to displace the Liberals in the Provisional Government.[15]

German leaders agreed that a Socialist takeover would facilitate peace but differed on the policy appropriate to encourage it. When it was reported that the Russian Socialists had been induced to take their initiative by the assurances of German Socialists, Bethmann concluded that an official German statement could "almost guarantee" negotiations for a separate peace with Russia. Concerned lest Bethmann demand conditions incompatible with the Kreuznach program, Ludendorff stipulated that any official pronouncement receive his prior approval. Bethmann was consequently obliged to confer with the High Command and Kaiser before making his Reichstag statement on Russia in mid-May. He managed to convince the Kaiser that negotiations required official German acceptance of the Russian Socialists' formula of "no annexations, no indemnities" but failed with Ludendorff, who assumed Bethmann was trying to take control of the negotiations Ludendorff was conducting at the front. In exchange for his agreement to the most general and thus ineffectual formulation, Ludendorff demanded that Bethmann commit himself publicly to the Kreuznach war aims. Bethmann accordingly was obliged to include in his Reichstag speech the contradictory and inconducive statement that he was at once "in complete accord" with the High Command on war aims but guaranteed Russia "an agreement founded on a mutually honorable understanding." With this renewed demonstration that his hands were tied as long as the possibility of total victory persisted, Bethmann postponed efforts to arrange peace with Russia.[16]

The prospect of peace with Russia in fact proved deceptive. The anticipated takeover by the moderate Socialists occurred the day after Bethmann's Reichstag speech. Although initially perceived as a proponent of peace, Socialist leader Alexander Kerensky conducted an even more belligerent policy than his predecessor, the "imperialist Miliukov;" not only did he discontinue front discussions but reestablished military discipline and initiated planning for a new offensive against Germany. Concluding that the only group interested in peace was Lenin's Radical Socialists, Zimmermann tried to fortify their opposition to Kerensky's war policy by communicating peace conditions to Lenin and issuing a press statement designed to force Kerensky's renunciation of an offensive and acceptance of a dictated peace. Events in Petrograd demonstrated, however, that even these hopes were unfounded and the High Command accordingly prohibited further "approaches" to Russia. This evaluation was borne out when Kerensky's power was demonstrated by a new Russian offensive at the beginning of July.[17]

Peace with France likewise seemed unlikely. The German hopes of early April were shattered by Anglo-French military successes and the devastation conducted as part of the German strategic withdrawals. Anticipating that the French would consider peace only when their spring offensive had failed, Bethmann merely maintained contact with potential intermediaries. German leaders also began to sense that a negotiated peace with France might be impractical since German retention of Alsace-Lorraine in any form would symbolize French defeat. All prospect of an understanding with either continental enemy accordingly appeared dim at the beginning of June.

* * * * *

Confronted with this renewed failure, Bethmann made a desperate attempt to regain control over policy in order to extricate Germany from the impasse in which he believed it was caught. The most serious and final confrontation between himself and the High Command was the unavoidable consequence.

The fundamental assumption of the High Command's policy was that Germany's continental hegemony could be guaranteed only by forcing English recognition. The generals had consequently demanded unlimited U-boat warfare which they hoped would make England surrender before American help arrived at the end of July and would thus convince England's allies, including the United States, to renounce further struggle. When the U-boats sank ever larger numbers of English ships through April and these expectations seemed to be valid, the High Command had confirmed its control over policy at the Kreuznach conference in late April. U-boat efficiency diminished, however, during May and Ludendorff confidentially postponed England's expected capitulation until the autumn. Lest any doubt arise as to the U-boat's ultimate success, he and Hindenburg publicly assured the German army and people that England's demise was more certain than ever.[19]

At the beginning of June the High Command made a fairly genuine reappraisal of its expectations for total victory. The impulse seems to have come from Colonel Hans Haeften, head of the military section of the Foreign Office and a confidant of Ludendorff. Having heard varying opinions on the U-boat's ability to achieve the anticipated results, Haeften reported to Ludendorff after extensive inquiries at the Admiralty, Foreign Office and General Staff that the U-boat's effectiveness had been exaggerated. Haeften therefore suggested that not only the U-boat but all means be applied to frighten England into concluding peace before the coming winter. Since he felt Bethmann lacked complete support at home, Haeften doubted the chancellor could direct the required "new orientation" of policy and should be replaced. Ludendorff's response was uncharacteristically tentative. He agreed to consider Haeften's advice but was as yet unsure that a new chancellor was necessary despite his reservations about Bethmann. When Admiral Henning von Holtzendorff, Chief of the Admiralty Staff, confirmed that the U-boat was producing less than expected, the news combined with unfavorable military, diplomatic and domestic prospects to make Ludendorff deeply pessimistic and responsive to some of Haeften's ideas. Anxious to maintain popular confidence in the High Command for what now seemed to be a protracted and less promising war, Ludendorff at once tried to persuade Bethmann to assume partial responsibility for the U-boat's diminished effectiveness but refused to admit that the U-boat had failed. If the German people demonstrated their determination to persevere, Ludendorff continued to hope that the U-boat would force England to renounce the policy of "encirclement and constriction" which it had always pursued toward Germany. While typically resorting to bellicosity when no more convincing tactic existed, the generals thereby indicated for the first time a slight awareness of the actual military situation and might have been brought around to a less rigid policy by cautious and clever persuasion.[20]

Bethmann chose instead to confront Hindenburg and Ludendorff in an effort to regain control over policy. When informed by Erzberger in mid-June of the High Command's pessimism, Bethmann at first temporized, perhaps on account of his renewed failure to shake the Kaiser's faith in the generals' judgment. Ludendorff's attempt to shift responsibility for popular disappointment in the U-boat, however, produced an indignant reaction from Bethmann, who may have been encouraged by a dispute between the High Command and Kaiser on spheres of authority. Bethmann sought to win back the Kaiser's support by demonstrating first the failure of the High Command's policy and then the favorable prospects for his own. He accused Ludendorff of duplicity in confidentially admitting the U-boat's failure while publicly encouraging exaggerated expectations and condemned the High Command's pursuit of a dictated peace on the basis of Foreign Office reports indicating that none of Germany's enemies could be forced to conclude peace quickly. Since Germany's unpromising situation made a rapid end to the war imperative, it was necessary to seek a negotiated peace. In spite of disastrous domestic conditions and little prospect of victory, neither France nor Russia were likely to accept a separate peace with Germany. Consequently England, "the soul of the war," had to be induced to negotiate by a combination of the U-boat's pressure and German demonstration of readiness. He believed that the moment was propitious because of the Anglo-French offensive's failure and Russian inability to revive militarily.[21] When he tried but failed to persuade the Kaiser, Bethmann reverted to the desperate recourse of presenting the Kaiser and High Command with a *fait accompli*. Indications of possible English responsiveness persuaded Bethmann to respond in a Reichstag speech. which would include a veiled attack on the High Command with the implied support of the Kaiser. Despite the repeated failures of the preceding months, Bethmann persisted in his hope that the Kaiser would support him if genuine negotiations were begun.[22]

Bethmann's attack had meanwhile induced the High Command to seek his removal. Bethmann's refusal to sacrifice himself for a "new orientation for strength" by assuming responsibility for popular disappointment in the U-boat convinced Ludendorff that Bethmann lacked the "personality necessary to lead." The High Command reiterated its denial that the U-boat had failed and claimed that all Germany's troubles stemmed instead from its civilian leaders' "faintheartedness." The generals reasserted that, far from being unfeasible, a dictated peace was the only possible outcome since a "negotiated" peace would occur only when one side collapsed and would thus be equivalent to a dictated peace. England could not be won by Bethmann's policy of moderation but only by power since, "more than anyone else, the English are impressed by single-minded determination." Bethmann consequently had to be replaced by a stronger leader who enjoyed the confidence of both people and army.[23]

The conflict was complicated and momentarily obscured by the Reichstag's intervention in foreign policy which was prompted by Erzberger's exposure of the U-boat's failure. The effects of Erzberger's move were mixed: in so far as it demonstrated that the High Command's policy of total victory was unpromising, the revelation strengthened Bethmann's poistion *vis-à-vis* the generals; but Erzberger's indication of the Central Powers' weakness might compromise Bethmann's efforts to bring England to the peace table. Bethmann consequently sought to square the circle by convincing the Kaiser of the U-boat's failure and Germany's need for peace while at the same time persuading England that Germany was strong but willing to discuss peace. When Bethmann tried to perpetuate the impression of the U-boat's effectiveness and refused to discuss the possibility of peace with England, members of the Reichstag accused him of opposing peace altogether and inventing excuses to stay in office.[24]

With contradictory motives, the Reichstag leaders and the High Command concluded an opportunistic alliance to bring about Bethmann's downfall. The generals claimed that he was not belligerent enough but actually feared that he might resume control over foreign policy. The parliamentarians criticized his belligerence but in fact felt that he was unable to stand up to the High Command. Disliking change and lacking a compatible substitute for Bethmann, the Kaiser at first refused to be influenced by the High Command or Reichstag and claimed—as he had when Bethmann had agitated for Hindenburg's appointment—that such questions were his own domain. The High Command's resort to its tried tactic of threatening to resign, however, forced the Kaiser to succumb and Bethmann resigned on July 13.

The Kaiser could not risk Hindenburg's resignation for the very reason Bethmann had given for appointing him: the dynasty might survive an unfavorable peace only if buttressed by Hindenburg's prestige. Hindenburg's appointment which Bethmann had hoped would serve his policy had not only complicated his task but ultimately caused his resignation.[25]

The crisis of July 1917 produced yet another reorientation of German policy. The basic objective remained what it had been during early 1917, namely, victory before the end of the year. This goal would thereafter be pursued through a separate understanding with England rather than Russia or France and the method of dividing the Entente altered in the process.

German perception of peace with England had already changed several times during the war. The breach of Belgian neutrality in August 1914 had provided England with the moral justification for a policy which its interests seemed to demand, i.e., preservation of the balance of power in Europe which in turn necessitated defense of French great power status. During the first few weeks of the war Bethmann had nonetheless hoped that some facile arrangement might permit Germany to win English acceptance of the Franco-Russian alliance's defeat and German continental hegemony.[1]

This hope proved illusory when the Entente powers announced in September 1914 their determination not to conclude peace separately. Bethmann initially contemplated a "war of existence" and "settling of accounts" with England to insure German security. Yet, when Falkenhayn recognized at the end of 1914 that Germany could not conquer on both fronts at once, Bethmann modified his attitude toward England. The projected separate peace with Russia might allow Germany to concentrate all its forces against the Anglo-French armies whose defeat would presumably force England to renounce French great power status and the balance of power; if not, the U-boat might produce English acquiescence. In either case Germany would have dealt a "shock to England's world hegemony" and established its own continental domination preparatory to an era of German world power. If on the contrary German military and naval power were insufficient to make England accede, Bethmann retained the option of a general peace on the basis of the *status quo ante bellum* since he assumed England was interested only in preserving the balance of power and not in destroying Germany. These views were not universally accepted in Berlin. Under the influence of the leading Anglophobe, Admiral Tirpitz, Falkenhayn perceived England as

Germany's most vicious and tenacious enemy whose defeat was the precondition of German security. Thus two conflicting policies toward England co-existed in Berlin from the beginning of the war.[2]

When the policy of concluding a separate peace with Russia or France failed at the end of 1915, another deviation occurred in German policy toward England. During 1915 the dissolution and defeat of the Franco-Russian alliance had been the main aim and English acceptance regarded as a mere byproduct. On Falkenhayn's prompting at the end of 1915, Bethmann decided, however, that England in fact preserved the Entente. Since Germany had virtually established its predominance over the continent, it remained only to make England renounce the continent by being abandoned by its allies. Even this recognition as Germany's main oppoinent did not induce Bethmann to conclude that England was commited to destroying Germany. When Falkenhayn suggested in early 1916 that unlimited U-boat warfare was the only way of defeating England, Bethmann con templated avoiding this eventuality by resort to a general peace with the Entente on the basis of the *status quo ante bellum*. He assumed that the war would require the total defeat of one side only if Germany threatened England's existence with the U-boat, until which time the issue would remain merely control over the continent. When Russia and France refused to renounce England, Falkenhayn's intention prevailed at the end of 1916: the Entente might collapse only if England were forced to abandon its allies.[3]

Inauguration of unlimited U-boat warfare at the beginning of 1917 constituted another revision of German policy toward England. The objective of dividing the Entente remained but the approach had changed. It had previously been assumed that abandonment by its allies would persuade England to accept German domination over the continent. The U-boat campaign was designed instead to force England to renounce its allies. In short, England was to be defeated rather than merely persuaded and separate peace with England would be the cause rather than the result of separate understandings with its allies. When it appeared in June 1917 that the U-boat could not in fact defeat England, Bethmann attempted to modify its purpose. If it could not defeat England, the U-boat might still demonstrate that the war was unprofitable and convince the English to negotiate. Bethmann was, however, unable to win support for a number of reasons. He failed to prove that his policy was necessary, i.e., that the U-boat could never defeat England. His means for inducing England to accept a compromise peace seemed unconvincing. Perhaps most important, he presented such a departure as an alternative to the High Command's policy and thus a diminution of its power. A reorientation of German policy toward England was possible only if it could be proven necessary, feasible and compatible with the High Command's authority.[4]

Bethmann's resignation turned out to be a victory bought at some cost by the High Command. Designed to conceal the U-boat's failure, Bethmann's removal publicized it instead. Members of the Reichstag attacked Bethmann because they believed he denied the U-boat's shortcomings and could not impose a realistic policy on the High Command and annexationists. When Ludendorff was unable to give the parliamentarians more than the vaguest assurances that either the U-boat or a land offensive could produce victory, they passed a Peace Resolution declaring that negotiated peace should replace total victory as Germany's objective. Although bitterly opposed, Ludendorff and Hindenburg did not respond with their usual threat of resignation as they had done to Bethmann's criticism. Thus, precisely at the moment of its most striking domestic triumph in removing Bethmann, the High Command was notably restrained, whereas the Reichstag claimed the right to be included in foreign policy formulation. While the Peace Resolution had little practical effect and the Reichstag little influence on foreign policy, there was a new climate which at once aided but complicated a diplomatic departure.[5]

* * * * *

Bethmann's successor, Georg Michaelis, was well suited to assume the role of interim administrator until a more permanent chancellor could be designated. A successful and conscientious bureaucrat, he had taken little interest in politics before becoming chancellor and might not have accepted the office had he been aware of the disagreements between the Reichstag and the High Command. During the hundred days of his tenure, he sought to delegate or avoid rather than solve political problems. It is frequently claimed that he was the tool of the High Command; Hindenburg and Ludendorff certainly saw in him a compatible, although not necessarily pliable, temperament and approved his appointment in the hope of interpreting their "military responsibility" even more broadly than they had during Bethmann's administration. But, in so far as Michaelis was manipulated by anyone, it was probably his new Foreign Secretary, Richard von Kühlmann, who used Michaelis to prepare a new diplomatic *démarche*.[6]

After Bethmann's departure, Kühlmann assumed control over foreign policy formulation. Enigmatic and devious, he impressed his colleagues with an air of *savoir faire* and, like many of his German contemporaries, favored the brilliant coup over piecemeal progress as the solution for international problems. These characteristics would color the final German efforts to split the opposing coalition.[7] Like those who had made policy immediately before him, Kühlmann had an *idée fixe*. Whereas Bethmann and Jagow had been primarily concerned with France and German domination over the continent and Zimmermann had regarded Russia as the most important consideration, Kühlmann's thinking was dominated by England and the problem of Germany's place as a world power next to the British Empire. Starting from the assumption that peace was necessary for Germany by autumn 1917, he viewed England as the determining factor since it was "the most important of our enemies." Like Bethmann but unlike the High Command, he assumed that no modern power could completely destroy another and that a compromise was consequently unavoidable. As unnegotiable preconditions for such an arrangement, England would require that France remain a "great power, independent and capable of being allied with," and that Belgium be reestablished as an "independent state." England might then renounce its allies expansive aspirations in order to conclude peace with Germany and perhaps even allow Germany concessions in return. After the Entente's front had been broken by such a separate peace with England, Germany should seek similar understandings with France and Russia. Assuming France was interested only in Alsace-Lorraine, it might make peace if Germany granted autonomy to the provinces and renounced annexations in both Briey-Longwy and Luxemburg. In the hope that "a separate understanding with Russia might be achieved later," Kühlmann also advised against extensive war aims in the east. Germany's allies (Austria-Hungary, Bulgaria and Turkey) and England other allies (Serbia and the "associated power," the United States) were not mentioned.[8]

Although suggesting the general policy which had caused Bethmann's fall, Kühlmann varied the details and presentation. He was more specific: England was to be bribed with fulfillment of its principal aims rather than merely informed of German readiness to discuss peace. The circumstances were made more propitious by the Reichstag's disclosure of the U-boat's failure and the Peace Resolution. Kühlmann's style was less abrasive than Bethmann's and he managed to present the policy without seeming to threaten the High Command's authority. The prospects for approval consequently seemed somewhat more favorable than they had for Bethmann. Kühlmann's policy constituted a new departure in German perceptions of peace with England. They had already tried isolating England through separate understandings with its allies and starving it into submission with the U-boat. Kühlmann was now advocating negotiation instead of isolation and starvation.

The Papacy's peace activities during the summer of 1917 functioned as a catalyst in accelerating but not fundamentally altering Kühlmann's policy. Papal Nuncio Pacelli had already sounded out Bethmann in June on the possibility of peace and seemed to be seeking an Anglo-German *rapprochement*. In the hope that the Reichstag Peace Resolution might have improved the possibility of peace, Pacelli returned to Berlin at the end of July but was now clearly advocating a general peace excluding Russia. Unprepared for this suggestion and ignorant of its implications, Michaelis implied that he was inclined to accept but consulted with Zimmermann and Erzberger. Zimmermann opposed even such a limited general peace and recommended bilateral negotiations with England instead. Michaelis accepted Zimmermann's advice which corresponded with the predilection of Kühlmann, who replaced Zimmermann as foreign secretary at the end of July.[9] The German Foreign Office accordingly sought to persuade the Papacy to suggest secret bi-lateral Anglo-German talks instead of making a public offer of mediation for a general peace. Anxious to avoid antagonizing either side, the Vatican proceeded to issue its public mediatory offer. Pacelli's subsequent efforts to gain German response for a general peace conference would remain unsuccessful. For their part, the Germans tried to use the Pope's suggestion to discredit the Entente governments and augment pacifism among the Entente populations.[10]

Although it did not correspond with Kühlmann's objectives, the Papal action provided a convenient means for unobtrusively ascertaining the views of his colleagues. On Kühlmann's prompting, Michaelis managed in a meeting on August 9 to extract from the High Command the recognition that the Belgian question was the "nucleus of the antagonism with England," i.e., that the war with England was not necessarily one of existence and might therefore be susceptible to compromise. If England could not be forced to renounce Belgium, the High Command recognized that German territorial demands in Belgium would have to be reduced. Michaelis and Kühlmann thereafter assumed that the general would agree to concessions in Belgium if peace with England were possible without a winter campaign.[11]

While quite prepared to exploit the Reichstag's Peace Resolution and other activities to win concessions from the High Command,

Kühlmann would probably not have discussed peace policy with the parliamentarians had the Papal move not forced him to do so. His main concern in discussions with the Reichstag leaders and representatives of the Bundesstaaten was retention of control over the formulation of a reply to the Papal offer. Both extremes of German public opinion had to be pacified. While Michaelis reassured the annexationists that Berlin had neither requested the Papal offer nor renounced territorial gains, Kühlmann placated those who favored negotiations by claiming that he would seek moderate conditions. To discourage further discussion of war aims altogether, Michaelis falsely asserted that the Pope had not asked for a specific answer. Able in this way to avoid commitments which would limit his "free hand," Kühlmann nonetheless realized that the supporters of the Peace Resolution could complicate or even destroy the prospects of success for his *démarche*.[12]

* * * * *

Concerned not only about an independent Reichstag initiative but also Austro-Hungarian inclination toward peace talks with the Entente, Kühlmann decided at the beginning of September to launch his own move. He recommended immediate action to Michaelis with the reminder that "we cannot end the war unless we somehow drive a wedge into the enemy coalition." Contrary to his earlier expectations, he doubted that an understanding with France was possible because "an ocean of hate divides us from France. . . [and] we therefore have nothing to offer it." Since France and Russia were in any case under British control, England was more than ever the critical element.[13] The moment was propitious for a move since a "significant domestic development was occurring" in England and augured well for an understanding. Supposed to have won the war at any price, Lloyd George had been no more successful than his "much maligned" predecessor, Asquith. An opposition group of Liberals and dissident Conservatives including Lord Lansdowne and Balfour was now reportedly gathering around Asquith. Without stating explicitly whether this group would seek to displace Lloyd George or merely press him to accept its views, Kühlmann argued that the critics were disinclined to continue the war through another winter just for the sake of far-reaching French war aims. If given "full assurance of specifically *English* aims" including the reestablishment of Belgium including the Channel coast, they might force the French into renouncing Alsace-Lorraine. Since France was dominated by England, "such an English 'wish' that France stick its Alsace-Lorraine desires into its pocket would have to be obeyed in Paris as an order, albeit with the gnashing of teeth." Kühlmann requested Michaelis' support in gaining authorization from the Kaiser and High Command for a confidential inquiry as to whether "important English states-men" believed "a completely clear, *official* German statement" on the future of Belgium would produce negotiations. If the English re-sponded, Germany would have to give "an unmistakeable, *open* state-ment on Belgium" as a counter-guarantee. Michaelis immediatedly concurred with Kühlmann's "intention to isolate France *vis-à-vis* England" in this war.[14]

Kühlmann's assumptions about England immediately seemed to be corroborated when Pacelli informed Berlin that London (appar-ently with the concurrence of Paris) was willing to negotiate if a "conciliatory answer" on Belgium were given by Berlin to the Papal mediatory offer. Himself inclined to comply, Michaelis deferred to the "expert knowledge in diplomatic affairs" of Kühlmann, who doubted a "serious feeler" would be transmitted in this way and again urged a secret sounding to establish "precisely what the whole thing was about." Pacelli's communication nonetheless provided Kühlmann with what could be viewed as renewed proof of English willingness to conclude peace and thus a convincing argument with which to seek authorization for his move from the Kaiser and High Command. At the same time his ability to use Belgium as a *quid pro quo* could be jeopardized if Pacelli's information became known to those Reich-stag members who advocated a public renunciation of Belgium in re-ply to the Papal offer. As both opportunity and threat, the Vatican's action seemed to reinforce the need for haste.[15]

To prepare for his meeting with the Kaiser, Michaelis was again briefed by Kühlmann. In return for a clear German statement on the "burning question of the moment," Belgium, England must promise negotiations in which Germany would be guaranteed its prewar terri-tory (including Alsace-Lorraine) and colonies. Germany's future as a world power depended on good relations with England, to which all other considerations should be subordinated. With this argument and the claim that England's "genuine peace feeler" through Pacelli justi-fied hope for its success, Michaelis won the Kaiser's approval for a "cautious" sounding since William "could not refuse an honorable peace merely because of the Flemish coast or other parts of Belgium." A representative of the Chancellor was simultaneously assured by Ludendorff that the Belgian coast was not a *sine qua non* for the High Command. A Crown Council with the High Command was con-sequently scheduled to establish German policy on Belgium.[16]

Kühlmann meanwhile devoted himself to the task of preserving his bargaining power over Belgium. Assuming that prior forfeiture of Belgium might remove the inducement for England to negotiate, he had to insure against renunciation in replying to the Pope's mediatory offer, as was demanded by some members of the Reichstag, particularly Socialist Philipp Scheidemann. Although Kühlmann did not inform the parliamentarians of Pacelli's communication and could thus claim that no explicit mention of Belgium was required, he did assert that England would negotiate only if it could reestablish Belgian independence in no other way. When this argument failed to convince all the Reichstag leaders, Kühlmann relied on his reputation as both a moderate in war aims and a friend of parliamentary government in order to win his point by threatening to resign. He was finally able in this way to avoid either reducing the anticipated effectiveness of Belgium or his own freedom.[17]

What seemed smooth sailing was suddenly threatened by the Navy. The Admiralty refused Kühlmann's request and blackmailed the Kaiser into rescinding his renunciation of the Belgian coast by threatening Tirpitz would publicly attack the Kaiser and Michaelis if the coast or some substitute were not obtained. Terrified by this prospect but unwilling to destroy the possibility of negotiations, the Kaiser typically tried to avoid a decision. He claimed that no chance of a compromise existed because Germany and England were committed to total war:

> Before one of us [i.e., England or Germany] stands alone on top, there will be no peace in the world! Great Britain will not allow condominium and must therefore be thrown out of Europe It is the same as in 1866 with Austria which was the precondition for 1870. Condominium with the Habsburgs in Germany was out of the question. The same with Napoleon [III?] in Europe. So it is also with England in the world.

If England requested peace, it was merely admitting defeat and should be treated firmly instead of being offered concessions. Since this confused and pitiful *volte face* destroyed the foundations of Kühlmann's policy, he decided to resign if the Kaiser confirmed it during the Crown Council. But the Kaiser characteristically proved consistent only in his inconsistency by reversing himself for a second time in two days during a conversation with Michaelis. After relieving himself of these emotions against England for frustrating his great designs, William again agreed to consider sounding the English for negotiations.[18]

The Crown Council of September 11 produced a tactical victory for Kühlman. Its specific topic for discussion was the "English peace feeler" conveyed confidentially by Pacelli rather than the public Papal mediatory offer which all present agreed should be answered vaguely. Starting from the premise that England wanted peace,

Kühlmann requested official authorization to establish whether it would negotiate in exchange for a German promise to reestablish Belgium; if it did, he believed that "promising peace negotiations could be brought about." Although they confirmed their willingness to forfeit the Belgian coast, Hindenburg and Ludendorff insisted on retaining the interior but Admiral Henning Holtzendorff, Chief of the Admiralty Staff, reiterated his demand for the coast. The Kaiser as usual tried to bridge dissension which was distasteful to him but ultimately granted Kühlmann's point that a "positive peace suggestion was at hand." The English request for peace was a "great success" for Germany because only England could "act as a wedge against the other powers." Since no annexation should be allowed to keep Germany from dividing the Entente, the Kaiser assumed the "new position" that "Belgium should be reestablished and the King of the Belgians could rule again." He tried to render this decision less unpalatable to the Admirality by making it contingent upon "compensations" and avoided a dispute with the High Command by merely noting its demand for eventual "economic incorporation" of Belgium. Imprecise and contradictory by normal standards, the decision's intent was made amply clear by the Kaiser after the Council when he told Kühlmann that he had "a free hand—show us whether you can produce peace before Christmas."[19]

This was the first time since Bethmann's public peace note in December 1916 that diplomatic objectives had received attention comparable with military and territorial considerations. Kühlmann and Michaelis had achieved the feat which had escaped Bethmann by making it seem necessary, practical and compatible with the High Command's prestige. The Kaiser's decision was sufficient for Kühlmann's purpose; indeed its very imprecision allowed Kühlmann more latitude than greater clarity might have done. However begrudging, the acquiescence of Hindenburg, Ludendorff and Holtzendorff encouraged Kühlmann to hope that they would in fact renounce their demands for acquisitions in Belgium if England was prepared to conclude peace before winter.[20]

Exploiting this hard-won authorization, Kühlmann immediately implemented his sounding. He had already refused Dutch and Danish intermediaries in preference for the Spanish envoy to the Low Countries, the Marquis Villalobar. Directly after the Crown Council, Kühlmann at first asked Villalobar to contact confidentially the "opposition group" around Asquith by going to London directly or via Madrid; he finally agreed that Villalobar should try instead through the English envoy in the Hague. Kühlmann authorized Villalobar to inform the English that Germany would promise publicly to reestablish Belgian integrity if guaranteed negotiations on favorable terms.[21]

It was meanwhile necessary to protect the prospects of success from domestic and diplomatic complications. In order to anticipate an independent initiative in the Belgian question by the Reichstag, Kühlmann answered the Pope's mediatory offer in vague terms. Despite Pacelli's urging, Belgium was not mentioned in the German reply since Kühlmann anticipated that firmness might discourage the English, whereas moderation might encourage them to assume that Belgium could be obtained without renouncing French aspirations for Alsace-Lorraine.[22] Kühlmann's efforts seemed to be jeopardized from another direction when it appeared that England might be forced to support French aspirations for Alsace-Lorraine by a French threat to conclude a separate peace with the Central Powers. Berlin had already discouraged a Viennese sounding which might have provided Paris with the means for putting this pressure on London.[23] Kühlmann was, however, less successful with his own subordinate, Lancken, head of the Political Section of the German occupation government in Brussels. Having continued to meet surreptitiously with intermediaries even after Kühlmann and Michaelis had ordered him to desist in August, Lancken was informed in mid-September that former French Premier Briand would meet him on September 21 if Lancken could obtain authorization to negotiate. Anticipating refusal, Lancken agreed to the meeting with the claim of having been authorized and in the hope of presenting his superiors with a *fait accompli*. When Lancken finally informed him, Kühlmann did in fact discourage the meeting with Briand since it might complicate his own sounding.[24]

Paradoxically, it was neither of these threats which compromised Kühlmann's move but rather Villalobar's lack of precisely that discretion for which Kühlmann had chosen him. Instead of privately approaching his British colleague in the Hague, Villalobar first communicated the sounding to Madrid by telegraph in order to ask his government's authorization. Madrid in turn passed on the German *démarche* to London and presented it as mere willingness to discuss peace rather than an offer of specific conditions in exchange for negotiations. The move thereby took on a different coloration and probably lost any appeal it might have had for the British.[24] The move was simultaneously jeopardized at home when the High Command intercepted Villalobar's telegrams to Madrid and concluded that Kühlmann's offer exaggerated Germany's need for peace. In order to dispel any illusion which might thereby be engendered in

London, Ludendorff persuaded Hindenburg to issue an army order stating that the High Command had renounced only the Belgian coast but not the hinterland, i.e., that Belgium would not be entirely reestablished. Although this pronouncement demonstrated the difficulty of extracting concessions from the High Command and was inconducive to arranging negotiations with England, Kühlmann remained confident that he would retain the Kaiser's support if peace were possible before Christmas.[25] The situation was further complicated when the French were informed. Kühlmann feared that Paris might persuade London that Berlin was desperate enough to grant complete restitution of Alsace-Lorraine as a pre-condition for negotiations. Villlobar's report of early October that London was "not yet ripe" for negotiations was interpreted by Kühlmann as the consequence of French pressure rather than British unwillingness to negotiate.[26]

A desperate departure seemed required to rescue the affair from failure. In particular, London apparently had to be deterred from acceding to a French demand that the return of Alsace-Lorraine be made a *quid pro quo* for negotiations. Kühlmann sensed that England could not conduct an independent policy after the move's exposure since the French could threaten to conclude a separate peace with the Central Powers. He decided that minor concessions in Alsace-Lorraine might be considered if they induced the British to force French acceptance of a compromise peace. In place of the bi-lateral negotiations which he had initially sought, he was now willing to include France from the start as long as prior guarantees insured German retention of the provinces. Kühlmann accordingly encouraged British pressure on France by stating in the Reichstag at the beginning of October that French demands for Alsace-Lorraine were the only obstacle to peace.[27]

Despite his elaborate preparations and last minute efforts to save it, Kühlmann's effort failed. Indeed his pronouncement in the Reichstag produced precisely the eventuality it was designed to prevent: Lloyd George announced that England would support French aspirations. Despite this rebuff, Kühlmann continued to seek talks with the British on the basis of limited German concessions in Alsace-Lorraine. The British, however, remained consistently unresponsive. The Germans realized by mid-December that stronger pressure would be necessary. In fact it seemed to be at hand.[28]

The immediate objectives of German policy changed again in November 1917 in response to the Bolshevik revolution which not only improved the prospects of an understanding with Russia but also provided the Germans with additional means of persuading England to compromise. The ultimate goal nonetheless remained what it had been since late 1914: to split the Entente through separate arrangements with its individual members.

Just when his policy of bribing England to conclude peace proved unfeasible, Kühlmann was provided with what seemed an even more effective inducement. After the failure of its offensive in July 1917, Russia had been largely discounted by Berlin as a military and diplomatic factor. Kühlmann had assumed that a peace with England would be succeeded immediately by an understanding with Russia; if not, the chaos within Russia was expected to become so serious that Germany could force Russia to make peace with the threat of defeat. These prognostications were borne out when the Bolsheviks suddenly assumed power in November 1917 and immediately advocated peace.[1]

Kühlmann tried to convert such a separate peace with Russia into the cause rather than the result of peace with England. He persisted in the belief that Germany's only chance to win the war was to shatter the Entente which was therefore "the most important war aim of our diplomacy." Despite his recent failure, only an understanding with England could achieve this result. Consequently a separate peace with Russia would be diplomatically significant only by achieving this objective. If peace with Russia conjured up the spectre of a Russo-German *rapprochement* and common front against the western powers, England might find it less disadvantageous to abandon France and conclude peace than to persevere in a protracted and unpromising struggle against such an imposing alliance. Kühlmann therefore sought to arrange at least an apparent reconciliation with Russia by avoiding extensive German annexations at Russian expense.[2]

He found support from German and Austro-Hungarian civilian leaders more easily than he had in September for his handling of the Belgian question. The Kaiser urged Kühlmann "to try to reach some kind of alliance or friendly relations with the Russians in spite of everything." Georg Hertling allowed Kühlmann even more latitude than had Michaelis, whom Hertling had succeeded as chancellor at the end of October. After putting Kühlmann in an awkward position because of his conversations with the French in September, Austro-Hungarian Foreign Minister Czernin became extremely anxious for an understanding with Russia and applauded Kühlmann's efforts. Czernin advocated a separate peace with Russia not only because it was necessary to preserve the Habsburg Monarchy but also because it was the only way Germany could achieve its precondition for peace, namely, dividing the Entente and military victory. The Reichstag was a potential threat which again proved harmless. The main supporters of the Peace Resolution who had jeopardized the Villalobar sounding again tried to affect the formulation of policy. They made a weak effort to cross-examine Kühlmann on his intentions and those who had been in contact with Russian Socialists since the previous spring even contemplated seeking negotiations over the head of their own government. The eastern situation had, however, altered drastically since the spring: whereas the Peace Resolution had been encouraged in part by the imminent Russian offensive, Russian military power had meanwhile collapsed and the Bolshevik government seemed inclined not only to conclude peace but also perhaps to concede annexations demanded by the High Command. Perhaps most important, the parliamentarians lacked any strong motivation to intervene since few were opposed to the territorial acquisitions which Kühlmann seemed to be seeking. The Reichstag ultimately caused Kühlmann little difficulty and encroached only very marginally on his control over negotiations.[3]

It was another story with the High Command. The Bolshevik revolution and increased likelihood of peace with Russia were interpreted quite differently by Kühlmann and the generals. The situation had changed since September when the High Command had reluctantly allowed its control over foreign policy to be qualified because they lacked a convincing alternative to Kühlmann's *démarche*. The possibility that Russia might leave the war immensely improved Germany's military position and revived the generals' conviction that the western powers could be defeated. Upon hearing of the Bolshevik takeover and request for peace, the High Command immediately decided in principle on a spring offensive on the western front. Hindenburg and Ludendorff simultaneously became more intransigent on the question of war aims since they were themselves committed to more extensive gains in the east than they were to the Belgian coast. Peace with Russia was thus envisaged by the High

Command at once as an opportunity for acquiring extensive territorial acquisitions and preparation for the final campaign in a total war against Germany's western enemies.[4]

A struggle for control over negotiations with Russia consequently erupted between Kühlmann and the High Command. In order to establish his mandate for the forthcoming peace talks with the Russians, Kühlmann requested a Crown Council in early December. Starting from the premise that a peace with Russia should be fashioned in terms of its effect on England, he argued that the Germans should seek to create the impression of a Russo-German *rapprochement* by minimizing territorial acquisitions and preserving the "fiction" of their independence as much as possible.[5] When the Kaiser granted Kühlmann's point and authorized him to conduct negotiations, the High Command became determined to thwart Kühlmann's plans and reassert control over policy. They demanded assurance that an understanding with Russia not lead to the peace with England which was Kühlmann's declared purpose and which they sought to prevent by insisting that U-boat operations be continued during eventual conversations with the British and by revoking their concession of the Belgian coast. The generals meanwhile initiated actual planning for a spring offensive on the western front. His negotiating authority again jeopardized, Kühlmann arranged for a second Crown Council on the eve of his departure for negotiations at Brest-Litovsk. The High Command reiterated its demands and declared flatly that no territorial concession to Russia would be countenanced; rather than a *rapprochement*, Hindenburg and Ludendorff expected another war with Russia.[6] Kühlmann persisted with his argument that annexations be kept to a minimum and presented in a manner which might foster the impression of Russian acquiescence. The Kaiser characteristically sought to conceal the dispute by giving another vague decision which he nonetheless claimed subsequently favored Kühlmann's policy. As had been the case in September, this vagueness suited Kühlmann's purpose since it allowed him maximal latitude. He continued to assume that the High Command's opposition could be overcome if he produced peace quickly.[7]

Kühlmann's victory was, however, brief. When the Kaiser made the mistake of praising Kuhlmann's policy during late January 1918, Hindenburg and Ludendorff forced William to back down with the threat of their resignation. Kühlmann's maneuvering room was thereby reduced but not entirely negated. In the realization that more annexations would have to be demanded, Kühlmann sought to render them as unobtrusive as possible. He meanwhile tried to prevent Reichstag criticism of such augmented aims by presenting them merely as a continuation of Bethmann's policy. His position *vis-à-vis* the High Command might have been improved had the Bolsheviks been more interested in concluding peace quickly than in precipitating revolution in Germany. When despite Kühlmann's appeals the Russians delayed negotiations in the hope that their assiduous propaganda would paralyze the Germany army, the High Command and Kaiser lost patience and served notice to the Russians at the beginning of February that German military operations would be resumed against Russia unless peace were concluded immediately on the High Command's terms. The High Command had effectively reestablished its control over policy.[8]

A windfall provided Kühlmann with an opportunity to wrest back control. Before the High Command's ultimatum could be presented, the chief Russian negotiator, Leon Trotsky, dramatically rebuffed the Germans by declaring that Russia would neither conduct war nor conclude peace. This announcement placed Berlin publicly before the alternatives of accepting a moderate peace or renewing eastern operations when troops were required for the impending western offensive. Kühlmann immediately repeated his admonition that territorial demands should be limited to areas already occupied which should be "dressed up" as autonomous states. He buttressed his diplomatic argument with the claim that German public opinion would resist resumption of hostilities designed to conquer territory beyond Germany's declared aims which might cause another war. The generals rejected each of these arguments and confirmed their power to determine policy. Perceiving Russia as defeated but irreconcilable, they insisted that Germany annex as much territory as possible in preparation for the next war with Russia. Rather than preventing resumption of German operations in the east, the projected western offensive made a rapid conclusion of peace with Russia all the more mandatory in order to clarify the situation and avoid protracted negotiations. When neither the Kaiser nor Hertling was able to meet these arguments, Ludendorff simply took the decision into his own hands and resumed operations in the east. He hoped in this way either to impose harsh terms on the Bolshevik government or to cause its collapse and then dominate the whole Russian state. The Bolsheviks were unable to meet such a military threat and submitted to the terms imposed on them by the High Command in the treaty of Brest-Litovsk.[9]

Although any possibility of creating the illusion of a Russo-German reconciliation was thereby destroyed, Kühlmann nonetheless sought as much as possible to draw Russia away from its former allies

and towards Germany. He worked to keep the Bolsheviks from being
displaced by a faction more sympathetic to the Entente. This policy
seemed to bear fruit by April 1918 when the Entente showed increasing hostility towards the Bolsheviks and Kühlmann again investigated the possibility of persuading England to renounce French
aspirations for Alsace-Lorraine in exchange for Belgium. In June the
Bolsheviks appeared willing to consider "an alliance in the near future." Even such a superficial eastern *détente* was, however, refused
by Ludendorff. The High Command still controlled policy and would
continue to do so as long as their objective of total victory on both
fronts seemed attainable.[10]

* * * * *

Kühlmann's efforts to arrange a separate peace with England had
failed. This failure was due above all to English policy. Although he
claimed to understand British motives, he had in fact greatly misunderstood them. He never really accepted the basic British precept
of opposing any state's attempt to dominate the continent. From
the British point of view, it was imperative in the existing situation
that the domination which Germany had virtually imposed militarily
be broken and that German power be reduced. Since England could
not do so alone, the Entente had to be preserved. Kühlmann's offer
to reestablish Belgium was consequently ineffective as long as England believed Germany sought continental hegemony and his claim
that Alsace-Lorraine prevented peace acted to unify rather than
divide the Entente.[11]

Kühlmann's perception of events in the east was no more accurate.
The threat of Russian defection and even *rapprochement* with Germany which Kühlmann hoped would induce England to support
France less actually made England need France more. At the end of
December Lloyd George declared publicly that Russia's leaving the
war would not cause England to conclude peace. The Allies' enmity
towards the Bolsheviks which encouraged Kühlmann to believe that
his policy might succeed in reality signified its failure by indicating
that the western powers were sufficiently confident or intransigent
to accept Russian defection and even hostility. Had the German
spring offensive of 1918 defeated France, England would probably
have persevered since, in place of its former continental allies, it
would still have had the United States, which had committed itself
to the destruction of German military power. It is therefore unlikely
that anything short of German defeat would have satisfied England
during the winter of 1918.[12]

Nonetheless shrewd and circumspect diplomacy on Berlin's part might have made conduct of the war more difficult and less promising for the Entente governments. The last opportunity for placing them publicly before the alternatives of a protracted stalemate or a compromise peace occurred in March 1918. Neither Kühlmann nor any other influential German civilian or military leader seriously considered a renunciatory peace, i.e., return to the *status quo ante bellum*. But neither would Entente statesmen. By extracting the refusal to compromise, the Germans might have complicated the task of the Entente governments *vis-à-vis* their own populations. A German statement of willingness to compromise could have been made cynically and disavowed when convenient. A moderate treaty with Russia could have been revoked after the western powers had been defeated; Brest-Litovsk could not be maintained unless the Allies were conquered, as events later in 1918 would demonstrate. Instead the High Command destroyed the possibility by imposing extreme conditions on Russia and launching its offensive in the west. The war consequently ended as it had begun—with German reliance on military strategy to the exclusion of diplomacy.[13]

CONCLUSIONS

This study argues that the major objective of German policy during World War I was to divide the Entente through the conclusion of separate understandings with its members in order to conquer the enemy powers individually and thereby establish the continental base for German world power. While the details of war aims received considerable attention and caused disagreements among German leaders, agreement existed on general objectives and war aims were subordinated to the goal of dividing the Entente. This study also suggests some conclusions on the influence of leaders' personalities and domestic politics on German policy. It likewise provides an insight into the nature and importance of the tension between German civilian and military authorities. The examination of German policy offers an opportunity to observe the process of policy-formulation and a vehicle for understanding not only the First World War but also the general phenomenon of modern warfare.

* * * * *

German policy during World War I has been the subject of so much dispute that it may justifiably be regarded as the major controversy in German and perhaps even European historiography during the last decade and a half. The opposing interpretations can briefly be summarized as aggression and anxiety. Led by the German historian Fritz Fischer, some have argued that Germany was motivated by aggression in consistently and consciously seeking to establish its dominance over Europe and thereby to achieve world power comparable with the British Empire and the United States. Others—most notably the German historians Gerhard Ritter, Egmont Zechlin and Hans Herzfeld—contended instead that Germany was driven more by anxiety engendered by the threat of encirclement and had no conscious or consistent aspiration for world power. This debate focused on the question of German war aims. Fischer and his supporters argued that German leaders and most Germans before and above all during the war projected explicit and extensive war aims programs which were pursued with only minor variations during the war. Fischer's opponents claimed that such aims were neither consistently sought nor generally accepted. Despite their obvious disagreements, the disputants directed attention to the issue of war aims and thereby established the general framework for evaluation of German policy.[1]

The present study suggests an alternate perspective on German policy. Since the motivations of aggressiveness and anxiety can both be demonstrated, any attempt to emphasize the one by excluding the other is unrealistic. In fact each tended to reinforce the other: German aggressiveness aroused opposition and thereby caused German anxiety; the resulting anxiety prompted reactions which inspired new aggression. Emotions which seem poles apart were actually closely related and probably symbiotic. They were reflected in assertions that Germany had to dominate Europe or collapse in the attempt. Thus a debate in terms of anxiety versus aggression misconstrues German motivations. The Germans were driven by both impulses which reinforced each other increasingly as the war progressed.

The concentration on war aims has contributed to our understanding but has in the process distorted German wartime policy. The significance of individual programs can and should continue to be debated but, taken together, they provide a relatively clear picture of German aspirations. Above all, they constitute what appears to this writer at least as undeniable evidence that the German government, ruling class and apparently most of the population desired expansion of German power to dominate the continent and exercise world power. But a distinction should be drawn between general and specific aims. While the general objectives remained largely the same and unquestioned throughout the war, the specific territorial, economic and other details varied considerably. These variations marked responses to changing conditions and policy considerations. They were a reflection rather than a determinant of general objectives, aspirations rather than commitments, symptoms rather than causes of German behavior. The debate over German war aims furthermore has tended to emphasize the disagreements and obscure the consensus among German leaders. The disagreements over details and degree were important; they are generally the stuff of politics and policy-making. In the process positions became overly rigid and polarized as their protagonists sought to win support and to disqualify their opponents. They thereby concealed the fundamental agreement among German leaders and public on the general goal of world power.

The concept of world power was seldom spelled out precisely and varied from time to time and individual to individual. At the very least it implied minimal territorial annexations but a commanding position on the continent and an end to the old balance of power system, including the Entente; at the most it envisaged a German-dominated *Mitteleuropa* from Spain to Russia and from Norway to the Balkans. The notion's essential element was establishment of a power base on the continent which would allow Germany to play a role comparable with the other world powers—the British Empire, the United States and the Russian Empire. This objective was regarded as indisputably necessary by most Germans since they assumed that the alternative was German decline to the status of a second class state like Switzerland. More important than the specific or momentary details was the currency of the concept among German leaders. For instance, Jagow argued against a general peace in summer 1915 with the claim that it would force Germany "to renounce its world power *[Weltpolitik]* for many years to come and to face very serious domestic financial difficulties."[2] Equally important for German efforts to arrange separate understandings with their opponents, Entente statesmen assumed world power was Germany's objective. Thus it was at once the basic German aim and the major stumbling block in German success.

The recent debate over German war aims has obscured the fact that the central problem for German policy-makers was not projecting but achieving them, less what Germany wanted than how it could be taken. As for all the belligerents, the operative question for the Germans was means rather than ends. This distinction became clear early in the war. German leaders began the conflict assuming that military means would suffice to defeat the Entente. When strategy proved inadequate by the end of 1914, Germany was confronted with a choice among the options of protracted stalemate, general peace and separate peace. The most attractive alternative seemed separate peace since stalemate implied eventual defeat and general peace meant perpetuation of the Entente, renunciation of world power and probably another war. Separate peace was of course not an end in itself but the means for dividing the Entente so as to conquer the remaining opponents and dominate the continent. Peace was thereby to function as a means of war comparable to military operations. When separate peace proved difficult to achieve, German leaders reverted to emphasis on military operations or combinations of diplomacy and strategy. The development and application of these means rather than the projection of war aims consequently was the critical issue for German wartime policy.

War means and war aims must be distinguished but were at the same time interrrelated. The ultimate aim of world power was the motivation for seeking successful means, namely, how to divide and conquer the Entente. But the search for effective means affected the details—though not the essence—of the ultimate aim. When separate peace was sought with one opponent, German demands from that opponent were reduced, while those at the expense of Germany's other enemies were augmented. Many German leaders recognized that the details of war aims would be determined by war means since the circumstances of victory would establish the conditions of peace. The Bavarian envoy in Berlin, Lerchenfeld, summed up the problem well in late 1914: "as long as the size of our victories is uncertain, no decision can be made on the size of our peace conditions."[3] For this reason among others, the details of German aspirations fluctuated and remained tentaive through much of the war. War aims required war means but the success of war means would determine the achievement of war aims.

The primary objective of German wartime policy between November 1914 and March 1918 was to divide the enemy alliance by separate understandings with its members. This goal was shared by most German leaders. Bethmann wrote Ballin in late December 1914 that "for us everything depends on shattering the [enemy] coalition, i.e., on [concluding] a separate peace with one of our enemies."[4] In August 1916 he advocated seeking a separate peace with Russia in order to "blow up the Entente" and thereby achieve "a final decision in this *Volkskrieg.*"[5] In April 1917 he reminded the Kaiser that "our objective will then as now have to be to achieve a separate peace with one of our enemies. . . . The main consideration [at eventual peace negotiations] will be to shatter the present coalition of our opponents and to bring one or several of them over to our side."[6] Jagow advocated the same goal. He wrote Grand Duke Ernest of Hesse in spring 1915 that "no means should remain untried since it must be our aim to split Russia [from its allies] if at all possible."[7] In April 1916 he advocated "blowing up the enemy coalition"[8] and in June stipulated that in eventual negotiations with France Germany would "seek the goal in the first place of shattering the [enemy] coalition through a separate peace and lasting understanding with France."[9] Romberg, the German envoy in Switzerland, shared this view when he advocated offering France easy conditions "for the service it would do us by shattering the enemy coalition;" in his view the main objective sought by the German army and Reichstag, including the Right, was "shattering the enemy coalition,"[10] Kühlmann agreed: he asserted in September 1917 that "we cannot end the war unless we somehow drive a wedge into the enemy coalition."[11] When peace with the Bolsheviks appeared possible in December 1917, he reiterated that "the disruption of the Entente and the subsequent creation of political combinations agreeable to us constitute the most important war aim of our diplomacy."[12]

Zimmermann, while less convinced that it was necessary, nonetheless acknowledged in November 1914 that it was desirable "to drive a wedge among our enemies and to arrange a separate peace as quickly as possible with one or another."[13] The Kaiser was inconsistent in his views but supported the efforts to divide the Entente with a separate peace with Russia and France; in backing Kühlmann's attempt to reach an understanding with England in September 1917, he designated its purpose "as a wedge against the other powers."[14] On an impulse from Tirpitz, Falkenhayn had been the first to urge a separate peace, first with Russia and then with France. While more inclined to seek total victory over all Germany's opponents, Hindenburg and Ludendorff had nonetheless advocated a separate peace with Russia in 1915 and again in spring 1917 and expected the U-boat to drive England out of the war. Kühlmann summed up the problem best in his testimony to the postwar Parliamentary Investigating Committee: in such a coalition war, "he would win who could first split the enemy coalition."[15] In one way or another, all German leaders sought to divide the Entente so as to conquer the continent and establish German world power.

* * * * *

Although applied by all German leaders form November 1914 through March 1918, this policy was frequently varied and redirected. Required primarily by diplomatic and military developments beyond German control, these adjustments were associated with the personalities of specific German leaders. Thus the role of personality in policy-making is implicated.

Much of the history of German and other wartime policy concentrates on the problem of personalities.[16] This approach implies that the personalities of leaders are an important or even critical element. Personality differences certainly existed, policies were often associated with individuals, and disagreements over policy were frequently attributed to personality conflicts. Bethmann, Ludendorff and Hindenburg were at first ranged against Falkenhayn; Bethmann and later Kühlmann opposed Hindenburg and Ludendorff. Falkenhayn's personality is presented as a factor first in his opposition toward an eastern reorientation of strategy and then blind commitment to the Verdun campaign. Bethmann's personality is regarded as influential in his decision to confront the High Command, his dismissal, his replacement by Michaelis and Kühlmann, the Reichstag's involvement, and the High Command's eventual domination. Michaelis and Hertling are frequently presented as tools of the High Command because of personality traits—Michaelis' inexperience with politics and bureaucratic mentality and Hertling's age. Kühlmann's policy is often painted as a result of personal bias in favor of England and the personal traits of egotism, duplicity, ambition, subtlety, etc. The existence of these characteristics is indisputable but does not prove their historical significance. Personality traits can be regarded as important if other personalities were both possible under the existing circumstances and likely to alter events. But, if no other type of individual was conceivable or if such individuals could probably not have significantly altered the outcome, then personalities were of little importance.

The debate over personalities often involved Bethmann. He might have remained in office if he had not confronted the High Command; but to have done so, he would probably have had to pursue a policy very much like that of Michaelis and Kühlmann, in which case the results would have been essentially the same. Thus the idiosyncrasies of Bethmann's personality were probably historically insignificant. The emphasis on personalities frequently appears in regard to Kühlmann. An individual who displayed less initiative was certainly possible and German policy would presumably have been less active if one had been appointed; in that case the unfeasibility of a separate understanding with England would not have been demonstrated. An equally active individual who pursued a different policy might have taken office; Zimmermann, for instance, might have sought a peace with Russia along the lines of Brest-Litovsk durng the summer of 1917 but it was unlikely until the Bolshevik revolution and then occurred even with Kühlmann in office. Another individual who pursued Kühlmann's policies might have taken office; Zimmermann in fact seems to have favored a separate peace with England during the summer of 1917 but was unlikely to succeed any better than Kühlmann. Thus Kühlmann's personality altered the course of events in no important degree.

Hindenburg and Ludendorff loom large during the last two years of the war. Their personalities were essential elements both in their desire to dominate and the policies they advocated. Their appointment had been urged by Bethmann and accepted by the Kaiser in large measure because of the personal characteristics of determination and charisma. These considerations were logical and perhaps necessary under the circumstances, namely, the need to maintain popular support for a longer war. This impulse fostered the contemporaneous emergence of comparable leaders such as Lloyd George, Wilson, Clemenceau and Lenin. Thus, in the sense that personalities like theirs were demanded by the circumstances, no other type of personality could emerge. Although they therefore revealed the total war character of the conflict during its final stage, they neither created nor fundamentally altered the situation. Hindenburg and Ludendorff were unlikely either to defeat the western powers by greater bellicosity or to divide them by less and thereby to change the war's outcome. But neither was any other German statesman or strategist liable to do so. The personalities of Hindenburg and Ludendorff were consequently only marginal factors in the course of events.

The view that personalities are important is nonetheless pervasive. It is encouraged by relations among German leaders. Their disputes over policy and their frustrations with failure tended to be transformed into personal terms, with the result that disagreements were often attributed to personal characteristics. It was then natural to assume that changes in personnel would change policies. This was the impulse for Bethmann's agitation to remove Falkenhayn; if he would not concentrate German forces against Russia, he should be replaced. The characteristics of determination and charisma likewise featured in Bethmann's advocacy of Hindenburg and Ludendorff. Later when Bethmann opposed them, the High Command demanded his replacement because he lacked "the personality to lead."[17] But Falkenhayn's replacement by Hindenburg and Ludendorff probably altered German policies little. The new High Command did not concentrate in the east as Bethmann had hoped and indeed showed sympathy for Falkenhayn's difficulties on the western front. Falkenhayn might very well have successfully advocated unlimited U-boat warfare in 1917 and an offensive on the western front in 1918. German leaders were fascinated by leadership but exaggerated its influence on events.

The emphasis on personality is probably further encouraged by the tendency of German policy-makers to regard individual Entente leaders as critical of their efforts to divide the enemy coalition. In the Russian case, the Tsar was seen as inclined to peace, while Grand Duke Nicholas, Sazonov, and the British ambassador in Petrograd were perceived as the primary stumbling blocks; German hopes rose when Sazonov and the Grand Duke were displaced by Stürmer and Protopopov and then Kerensky and Lenin. Similar assumptions were made about France: French determination to persevere was identified with individuals like Poincaré and opposition with personalities like Caillaux; the significance of personality was twisted to suit assumptions, as when Clemenceau's appointment was interpreted as favorable to peace because he would encourage false hopes. In Kühlmann's efforts to arrange a separate peace with England, the British political scene was perceived in terms of individuals—perseverance was identified with Lloyd George and opposition with Asquith, Landsdowne and Balfour. American mediatory efforts were explained by Wilson's idiosyncracies. The essence of German secret diplomacy was the assumption that individuals could be isolated from their colleagues and constituents. The personalities of individual enemy leaders were viewed as critical, as if they could act in a vacuum. In fact, although they were different personalities and advocated varying approaches, all Entente statesmen who had a realistic chance to take power shared the determination to win the war; however much they might disagree on means, they were unanimous on ends. A striking feature of the war is precisely the continuity of all the belligerents' policies despite the variety of their leaders' personalities. Yet the emphasis on personality is a symptom of the war; trapped as they all were in a frustrating stalemate, the belligerents searched desperately for a messiah who could save them. None was found because no single leader could alter the basic facts of the war and the policies they required.

* * * * *

The recent debate's focus on war aims has tended to illuminate the role of domestic politics in foreign policy. Fischer and his supporters argue that extensive war aims were demanded by virtually all Germans, whereas his opponents claim that only relatively small and eccentric groups favored extreme aims. Fischer and his supporters perceive German leaders as willing and convinced advocates of extreme aims, while his opponents believe German leaders before Hindenburg and Ludendorff were reluctant and acceded only under pressure. Despite these differing interpretations, the disputants agree that the essential impulse for war aims and thus for German policy came from domestic politics. This impulse was conditioned by domestic considerations, above all, the desire either to preserve or change the internal structure. In this writer's view, domestic politics did supply a basic motivation for German pursuit of world power.

This interpretation of the relationship between domestic politics and foreign policy can, however, misconstrue policy. Although an important consideration in the German aspiration for world power, politics did not significantly influence the actual formulation or application of German wartime policy. However much they shared their public's aspirations, virtually all German leaders sought to isolate public opinion from policy-making by disregarding it when they could and minimizing it when they could not. This attitude is attributable in part to the German patricianal tradition of allowing the elite and experts to decide especially in such specialized areas as foreign policy where it was widely assumed that the government knew what was best for the country. Most German leaders felt that consultation was in any case superfluous since they pursued what they assumed were national aspirations. At the same time they recognized that war aims had become entwined with acrimonious domestic issues and thus sought to avoid public discussion of foreign policy in order to reduce dissension and preserve the national unity essential to continuing the war. But they excluded politics for tactical reasons: since peace conditions would depend on the extent of victory and victory required dissolution of the Entente through separate understandings, German policy would have to remain flexible by avoiding public commitments. In short, it appeared desirable for both positive and negative considerations to exclude domestic influences from foreign policy formulation.

Domestic politics increasingly threatened to encroach on policy making as the war progressed but German leaders generally managed to minimize its influence. Demands from the Reichstag and unofficial groups were sometimes acknowledged but never accepted as a commitment by the government. The Reichstag's involvement in Bethmann's resignation and above all its Peace Resolution seemed to promise greater parliamentary influence. But, while disagreeing on policy, Kühlmann and the High Command were at one in preventing the Reichstag from assuming a genuine role in policy-making. The High Command's campaign to organize for total war by mobilizing manpower and morale implied that public opinion was essential but in fact the generals assumed that the masses were passive and allowed them no influence on policy.

German leaders reversed the equation in regard to their opponents. They assumed that enemy public opinion could be sufficiently discouraged to force enemy governments to sue for peace; this was the objective of their propaganda, contacts with enemy politicians, the Verdun campaign, the peace offer at the end of 1916 and unlimited U-boat warfare. The core of the total war concept was the assumption that victory would go to the side whose people persevered longer. Thus German leaders regarded enemy public opinon as an active element but their own population as relatively passive.

*   *   *   *   *

Studies of German wartime policy often conentrate on the conflict between civil and military authorities. Indeed the takeover of Hindenburg and Ludendorff is sometimes viewed as the classic case of militarism.[18] On one level this is a useful approach. It is undeniable that distinguishable civilian and military groups existed, that they felt mutual antipathies, and that policy disagreements repeatedly took the form of civil-versus-military. Struggles over respective areas of authority occurred from the war's outbreak to its conclusion over such questions as the formulation of war aims and conduct of peace negotiations. Mutual distrust grew as each suspected the other of seeking to shift responsiblity for awkward decisions and failures. Each side sought to trump the other by *faits accomplis* and threats to resign. Alternations between strategy and politics created the appearence that they were mutually exclusive: when diplomacy failed during the July crisis of 1914, German leaders resorted to strategy; strategy's failure by the end of 1914 caused diplomacy's revival; diplomacy and strategy were unable to separate Russia or France in 1915 and the Verdun campaign seemed the best recourse; when France persevered, diplomacy was tested again at the end of 1916; the Entente rejection of peace cleared the way for unrestricted U-boat warfare which did not force England out of the war and diplomatic means again seemed appropriate; the renewed failure of diplomacy seemed to justify a final offensive in March 1918. Each of these failures produced frustration, disagreement, personal antipathies and struggles over authority which often took the form of civil-military rivalry. The relative power of the two elements shifted with the changes of policy: strategists tended to dominate when strategy promised success and statesmen prevailed when policy was the determinant. There was, however, a rapid lurch toward the military—in the persons of Hindenburg and Ludendorff—after 1917. The wartime tensions perpetuated the traditions of constitutional, practical and personal rivalries which had characterized German politics for centuries. The conflict was consequently an undeniably important feature of German policy-formulation.

The civil-military distinction can, however, be overemphasized. Despite appearances, it became less rather than more relevant during the war. German civilian and military leaders were agreed on the ultimate goal of world power, while their disagreements over aims and means are not clearly explicable in terms of civil-military categories: Hindenburg and Ludendorff joined Bethmann against Falkenhayn and many civilians shared the extensive aims of the High Command, while some soldiers advocated more moderate aims. Although civil-military tensions certainly existed, periods of toleration and even cooperation occurred: Falkenhayn applied the eastern strategy desired by Bethmann during the summer of 1915; the Verdun campaign exerted the pressure on France which Bethmann had hoped for; Falkenhayn's Rumanian offensive seemed the precondition for a separate peace with Russia in late 1916; Bethmann, Hindenburg and Ludendorff all sought separate understandings with Russia in the spring of 1917; the High Command approved Kühlmann's initial efforts to arrange peace with England in the autumn of 1917. More important, strategy and policy became increasingly interdependent: at the end of 1914, most German leaders recognized that strategy could not succeed without the assistance of policy in dividing the Entente but it soon became clear that a separate peace was unlikely unless strategy defeated at least one opponent. In short, military success required diplomacy and diplomatic success required strategy.

This interdependence had paradoxical results. Soldiers called on statecraft to resolve their military problems and thereby implied that it was the critical element, while statesmen looked to strategy as the solution for their dilemma and implied that it was the crucial factor. Each regarded the ultimate determinant of the war as the other's speciality: first Falkenhayn and later Hindenburg and Ludendorff perceived political, economic and psychological considerations as critical, while Bethmann and other civilians argued that the war would be won through military and diplomatic means. At the same time, each intimated that the other's problems were less complex: Falkenhayn thought a separate peace with Russia was simple, while Bethmann sought to produce Russian defeat by merely altering strategy. When failures occurred, each side tended to blame the other and thereby to suggest that it held the key to success.

The takeover by Hindenburg and Ludendorff is generally interpreted as a victory for the military. It is undeniable that the two men were soldiers, interpreted civilian problems in paramilitary terms, and despised civilians as a group. It is, however, doubtful whether military status is the explanation either for their domination or policies. The major consideration in their appointment and power was the public image of Hindenburg, i.e., essentially a political and psychological concern. Another element was their conception of the war as total which corresponded more closely with reality than did the limited war assumptions of Bethmann and Kühlmann. Yet the total war notion is not specifically a military point of view: most military men preferred to see the war in more limited and thus controllable terms, whereas many civilians—e.g., Lloyd George, Clemenceau, Lenin, and perhaps Wilson—viewed it as total. To the extent that it was either, the total war concept was more civilian than military since it saw the critical element as the whole society rather than merely its army. In fact it is probably most accurate to perceive war as the integration rather than isolation of civil and military aspects. The victory of Hindenburg and Ludendorff is consequently misunderstood if regarded exclusively in civil-military terms.

The civil-military issue is frequently construed morally, namely, as "good" civilians versus "bad" soldiers. This formulation is probably due to a number of factors. Generally civilians, most historians find the civilian point of view more compatible; those who are committed to the liberal standpoint usually believe civilian authority should prevail over military. As personalities, the German civilian leaders were perhaps more attractive than their military counterparts, although the contrast is less clear in the case of Falkenhayn and Bethmann than it is between Bethmann on the one hand and Ludendorff or Hindenburg on the other. For Anglo-American historians there exists the additional distinction that the civilians generally opposed the U-boat, whereas the military generally advocated it. Perhaps above all, it is widely assumed that the civilians pursued moderate objectives and favored peace, whereas the soldiers had extreme goals and favored war. These biases are misleading. Like the proponents of unlimited U-boat warfare, the opponents considered it in pragmatic rather than moral terms. Both civilians and military advocated world power and accepted the necessity of war to achieve it. Both sought to use peace as a means of war and were motivated by political rather than humanitarian considerations. In moderating their war aims, the civilian leaders were motivated by concerns for practicality rather than morality. Thus no moral distinction should be drawn between German soldiers and statesmen.

The soldiers' policies are frequently compared unfavorably with those of the statesmen in terms of realism and consistency. Falkenhayn's attack on Verdun is often crticized because it did not produce French defeat; but its objective was less defeat than attrition to produce French collapse. The alternatives to attrition were no more practical granted the assumptions prevailing among German leaders: a general, compromise peace was seriously entertained by no German leader at the time, while a general, defensive strategy was unacceptable because the alternative of continuing the war seemed less onerous to France, i.e., because of political and diplomatic rather than military considerations. Falkenhayn's strategy was thus consistent with German aspirations and failed not because of its conception but because of German weakness and French tenacity. The hopes of Bethmann and Jagow that France could somehow be bribed or cajoled into peace were less realistic.

Ludendorff's policies are also usually regarded as less realistic and consistent than those of Bethmann and Kühlmann. This evaluation is due primarily to the fact that Bethmann and Kühlmann specifically committed themselves to less extensive territorial aims. But this distinction is deceptive since all sought the goal of world power. The question therefore reduces to the relative consistency and realism of their means. On the surface, the civilians' means seem more realistic because of their subtlety and duplicity which contrast sharply with Ludendorff's rough and candid approach. But the civilians' policy was based on the fundamental contradiction that it sought the total end of world power with the limited means of negotiating separate understandings. In fact the Entente powers would not conclude a separate peace if they could continue fighting and would only if they were defeated—in which case the negotiations were a formality, as demonstrated by the treaty of Brest-Litovsk. The civilians' policy was consequently caught in a trap: separate peace was feasible only when it had become unnecessary but was unfeasible when it was necessary. The German civilians tried to escape this dilemma by concealing their ultimate objective or hoping that their enemies preferred German domination to continued war. Ludendorff on the other hand advocated total means to achieve total ends and accurately surmised that Germany's enemies recognized the implications of German victory and would therefore reject separate peace until defeated. In this sense Ludendorff was more realistic than Bethmann and Kühlmann. Ludendorff's problem that German power was insufficient to defeat all its opponents was not his alone but shared by all German leaders. Since they could not increase German power, they could only reduce German aspirations. No German statesman seriously considered renouncing the pursuit of world power and thus all were caught in the same contradiction.

The implication of German leaders' policies are different from what they sometimes appear. Because of their reputedly moderate ends and their subtle means, the civilians are usually seen as less dangerous than Hindenburg and Ludendorff. Since all sought the same end of German world power, any distinction among them must lie in the area of means. But neither was able to achieve the goal of world power and this distinction probably made little difference; the takeover by Hindenburg and Ludendorff is therefore of little historical significance. Yet, to the extent that the differences between civilian and military means affected events, those of Bethmann and Kühlmann were more likely to conceal German objectives and thus divide the

Entente. The civilians' policies were thus potentially more rather than less dangerous than those of the soldiers.

* * * * *

In their efforts to divide the Entente, German leaders acted upon certain assumptions about France, Russia, and England. These assumptions were also reflected in German perceptions of Germany's major ally, Austria-Hungary, and major non-European enemy, the United States.

The German view of Austria-Hungary was thoroughly functional and unencumbered by sentiment or principle. The essential objective was maintenance of the Habsburg Empire as a diversion for Russia. This had been the most important motivation for German support during the July crisis of 1914 and remained so throughout the war. The Germans consequently sought to prevent Austro-Hungarian defection by a combination of pacification and dissimulation. This approach characterized their discussion of war aims and the possibility of a postwar union. Extensive German aims at Habsburg expense— including the possibility of virtual absorption into a German-dominated *Mitteleuropa*—were concealed behind more moderate schemes and dilatory or vague answers whenever disagreements emerged. The same procedure was applied to Austria-Hungary in regard to separate peace efforts. Consultation occurred when it seemed necessary to reduce the risk of Austro-Hungarian defection. The allies in fact agreed during 1915 on the desirability of a separate peace with Russia and the Germans kept Vienna informed on the general progress of negotiations. Although primarily designed to divide the Entente, the German peace offer of December 1916 was also inspired by the desire to shore up the alliance by giving the impression of sharing Vienna's hope for a general compromise peace. Bethmann and Kühlmann worked during 1917 to persuade Vienna that they were not unalterably opposed to a general peace. The possibility of a separate peace with Bolshevik Russia again brought German and Austro-Hungarian policies into seeming accord and Kühlmann observed the formality of consulting with Czernin in connection with negotiations at Brest-Litovsk. The appearance of agreement was thus fostered by the German government.

In reality genuine cooperation was impossible because the allies pursued incompatible objectives. Austria-Hungary wanted to rescue its great power status without being dominated by Germany, whereas Germany would rescue Austria-Hungary only if it could impose its domination. This conflict of interests emerged increasingly after 1917 because of growing Austro-Hungarian weakness, the candor of

Hindenburg and Ludendorff, and the prospects of annexations in the east. It affected the German pursuit of separate understandings with the Entente. The Germans recognized that differences would develop in a separate peace with Russia, and regarded understandings with France and England as their exclusive preserve. Their general agreement on the desirability of a separate understanding with Russia in 1915 would probably have been short-lived if the Russians had responded since disputes would have occurred over territorial aspirations and Austria-Hungary, having achieved its major aim, might have either concentrated against Italy or even left the war. Little coordination of peace policy existed in early 1916 when German attention was rigidly fixed on Verdun. Seeing Austro-Hungarian agitation for a general peace in 1917 as a threat to their efforts to divide the Entente, Bethmann and Kühlmann were more concerned to restrain than consult. The domination of Hindenburg and Ludendorff combined with Austro-Hungarian decline in 1918 to subordinate Vienna increasingly to Berlin. The peace of Brest-Litovsk and the German spring offensive were decided upon without genuine concern for Austro-Hungarian interests. Consultation with allies was no more important than negotiations with enemies as long as total victory seemed possible on the battlefield.

The main German concern in regard to the United States was to limit its effect on the war. Berlin pursued this objective in practical terms by working to preserve American neutrality as long as possible. The Germans thereby demonstrated some awareness of American economic and military potential but were motivated equally by the fear that American entry would persuade the European neutrals to join the ranks of their enemies. Thus German leaders—particularly the civilians—opposed unlimited U-boat warfare and sought to pacify the Americans. But more characteristically German leaders limited American influence by the mental device of minimizing its importance. Even opponents of the U-boat such as Bethmann were less concerned about its effect on the United States than on England, which it would force to continue the war rather than reconcile itself to German continental domination. Most German leaders felt that the Americans were aiding the Entente as much as they could and that American military assistance would be minimal and tardy. Above all, the American reaction had to be subordinated to the calculation that the U-boat was the only means of producing a German victory by the end of 1917. Even if it had been possible, foreknowledge of the Russian revolution would probably not have altered German behavior. The revolution initially produced more rather than less Russian commitment to war and the Bolshevik takeover was far from certain. Furthermore the U-boat was most successful in the spring of 1917 when it would have had to be postponed to avoid American entry. Most important for their efforts to divide the Entente, German leaders disregarded the psychological impact of American entry which erased Entente hopelessness and thereby any chance of German success. Hindenburg and Ludendorff likewise dismissed the United States as a significant factor in their 1918 campaign.

This attitude toward the United States provides a further insight into German thinking. The Germans negated the United States because it would otherwise have constituted an insurmountable obstacle to their aspirations. Had they recognized that American entry prevented French or British surrender, the Germans would have had to renounce their efforts to divide the Entente. But, since the Entente's dissolution was necessary to German continental domination, it was essential to dismiss the psychological effect of American entry. The Germans had to minimize the likelihood of large-scale American involvement in Europe for the same reason: German continental domination would become impractical if the United States became deeply involved. American power likewise had to be regarded as limited since German aspirations for world power would have to be forsaken if it was admitted that American power overshadowed a continent under German control. German aspirations consequently demanded the assumption that American entry was not critical.

* * * * *

German policy was conditioned not only by individuals and elements of the German government and society but also by the process of its formulation. The efforts to divide the Entente were based on assumptions about Germany's enemies which were related to the intelligence gathered and interpreted by the German government.

The sources of German information were affected by the war. Since the basic elements of enemy societies persisted into the war, the primary facts were based on prewar experience. But predictions of future behavior demanded sources of fresh information. The main source remained the enemy press whose importance was augmented by the disappearance of the other major source, namely, formal diplomatic relations. These official contacts were replaced by unofficial channels through individuals who presented themselves as intermediaries. Another prewar source which persisted and indeed became more important was the neutrals, above all, Switzerland and Denmark. German information might have been improved by greater

coordination among the various departments of the German government, especially the Foreign Office, General Staff and Admiralty.
The lack of mutual confidence and frequent antipathy discouraged
sharing and promoted the development of autonomous intelligence
operations. The ultimate effect, however, was probably minimal
since all departments relied primarily on the enemy press and no
information which was available but not shared would have significantly altered German policy.

The accuracy of German information varied according to its source.
Although censored and converted into propaganda organs to greater
or lesser degree, the enemy press remained the best source in terms
of quantity and validity. Above all, it reflected the basic facts of
enemy societies: the stresses of war but the determination to persevere. Neutral governments were the next most dependable source.
All were influenced by their perceptions of their own national interests, above all, by the dual motives of encouraging a compromise
peace to preserve the balance of power but of preparing for the
eventuality of one side's victory. Each had its particular concerns:
Denmark, for instance, feeling trapped between Germany and England, worked for an Anglo-German *rapprochement*. Information related to a neutral's interests was consequently likely to be distorted
but otherwise was relatively accurate. The least reliable source was
the unofficial contacts whose authority was difficult if not impossible
to ascertain. Some were doubtless enemy agents whose task it was to
produce misleading information. Those who were not frequently exaggerated their role for psychological, financial or humanitarian
reasons and often reported what they sensed the Germans wanted to
hear in order to preserve their appeal as contacts. As a result, these
individuals so perverted their information that the medium may be
said to have become the message. These were not specifically German
problems and German information was probably not significantly
worse or better than that of the other belligerents.

The basic intelligence problem for the Germans as well as the
other belligerents was less information than interpretation. They had
sufficient information and experience to make realistic judgments on
the prospects for dividing the Entente. The bulk of information at
their disposal in terms of both quantity and quality indicated that
separate understandings were unlikely, while only occasional and
usually unreliable sources suggested the contrary. Yet the Germans
chose the less reliable information and disregarded or explained away
the rest. Information was interpreted to fit preconceived assumptions.

Assumptions about their opponents' behavior were thus the primary determinants of German policy. It was assumed that the disappointment of Entente hopes for military victory would produce defeatism and the realization that territory occupied by Germany could be liberated only by an accommodation with Germany. The Germans were correct in expecting Entente military failures and German military successes to produce Entente disappointment but Entente defeatism remained limited and insufficient to cause demands for peace until the Bolsheviks did so in 1918. The Germans might have concluded that their assumptions were fallacious and renounced any hope of dividing the Entente. But dissolution of the Entente was the precondition for German world power. Since they did not want to sacrifice their aspiration, the Germans had to maintain the assumption that the enemy alliance could be shattered. Their aspiration necessitated their assumption.

These preconceptions determined German perceptions of their enemies. Because separate peace was essential, it seemed possible. Rather than first finding evidence for enemy inclination to conclude separate understandings, the Germans decided that they were possible and proceeded to find proof. Groups and events were consequently distorted to accommodate assumptions: enemy advocates of perseverance were dismissed as unrepresentative, enemy disappointment was exaggerated into defeatism, and enemy domestic political disagreements magnified into imminent revolution. Domestic criticism of enemy conduct of the war was distorted into condemnation of the war altogether. Disaffection among the Entente was blown up into alliance crises. Enemy responses were perceived less in terms of enemy interests than of German expectations: when they themselves took the offensive, the Germans assumed that the threat of defeat would cause their opponents to sue for peace; when they repelled Entente offensives, the Germans assumed that Entente disappointment would cause defeatism. Larger considerations were subordinated to details: the personalities of individuals like the Tsar and Caillaux seemed critical, whereas widespread Russian and French determination to preserve their great power status and thus their alliance was regarded as marginal. Enemy leaders were dehumanized and converted into two dimensional stereotypes: the Tsar, for instance, was viewed as peace-loving but deceived by bellicose advisers and unscrupulous allies. When events were susceptible to a number of interpretations, the most favorable was frequently chosen, whereas the least favorable was usually more accurate. In short, reality was adjusted to aspirations and German perceptions tell more about how German leaders wished the world to be than how it actually was. Their behavior shows the extent to which men can delude themselves under the compulsion of necessity.

* * * * *

The present study's focus implies that German policy-making was both rational and significant. This was the basic assumption of German and other wartime leaders. Rational policy-making presumes that the interrelationships among events can be comprehended. German leaders reflected this assumption in their memoranda and discussions by isolating and analyzing factors which they felt influenced or determined the course of events. Rational policy-making further presumes that policy-makers can be sufficiently unprejudiced to project policies which are appropriate to the circumstances. While often condemning their opponents, German leaders acted on the assumption that their own poicies fit the situation. Finally the results of policies must be predictable it policy-making is to be rational. In arguing for their particular policies, German leaders necessarily anticipated favorable results and thus assumed that events could be predicted. Policy-making is significant if it controls events in the sense of producing desired results. The policy disputes among German leaders demonstrated that they made this assumption: the right decision would produce the desired result, the wrong decision would not. Thus German leaders assumed that their policy-making was both rational and significant. Indeed all great power leaders made the same assumption.

This view of policy-making was reflected in the notion of a "key" factor or moment. German leaders regarded the Entente's dissolution as critical to their success. In arguing for a separate peace with this or that opponent, German leaders usually asserted that it was "the keystone" or "soul" of the Entente. The conclusion of an understanding with Russia was believed to depend on some specific detail: various Russian war aims (such as the Dardanelles or Poland), the defeat of Russia allies (Serbia and Rumania), military setbacks, personalities (the Tsar, Grand Duke Nicholas, Sazonov, Stürmer, Miliukov, Lenin, etc.), or a particular event or moment (e.g., the fall of Bucharest). The key to peace with France was variously seen to be French military defeats or setbacks, attrition (as at Verdun), domestic strife or change of government, popular defeatism, disappointment with France's allies, or specific aims (especially Alsace-Lorraine). England's willingness to renounce its allies was assumed to depend on Belgium, the threat of starvation through the U-boat, disappointment with its allies, or German moderation toward France and/or

Russia; the "propitious moment" for peace with England was seen first as early 1917, then as the autumn of 1917. Many German leaders believed that German aims were the key to separate understandings with their opponents. The advocates of concentrating on one front or another claimed that it was critical to German victory. Similar thinking pervaded Entente discussions in which statesmen and soldiers asserted that this or that element, person, strategy or moment was the key to success. Such claims assumed that their advocates could comprehend events and that their strategies could control events. In short, policy-making was assumed to be rational and significant.

This assumption was seldom borne out by events. German leaders infrequently understood events because of the war's complexity and their own preconceptions. They were consequently unable in general to develop realistic policies. The complexity of events made the results of decisions virtually impossible to predict. They were therefore unable to influence events in the desired direction. Rather than the determinant of events, German policy was more often the victim. It frequently developed in response to previous setbacks: the failure of military means caused resort to diplomatic and the insufficiency of diplomatic means recourse to military; the failure to conclude peace with one opponent led to attempts with another. Policies and strategies seldom produced the anticipated results: the Schlieffen plan, the Verdun campaign, the U-boat and the March 1918 offensives did not produce victory but the summer offensive of 1915 against Russia was unexpectedly successful. The 1915 campaign in fact offers a useful example: developing out of a supposedly limited operation designed to rescue Austria-Hungary but to avoid large-scale German reinforcements, it produced a major success and resulted in German concentration in the east. The problem was insightfully summarized by Wild von Hohenborn, Prussian Minister of War:

> At first, Falkenhayn wanted to go only to the San, then he was driven to Lemburg, then the push along the Bug occurred. All developed historically, as if by itself, each event out of the previous. At first, no one here [in the General Staff] thought about the great, final operation [i.e., to defeat Russia completely]. Only later will the events be presented in history as a "plan of genius." Anyone who has had first hand experience, however, knows that strategy is a simple thing. One limited goal follows another. What the layman thinks about it, God only knows.[19]

In short, policy was less a matter of shaping than of probing and responding to events.

Pragmatism was thus the essence of German diplomacy and is particularly evident in the efforts to divide the Entente. Perhaps the most salient feature of these attempts was their oscillations: the

Germans sought understandings first with one opponent, then with another, and sometimes with two at once. Their behavior can be perceived as inconsistency or indecision as to which enemy was most important. It is better interpreted as evidence of the German conviction that their main objective was less the defeat of any particular enemy than the dissolution of the Entente. German policy was adjusted as the prospects of separate understandings with their opponents fluctuated. Thus, rather than being inconsistent or indecisive, the Germans persistently and consciously pursued their objective. Their means of pursuing it were, however, repeatedly changed in response to unforeseen events.

This pragmatism is revealed by the amoral character of German policy as exemplified by the German perception of peace. Those who advocated peace during the First World War were sometimes presented as humanitarian and thus morally "good," whereas those who opposed it were seen as "bad." This framework was often associated with the civil-military distinction—the civilians being seen as advocates of peace, the soldiers of war. The issue was raised after the war as a way of attributing responsibility for prolonging the terrible ordeal. Moral and humanitarian considerations motivated some historians, private individuals and neutral statesmen but few leaders of belligerent states. The Germans and their opponents evaluated peace solely in terms of a political calculation: Bethmann, for instance, argued in November 1914 that a separate peace with Russia would offer the benefit of allowing Germany to defeat the western powers "at the cost" of German renunciation of war aims in the east.[20] This attitude was neither exceptional nor illogical but virtually demanded by the role of wartime statesman. No leader could retain office if he placed the humanitarian demands of peace over the demands of national interest as perceived by his colleagues and constituents. In short, peace had become a means of war.

The non-ideology of German policy likewise reflected its pragmatism. German leaders were ideologically committed at home in their determination to preserve the existing social and political structure; indeed this was to be the main function of victory. Although their aspirations would revolutionize the European state system, German leaders perceived it in essentially traditional terms and the war was seen as the struggle between traditional coalitions. They relied overwhelmingly on traditional means to divide the Entente: most of their efforts were directed toward official governments and rulers; when these proved unresponsive or negative, traditional opposition groups were sought out in order to encourage a change of government and thus policy. Less traditional methods and groups were meanwhile investigated—disruptive and even revolutionary elements which might frighten the ruling classes, slow or disrupt the war effort, or even produce open insurrection and perhaps cause the takeover by parties which would conclude separate understandings with Germany. The Germans sought to encourage such dissidents with financial aid and most successfully by expediting Lenin's return to Russia; despite its extreme conditions, the treaty of Brest-Litovsk in fact helped the Bolsheviks remain in power. The ideologically bizarre situation thereby developed that a reactionary German government encouraged international revolution. The contradiction is of course explained by the opportunism of German policy. In their choice of partners for separate understandings, German leaders were unaffected by ideological considerations. They generally approached traditional elements not because they were conservative but because they were in power and could make peace. When the Bolsheviks took over, the Germans had no hesitation in dealing with them. Whatever seemed useful in dividing the Entente—dynastic solidarity, sympathy toward reform or encouragement to revolution—was appropriate.

The historical significance of German decision-making should be evaluated in the light of its pragmatic character. The present work's orientation implies that decision-making is historically important. This is generally the assumption of statesmen and diplomatic historians. It can certainly be argued that a few decisions—such as the campaigns of 1914, 1916 and 1918 and the U-boat—were important in that they altered the course of events. Yet decisions and decision-making should be distinguished. Decision-making involves the decision-maker's analysis of the situation, development of policy, prediction of results, and power to produce desired effects. Policy-making can be regarded as important if analyses are relatively accurate, appropriate policies are chosen, results are predictable, and the power is available. In short, the development of policy is historically important if a significant correlation exists between what decision-makers perceive and desire and what actually happens. There was in fact very little relationship. Events were too complex to comprehend, policies were largely inappropriate to the circumstances, results were unpredictable, and the power to achieve objectives was usually lacking. Thus, while some decisions proved important in altering the course of events, the decision-making behind them was generally not historically influential. Wartime decision-making was often intersting but seldom relevant to the war's progress.

The relative success and failure of German policy-making must be judged in this context. On one level German diplomacy can be said to have failed since it did not divide the Entente. Critics of German policy attribute this failure to exorbitant war aims which they argue complicated or even precluded separate understandings; this is the basic assumption for the view that German war aims were historically significant. These aims certainly existed and thus hypothetically could have been reduced or even renounced; in fact this was unlikely because of the aspirations of German leaders and the demands of their colleagues and constituents. But the existence of aims does not prove their importance. The argument that they precluded separate understandings assumes that Germany's opponents would have concluded peace if moderate conditions had been offered. It was, however, unlikely that the Entente governments would have responded: not the conditions of peace but the preservation of their great power status was their main concern and required maintenance of their alliance. The details of German war aims were therefore irrelevant to the success of German policy. Such a conclusion suggests that German policy could not have succeeded however it had been formulated. The critical determinant was less German policy than German power: as long as Germany could threaten the great power status of the other powers, they would have to maintain their alliance, thus reject German separate peace offers, and thereby insure the failure of German policy. But, if German policy could not succeed, it is misleading to describe it as unsuccessful and more accurate to regard it as impractical.

* * * * *

Although German and other policy-making can be regarded as historically insignificant, it nonetheless provides useful insights into the war's character. The coalition dimension, the forces released by the war, the constraints on war leadership, and the nature of the European state system were thereby revealed.

German efforts to divide the Entente suggested the ambiguous quality of alliances. While the Germans devalued alliances in that they consulted their allies little and often implied that the Entente could easily be shattered, their persistent and sometimes compulsive attempts to conclude separate understandings demonstrate that they believed alliances were crucial. The alliances were important but had different implications for each side: it was desirable for the Germans to maintain their own alliance but necessary to divide their opponents, whereas it was essential for the Entente to preserve their alliance but advantageous to isolate Germany. However predictable, the Entente's importance would not have been conclusively proven had the Germans not tested it. The altered significance of alliances simultaneously illustrated the war's evolution: the war began as a relatively limited conflict in which alliance politics and diplomacy seemed crucial but ended as a total and revolutionary struggle in which traditional alliances and diplomacy became peripheral.

German policy indicated the revolutionary forces released by the war. The war required the mobilization of the masses which confronted policy-makers with a profound problem of winning mass support without granting the masses influence over policy. German and other leaders succeeded at the cost of mortgaging their power: they maintained control over policy-making by promising victory. Yet the human costs of the war and need to maintain mass morale required the prospects of ever-greater rewards. Thus, as their promises increased, governmental power to fulfill them decreased and the prospect of domestic revolution consequently grew as the war continued. German policy also fostered international revolution. However traditional their perceptions and methods, German efforts to divide the Entente, dominate the continent, and establish world power implied the end of the European state system. Although they could not achieve this objective, the Germans obliged their opponents to commit such extensive resources that the great power system was profoundly weakened. Above all, the inability of policy-makers to comprehend and control events demonstrated the war's complexity. Total and revolutionary rather than limited and traditional, the war's outcome depended on societies as a whole rather than merely strategy or diplomacy and thus on forces which were beyond the understanding or influence of leaders.

German policy demonstrated the constraints on war leadership. Internal developments radically augmented governmental power: administration was centralized, the economy controlled, legal restraints on government reduced, the press censored, and opposition generally paralyzed or coopted. Above all, the masses were not only willing to accept leadership but desperately sought a savior to whom they could submit. Yet governments could not produce victory and the paradox emerged that governments were less potent as their powers increased. A messiah became more desirable as he became less likely to succeed.

Finally German policy provides insights into the nature of great power status and the European state system. In their efforts to dominate the continent, the Germans assumed the traditional role of hegemonic power. Trapped between their power and aspirations, they had sufficient strength to try but not enough to succeed. Like their predecessors, the Germans were driven by anxiety and arrogance:

the fear that their opportunity might pass but the determination to exploit it. Hypothetically, the Germans could have rejected this role but their assumption of it was virtually demanded by the imperative that great powers defend and augment their power. The Entente powers chose to defend their great power status for the same reason and thereby played the traditional role of defenders of the balance of power and state system. Hypothetically, they too might have rejected the function and concluded—as the Germans hoped—that it was preferable to be dominated by Germany than decimated by war. But none of the Entente powers seriously considered this alternative because the urge to preserve their great power status was too compelling. Thus German policy not only activated the European state system but also began the process of its destruction.

FOOTNOTES

Introduction

1. John A. Moses (ed.), *The War Aims of Imperial Germany: Professor Fritz Fischer and His Critics*, St. Lucia (Queensland, Australia) 1968; Ernst W. Graf Lynar (ed.), *Deutsche Kriegsziele, 1914-1918*, Frankfurt/Berlin, 1964. Fischer's position is most succinctly put in: *World Power or Decline*, New York, 1974. Translation and introduction by L. L. Farrar, Jr.

Chapter I

1. For details of the author's views on European diplomacy before 1914, see: L. L. Farrar, Jr., "Impotence of Omnipotence: The Paralysis of the European Great Power System, 1870-1914," *International Review of History and Political Science*, February, 1972, pp. 13-44.

2. For details of the author's views on the July crisis, see: L. L. Farrar, Jr., "Limits of Choice: July 1914 Reconsidered," *Journal of Conflict Resolution*, March, 1972, pp. 1-23.

3. For details of the author's views, see: L. L. Farrar, Jr., "The Short-War Illusion: The Syndrome of German Military Strategy, August-December, 1914, *Militärgeschichtliche Mitteilungen*, October, 1972, pp. 39-44 (hereafter Farrar, "Illusion"); L. L. Farrar, Jr., *The Short-War Illusion: An Analysis of German Policy, Strategy and Domestic Affairs, August-December, 1914*. Foreword by James Joll. Santa Barbara, 1973 (hereafter Farrar, *Illusion*).

4. Farrar, "Illusion," pp. 44-50; Farrar, *Illusion*, pp. 7-12; Gerhard Ritter, *The Schlieffen Plan*, London, 1958 (hereafter Ritter, *Plan*). Erich von Falkenhayn, *Die Oberste Heeresleitung 1914-19 in ihren wichtigsten Entschliessungen*, Berlin, 1920, pp. 14-20 (hereafter Falkenhayn, *Heeresleitung*).

5. Farrar, "Illusion," pp. 44-45; Farrar, *Illusion*, pp. 19-37; Ritter, *Plan*, p. 94.

6. Farrar, *Illusion*, pp. 31-33, 89-94.

7. Ibid., pp. 60-66, 94-101.

8. Ibid., pp. 19-31, 57-59.

9. Ibid., p. 68; Document A 16470, A 16746, 19228, German Foreign Office File WK2.

10. Farrar, *Illusion*, pp. 68-71, 106-11; A 16086, A 17761, A 31349, A 34380, WK 2; AS 2369, AS 2708, AS 2724, zu 2793, AS 2796, zu A 35684, WK 2 geh; André Scherer and Jacques Grunewald (eds.), *L'Allemagne et les problèmes de la paix pendant la première guerre mondiale*, Paris, 1962, Volume I (hereafter Scherer, *L'Allemagne*); Edward House, *The Intimate Papers of Colonel House*, ed. C. Seymour, London, 1926, Volume I, pp. 328-45 (hereafter House, *Papers*); *Papers Relating to the Foreign Relations of the United States, 1914*, Washington, D. C., p. 98 (hereafter *Papers*); Cecil Spring-Rice, *Letters and Friendships of Sir Cecil Spring-Rice*, London, 1929, Volume II, p. 222 (hereafter Spring-Rice, *Letters*); Oskar Strauss, *Under Four Administrations*, Boston, 1922, p. 384; Ester Caukin, "Peace Proposals of Germany and Austria-Hungary, 1914-1918," unpublished Ph.D. dissertation, Stanford University, 1927, p. 4 (hereafter Caukin, "Proposals"); Rudolf Stadelmann, "Friedensversuche in den ersten Jahren des Weltkrieges," *Historische Zeitschrift*, October, 1937, p. 498 (hereafter Stadelmann, "Friedensversuche"); Kent Forster, *The Failures of Peace*, Washington, D. C., 1941, p. 62 (hereafter Forster, *Failures*); Johann H. Bernstorff, *My Three Years in America*, London, 1920, pp. 57-58 (hereafter Bernstorff, *Years*); Hans W. Gatzke, *Germany's Drive to the West: A Study of Germany's Western War Aims during the First World War*, Baltimore, 1950, pp. 16-17 (hereafter Gatzke, *Drive*); Dieter Ahlswede, "Friedensbemühungen zwischen dem Deutschen Reich und Grossbritannien 1914-1918," unpublished Ph.D. dissertation, University of Bonn, 1959, pp. 20-28 (hereafter Ahlswede, "Friedensbemühungen"); James W. Gerard, *My Four Years in Germany*, New York, 1917, pp. 162-73 (hereafter Gerard, *Years*); Klaus Epstein, *Matthias Erzberger and the Dilemma of German Democracy*, Princeton, 1959, pp. 210ff (hereafter Epstein, *Erzberger*); Theobald von Bethmann-Hollweg, *Betrachtungen zum Weltkriege*, Berlin 1922, Volume II, pp. 26-27 (hereafter Bethmann, *Betrachtungen*).

11. Memoranda collected in WK 15; Erich O. Volkmann (ed.), *Die Annexionsfragen des Weltkrieges. Das Werk des Untersuchungsausschusses*, Reihe 4, Volume XII, Part 1, Berlin, 1929, pp. 35ff (hereafter Volkmann, *Annexionsfragen*); Gatzke, *Drive*; Farrar, *Illusion*, pp. 20-22; Fritz Fischer, "Deutsche Kriegsziele, Revolutionierung und Separatfrieden im Osten, 1914-1918," *Historische Zeitschrift*, 188, pp. 249-310 (hereafter Fischer, "Kriegziele"); Fritz Fischer, *Griff nach der Weltmacht*, Düsseldorf, 1964, pp. 109-37 (hereafter Fischer, *Griff*); Gerhard Ritter, *Staatskunst und Kriegshandwerk*, Munich, 1964, Volume III, pp. 15-54 (hereafter Ritter, *Staatskunst*); Egmont Zechlin, "Deutschland zwischen Kabinettskrieg

und Wirtschaftskrieg," *Historische Zeitschrift*, 199, pp. 347-458 (hereafter Zechlin, "Deutschland").

12. Farrar, *Illusion*, pp. 22-28; Fischer, "Kriegsziele," pp. 255-56; Fischer, *Griff*, pp. 113-19; Ritter, *Staatskunst*, pp. 44-47; Werner Conze, *Polnische Nation und deutsche Politik im ersten Weltkrieg*, Cologne, 1958, p. 67 (hereafter Conze, *Nation*).

13. Farrar, *Illusion*, pp. 27-28; Bernstorff, *Years*, p. 33; Alfred von Tirpitz (ed.) *Politische Dokumente*, Berlin, 1926, Volume II, p. 43 (hereafter Tirpitz, *Dokumente*); Edward Grey, *Twenty-Five Years, 1892-1916*, New York, 1925, Volume II, pp. 161-63 (hereafter Grey, *Years*); Gerard, *Years*, p. 210; A 21227, A 21692, WK 2; AS 2724, WK 2 geh.

14. Farrar, *Illusion*, pp. 28-31; Fischer, *Griff*, pp. 120-38.

15. Farrar, *Illusion*, pp. 14-18, 75-78; *Der Weltkrieg 1914-1918*, published by the Reichsarchiv, Berlin, 1929, Volumes V-VI (hereafter *Weltkrieg*); Falkenhayn, *Heeresleitung*, p. 26; Tirpitz, *Dokumente*, II, pp. 160-68.

16. *Weltkrieg*, VI, pp. 95-97; Tirpitz, *Dokumente*, II, pp. 160-68; AS 2575, AS 2585, WK 2 geh.

17. Zu AH 2344, File 21; AS 2769, WK 2 geh; Paul R. Sweet, "Leaders and Policies: Germany in the winter of 1914/15," *Journal of Central European Affairs*, October 1956, pp. 229-53 (hereafter Sweet, "Leaders").

18. AS 2735, AS 2743, AS 2758, AS 2783, zu AS 2793, AS 2809, AS 2828, WK 2 geh.

19 Conze, *Nation*, p. 67; Luigi Albertini, *The Origins of the War of 1914*, London, 1957, Volume III, p. 23; Sweet, "Leaders," p. 233; AS 2769, WK 2 geh; 638, WK 15 geh; Volkmann, *Annexionsfragen* p. 193; George P. Gooch, *Recent Revelations in European Diplomacy*, London, 1927, pp. 2-3 (hereafter Gooch, *Revelations*).

20. H. P. Hanssen, *Diary of a Dying Empire*, ed. R. H. Lutz, Bloomington, 1955, pp. 83-84 (hereafter Hanssen, *Diary*); *Weltkrieg*, VI, pp. 415-16; C.R.M.F. Cruttwell, *A History of the Great War 1914-1918*, Oxford, 1934, pp. 83-87 (hereafter Cruttwell, *History*); Sweet, "Leaders," p. 244; Friedrich Thimme, *Bethmann Hollwegs Kriegsreden*, Stuttgart, 1919, pp. 14-21 (hereafter Thimme, *Kriegsreden*).

21. AS 2809, AS 2834, WK 2 geh; Franz Conrad von Hötzendorff *Aus Meiner Dienstzeit*, Vienna/Leipzig/Munich, 1925, Volume V, pp. 651-56, 817-20, 849 (hereafter Conrad, *Dienstzeit*).

22. Karl H. Janssen, "Der Wechsel in der Obersten Heeresleitung im Jahre 1916," *Vierteljahreshefte für Zeitgeschichte*, October 1959,

p. 341 (hereafter Janssen, "Wechsel"); Karl H. Janssen, *Der Kanzler und der General: Die Führungskrise um Bethmann Hollwegs und Falkenhayn 1914-1916*, Göttingen, 1967 (hereafter Janssen,*Kanzler*); John W. Wheeler-Bennett, *The Wooden Titan*, London, 1936, pp. 29-30 (hereafter Wheeler-Bennett, *Titan*); Bethmann, *Betrachtungen*, II, p. 46; Ritter, *Staatskunst*, III, pp. 55-65.

23. Fischer, "Kriegsziele," pp. 249-310; Egmont Zechlin, "Friedensbestrebungen und Revolutionierungsversuche: Deutsche Bemühungen zur Ausschaltung Russlands im ersten Weltkrieg," Beilagen zu *Das Parlament. Aus Politik und Zeitgeschichte*, 17 May 1961, 14 June 1961, 21 June 1961, 15 May 1963 (hereafter Zechlin, "Friedensbestrebungen").

24. Gatzke, *Drive*, p. 1.

25. For details of the author's view on war aims and diplomacy, see L. L. Farrar, Jr., "Ends and Means: German Policy July-December 1914 as a Case Study of Decision-making in Wartime," *International Review of History and Political Science*, November, 1973, pp. 34-58.

26. Farrar, *Illusion*, pp. 132-34, 139-47.

Chapter II

1. 2418, WK 1, Volume 4; A 31432, AS 2793, AS 2927, WK 2 geh.

2. Zu AS 2793, AS 2828, AS 2826, WK 2 geh.

3. AS 2877, AS 3042, AS 3093, AS 3116, AS 15 (1915), zu AS 15, AS 20, AS 24, AS 41, WK 2 geh.

4. A 27791, A 28166, A 28234, AS 2853, AS 2870, AS 3042, AS 3061, AS 3082, AS 3115, zu AS 15 (1915), AS 80, WK 2 geh; A 34780, WK 2; A. Klein, "Der Einfluss des Grafen Witte auf die deutsche-russischen Beziehungen," unpublished Ph.D. dissertation, University of Münster, 1933, pp. 9, 99; Maurice Paleologue, *La Russie des tsars pendant la grande guerre*, Paris, 1921, Volume I, pp. 120 (hereafter Paleologue, *Russie*); Stadelmann, "Friedensversuche," 493; George Buchanan, *My Mission to Russia and Other Diplomatic Memories*, Boston, 1923, Volume I, p. 22 (hereafter, Buchanan, *Mission*).

5. Ritter, *Staatskunst*, pp. 64-72, 599, n. 36; Cruttwell, *History*, p. 149; Schulthess' *Europäischer Geschichtskalender, 1915*, Munich, 1918, pp. 13-14, 636 (hereafter, Schulthess, *Geschichtskalender*).

6. *Weltkrieg*, Volume VII, pp. 1-15, 74-300; Cruttwell, *History*, pp. 171-72; Schulthess, *Geschichtskalender*, pp. xxiii-vii, 96-96a, 101. A 828 (1915), AS 1196, A 1306, A 1726, AS 224, zu AS 224, AS 264.

7. AS 284, AS 321, AS 619, AS 935, WK 2 geh; *Die Internationalen Beziehungen im Zeitlalter des Imperialismus*, M. N. Prokowski (editor), Series III, 1,2, Berlin, 1933-43, Volume II, p. 37 (hereafter, IB).

8. AS 265, AS 270, AS 339, AS 346, zu AS 346, AS 431, zu AS 431, AS 485, zu AS 485, AS 641, zu A 6215, AS 715, AS 725, AS 935, WK 2 geh; K. D. Erdmann, "Zur Beurteilung Bethmann Hollwegs," *Geschichte in Wissenschaft und Unterricht*, September, 1964, p. 527 (hereafter, Erdmann, "Beurteilung").

9. *Weltkrieg*, Volume VII, pp. 16-73, 297-300, 346-65; Cruttwell, *History*, pp. 147-70, 204-27; Paul Guinn, *British Strategy and Politics, 1914-1918*, Oxford, 1965, pp. 48-75 (hereafter, Guinn, *Strategy*); Gerard E. Silberstein, *The Troubled Alliance: German-Austrian Relations, 1914-1917*, Lexington, Kentucky, 1970, passim (hereafter, Silberstein, *Alliance*),; Egmont Zechlin, "Das 'schlesische Angebot' und die italienische Krigsgefahr 1915," *Geschichte in Wissenschaft und Unterricht*, September, 1963, p. 547 (hereafter, Zechlin, "Angebot"); Karl E. Birnbaum, *Peace Moves and U-boat Warfare*, Stockholm, 1958, pp. 22-27 (hereafter, Birnbaum, *Moves*); Schulthess, *Geschichtskalender*, p. vii.

10. Zechlin, "Angebot," p. 547; Janssen, "Wechsel," p. 341; Cruttwell, *History*, pp. 139, 171; Alfred Tirpitz, *Erinnerungen*, Leipzig, 1929, pp. 446, 457 (hereafter, Tirpitz, *Erinnerungen*); Conrad Haussmann, *Schlaglichter: Reichstagbriefe und Aufzeichnungen*, Frankfurt, 1924, p. 28 (hereafter, Haussmann, *Schlaglichter*).

11. AS 957, AS 979, AS 1008, AS 1025, AS 1040, zu AS 1130, zu AS 1145, zu AS 1151, AS 1177, AS 1305, AS 1272, AS 1273, AS 1305, AS 1567, AS 1742, AS 1887, WK 2 geh; Scherer, *L'Allemagne*, p. 94; G. Frantz, "Friedensfühler bis Ende 1915: ein Beitrag nach russischen Quellen," *Berliner Monatshefte*, November, 1933, p. 586 (hereafter, Frantz, "Friedensfühler").

13. AS 1535, AS 1571, AS 1616, AS 1690, AS 2237, WK 2 geh; Frantz, "Friedensfühler,", p. 587; Scherer, *L'Allemagne*, pp. 94-95; Alexandra, *Lettres de l'Impératrice Alexandra Feodorovna à L'Empereur Nicholas II*, Paris, 1924, p. 102 (hereafter, Alexandra. *Lettres*).

14. AS 2656, AS 2696, AS 2761, zu AS 2761, AS 2800, WK 2 geh; Scherer, *L'Allemagne*, p. 99; IB, Volume IV, pp. 291-96.

15. AS 2833, WK 2 geh; Scherer, *L'Allemagne*, pp. 115-16; Alexandra, *Lettres*, p. 102.

16. Janssen, "Wechsel," p. 342; *Weltkrieg*, Volume VIII, p. 1, 598, 602; Cruttwell, *History*, pp. 171, 174; G. A. Müller, *Regierte der Kaiser?* Göttingen, 1959, pp. 96-97 (hereafter, Müller, *Kaiser*).

17. *Weltkrieg*, Volume VIII, pp. 599-600, 606; Birnbaum, *Moves*, pp. 27-28; Silberstein, *Alliance*, passim.

18. AS 2851, WK 2 geh; AS 3066, WK 15 geh; *Weltkrieg*, Volume VIII, pp. 202, 604.

19. AS 3226, WK 2 geh.

20. Zu AS 2851, AS 2905, AS 3066, zu AS 3066, AS 3116, WK 2 geh.

21. AS 3554, WK 2 geh; *Weltkrieg*, Volume VIII, pp. 100, 315, 600-603; Silberstein, *Alliance*, passim; Birnbaum, *Moves*, pp. 28-31; Cruttwell, pp. 158-61.

22. AS 2890, AS 2923, AS 3171, AS 3247, zu AS 3247, AS 3302, AS 3311, AS 3336, AS 3374, AS 3399, AS 3400, AS 3422, AS 3488, AS 3555, AS 3585, AS 3611, AS 3617, AS 3636, AS 3650, AS 3680, AS 3686, WK 2 geh.

23. AS 3840, WK 2 geh; *Weltkrieg*, Volume VIII, p. 610.

24. AS 3601, zu AS 3750, AS 3760, zu AS 3840, zu AS 3945, WK 2 geh.

25. AS 3904, WK 2 geh; for discussion of German war aims at Russian expense during this period, see: Fischer, *Griff*, pp. 236-57; Imanuel Geiss, *Der polnische Grenzstreifen, 1914-1918*, Lübeck/Hamburg, 1960, pp. 78-96 (hereafter, Geiss, *Grenzstreifen*); Werner Basler, *Deutschlands Annexionspolitik im Polen und im Baltikum 1914-1918*, Berlin, 1962, passim (hereafter, Basler, *Annexionspolitik*).

26. Zu AS 3840/3945 III, WK 2 geh.

27. AS 3945, WK 2 geh; Frantz, "Friedensfühler," pp. 579, 599; A. Polovinov, *Memoiren*, Merkur, 1924, p. 187 (hereafter, Polovinov, *Memoiren*); Theobald von Bethmann Hollweg, "Das Friedensangebot vom 1915," *Preussische Jahrbücher*, 1919, p. 115 (hereafter, Bethmann, "Friedenangebot").

28. AS 3972, WK 2 geh.

29. Zu AS 3840/3945 III, AS 3972, WK 2 geh.

30. *Weltkrieg*, Volume VIII, pp. 607, 611; Silberstein, *Alliance*, passim.

31. Zu AS 3750/3760, zu AS 3840/3945 I & III, AS 5026, WK 2 geh.

32. AS 4622, AS 4924, AS 5026, AS 5042, AS 5046, AS 5111, AS 5148, AS 5267, AS 5820, AS 5912, AS 5967, AS 5993, WK 2 geh; Franz, "Friedensfühler," p. 539; Paleologue, *Russie*, Volume II, pp. 139-41; M. V. Rudzianko, *The Reign of Rasputin: An Empire's Collapse*, London, 1927, pp. 169-70 (hereafter, Rudzianko, *Reign*); E. A. Adamov, (editor), *Die Europäischen Mächte und die Türkei während des Weltkrieges: Konstantinopel und die Meerengen*, Dresden, 1930, Volume IV, p. 141 (hereafter, Adamov, *Mächte*).

33. Zu AS 2769, WK 2 geh.

34. Moltke's advocacy of revolution to aid military operations: on 2 August, *Die deutschen Dokumente zum Kriegsausbruch 1914*, Karl Kautsky, (ed.), Berlin, 1924, Volume III, Number 662, pp. 133ff; on 5 August 1914, ibid., Volume IV, Number 876, pp. 94ff. (hereafter, Kautsky, *Dokumente*). Falkenhayn's advocacy of a Finnigh legion: in January 1915, Zechlin, "Friedensbestrebungen," 14 June 1961, p. 333. Advocacy by Hindenburg and Ludendorff of a Polish legion: in October 1916, see below, p. 65.. Jagow's outline of revolution as both means and end: on 11 August 1914, WK 11a geh.

35. Bethmann in the Reichstag: on 4 August 1914, Schulthess, *Geschichtskalender, 1914*, Volume I, p. 384. Moltke's statement: 2 August 1914, Kautsky, *Dokumente*, Volume III, Number 662, p. 133. Rantzau's statement: 6 December 1915, Deutschland 131 geh. Jagow on the Russian "nightmare," etc.: 2 September 1915, Deutschland 180 geh; 25 October 1915, WK 20c geh. The Kaiser's condemnation of Germany's enemies: Ulrich Gehrke, *Persien in der deutschen Orientpolitik während des Ersten Weltkrieges*, Berlin, 1960, Volume I, pp. 133-34 (hereafter, Gehrke, *Persien*). Tschirsschky's criticism of Berchtold: 10 August 1914, WK 11a. Rantzau's rejection of constraints: 14 August 1915, WK 11c. Jagow's condemnation of the Romanovs: 2 September, Deutschland 180 geh; 25 October 1915, WK 20c geh. Rantzau's condemnation: 6 December 1915, Deutschland 131 geh. Rantzau recognizes risk: 14 August 1915, WK 11c geh.

36. Bethmann: 6 August 1914, WK 11c geh; 13 January 1915, WK 2 geh; 4 October 1915, Russland 61. Zimmermann: 3 August 1914, WK 11. Michaelis: 26 July 1917, WK 2 geh. Kühlmann: 29 September 1917, Russland 63 Nr. 1 geh. Moltke: 2 August 1914, Kautsky, *Dokumente*, Volume III, Number 662, pp. 133ff; 5 August 1914, ibid., Volume IV, Number 876, pp. 94ff. Falkenhayn: Zechlin, "Friedensbestrebungen," 14 June 1961, p. 333. Hindenburg and Ludendorff: see below, p. 65; 25 March 1917, WK 2 geh; 16 December 1917, Russland Politisches Nr. 1. German leaflets: Graf Bogdan Hutten-Czapski, *Sechzig Jahre Politik und Gesellschaft*, Berlin, 1936, Volume II, p. 156 (hereafter, Hutten-Czapski, *Jahre*). Rantzau: see footnote 35. Romberg: 5 October 1914, WK 11 adh 1; 30 September 1915, Russland Nr. 61; 24 August 1916, WK 11c geh. Lucius: 15 June 1917, WK 2 geh. Bussche: 26 December 1915, WK c geh. Mirbach: 13 May 1918, Russland 61. Bergen: Z. A. B. Zeman (ed.) *Germany and the Revolution in Russia, 1915-1918*, London,

1958, p. ix (hereafter, Zeman, *Germany*); 28 November, WK 11c geh. Oppenheim: Fischer, *Griff*, p. 142. Riezler: 13 January 1915, WK 11c geh; 26 November 1917, Russland Nr. 61. On the parties: Fischer, *Griff*, pp. 157-58. Jagow's scepticism: Rantzau to Zimmermann, 2 April 1917, WK 2 geh. Hefferich: 26 December 1915, WK 11c geh.

37. Zechlin, "Friedensbestrebungen," 14 June 1961, pp. 325-29.

38. Zeman, *Germany*, pp. vii-viii, 23.

39. Fischer, *Griff*, p. 156. Zechlin, "Friedensbestrebungen," 14 June 1961, pp. 333-37. Conze, *Nation*, passim.

40. Zechlin, "Friedensbestrebungen," 21 June 1961, pp. 342-48.

41. Ibid., 14 June 1961, pp. 331-33, 336. W. M. Carlgren, *Neutralität oder Allianz: Deutschlands Beziehungen zu Schweden in den Anfangsjahren des ersten Weltkrieges*, Stockholm/Göteborg/Uppsala, 1962, passim.

42. Zechlin, "Friedensbestrebungen," 21 June 1961, pp. 348-53. Hans Beyer, *Die Mittelmächte und die Ukraine*, Munich, 1956, passim.

43. Zechlin, "Friedensbestrebungen," 21 June 1961, pp. 353-60.

44. 9 January 1915, 26 March 1915, 6 July 1915, 14 August 1915, 26 December 1915, WK 11c geh. Z. A. B. Zeman and W. B. Scharlau, *The Merchant of Revolution: The Life of Alexander I. Helphand (Parvus)*, Oxford, 1965, passim.

45. 39 September 1915, Russland Nr. 61.

46. 23 January 1916, WK 11c geh. Zeman, *Germany*, p. 23.

47. Zeman, *Germany*, pp. 25-139. Fischer, *Griff*, p. 182. Werner Hahlweg (ed.), *Lenins Rückkehr nach Russland 1917,* Leiden, 1957, passim.

48. Rantzau: 14 August 1915, WK 11c geh; 6 December 1915, Deutschland 131 geh. Zimmermann: Zechlin, "Friedensbestrebungen," 21 June 1961, p. 362; Zeman, *Germany*, p. ix. Romberg: 30 September 1915, Russland Nr. 61; 24 August 1916, WK 11c geh. Jagow: Rantzau to Zimmermann, 2 April 1917, WK 2 geh. Helfferich: 26 December 1915, WK 11c geh. Bolshevik survival: Zeman, *Germany*, pp. 72-139.

49. Funds: Fischer, *Griff*, p. 182. Rantzau on Jagow: 2 April 1917, WK 2 geh.

50. Agent claims: 21 December 1915, WK 11c geh. Helphand's organization: Fischer, *Griff*, p. 182. Rantzau: 2 April 1917, WK 2 geh. Kühlmann: 29 September 1917, Russland 63 Nr. 1 geh.; 3 December 1917, Deutschland Nr. 131 geh. Funds: Fischer, *Griff*, p. 182; Zeman, *Germany*, p. 23. Bolsheviks not German agents: Zeman, *Germany*, pp. x-xi.

51. 25 December 1914, WK 11c geh.

Chapter III

1. Tirpitz, *Erinnerungen*, p. 427; Sweet, "Leaders," pp. 229-33; Fischer, *Griff*, pp. 223-33; Ritter, *Staatskunst*, Volume III, pp. 55-63; AS 2769, zu AS 2769, WK 2 geh; Scherer, *L'Allemagne*, Volume I, pp. 15-19, 26-29.

2. Schulthess, *Geschichtskalender, 1914*, p. 436; Sweet, "Leaders," p. 244; Thimme, *Kriegsreden*, pp. 14-21.

3. Sweet, "Leaders," p. 245.

4. AS 2489, AS 2618, AS 2656, AS 2687, AS 2743, AS 2762, AS 2762, AS 2846, AS 2866 II, AS 2897, AS 2911, zu AS 2911, AS 2917, zu AS 2917, AS 2923, AS 2934, AS 2938, AS 2949, AS 2980, A 34554 (all 1914); AS 1423, A 10062 (1915), WK 2 geh and WK 2 Spez Blitz; AS 2413, WK 1, Volume V; G. Adams, *Treason and Tragedy: An Account of French War Trials*, London, 1929 (hereafter, Adams, *Treason*); W. O. Lancken, *Meine Dreisig Dienstjahre*, Berlin, 1931 (hereafter, Lancken, *Dienstjahre*).

5. AS 48, WK 2 geh.

6. Zechlin, "Friedensbestrebungen," 20 May 1963, p. 24. A 28659, zu A 28659, Russland Nr. 61; Zeman, *Germany*, p. 608;

7. See Footnote 8.

8. Raymond Poincaré, *Au Service de la France*, Paris, 1928, Volumes V-VIII (hereafter, Poincaré, *Service*); Joseph J. C. Joffre, *Memoirs*, New York, 1932, Volume I (hereafter, Joffre, *Memoirs*); Albert Pingaud, *Histoire diplomatique de la France pendant la grande guerre*, Paris, 1940, Volume I (hereafter, Pingaud, *Histoire*); Jere C. King, *Generals and Politicians*, Berkeley, 1951 (hereafter, King, *Generals*); Pierre Renouvin, "Les Buts de guerre du gouvernement français (1914-1918)," *Revue historique*, January-March, 1966, pp. 1-38 (hereafter, Renouvin, "Buts").

9. Ritter, *Staatskunst*, Volume III, pp. 64-72, 599 (footnote 36); Cruttwell, *History*, p. 149; Schulthess, *Geschichtskalender, 1915*, pp. 13-14, 363; Zechlin, "Friedensbestrebungen," 15 May 1963, p. 24 (footnote 59).

10. Janssen, "Wechsel," p. 341.

11. AS 759, A 7469, AS 794, A 7572, AS 825, AS 849, AS 855, AS 1017, AS 1093, AS 1261, AS 1264II, AS 1336, WK 2 geh.

12. AS 1174, A 10205, AS 1295, AS 1498, WK 2 geh; Scherer, *L'Allemagne*, pp. 78, 84, 90-91.

13. For contacts with dissident politicians, see: A 10028, A 13244, WK 2 geh. For contacts with Bolo and the ex-Khedive of Egypt, see: AS 794, AS 825, AS 1017, AS 1261, AS 1264 II, AS 1336, WK 2 geh; Scherer, *L'Allemagne*, pp. 68-69, 78-80.

14. AS 855, AS 1093, AS 1192, A 138, WK 2 geh.

15. For efforts to purchase French papers through Lenoir, see: AS 2191, AS 2247, AS 2280, AS 2343, AS 2387, AS 2621, AS 2878, AS 3334, AS 3506, AS 3559, AS 3601, AS 3737, WK 2 geh. For efforts to purchase papers through the ex-Khedive and Bolo, see: AS 2255, AS 2467, AS 2712 , AS 2993, zu AS 2993; Scherer, *L'Allemagne*, pp. 101, 120-21. For German efforts to contact Caillaux through Lipscher and Ceccaldi, see: AS 3280, AS 3373, WK 2 geh. For German contacts with the Radical Socialists Turmel, Lethal and Artemont, see: A 10028, A 12442, A 13244, AS 1613, zu AS 1613, AS 1640, AS 1733, AS 1743, zu AS 1733/1743, WK 2 geh. For the views of Jagow and Falkenhayn, see: zu AS 1733, AS 1743, zu AS 1733/1743, zu AS 3760/3779 II, WK 2 geh; *Weltkrieg*, Volume VIII, pp. 243-48, 609-10.

16. For contacts through Haussmann, see: Haussmann, *Schlaglichter*, p. 44, AS 3803, AS 4089, zu AS 4089, AS 4342, AS 4396, AS 5065, WK 2 geh. For contacts through Erzberger, see: AS 3920, AS 4180, AS 4944, WK 2 geh.

17. For contacts through Judet (code name "Blitz"), see: A 24235, AS 4435, zu AS 4435, AS 5033, zu AS 5033, AS 5249, AS 5314, AS 5510, WK 2 geh Spez Blitz; Scherer, *L'Allemagne*, pp. 163, 189-90; Georges Wormser, "Les Sondages de L'Allemagne en 1915 et 1916 en vue d'une paix separée avec la France," *Académie des Sciences Morales et Politiques*, 1963, pp. 257-59 (hereafter, Wormser, "Sondages"). For contacts with French Radical Socialists, see: AS 4724, WK 2 geh. For discussion of using Lenin's plans, see: A 28659, zu A 28659, Russland Nr. 61; Z. A. B. Zeman, *Germany and the Revolution in Russia, 1915-1918*, London, 1958, p. 608 Hahlweg, *Ruckkehr*, pp. 40-43. For contact with Duval, see: AS 4724, AS 5086, WK 2 geh; Adams, *Treason*, pp. 52-70.

18. AS 5139, WK 2 geh; Scherer, *L'Allemagne*, p. 204. AS 3280, AS 3373, zu AS 5139, AS 5169, AS 5308, AS 5454, zu AS 5454, AS 5460, AS 5509, AS 5542, AS 5596, AS 5975, AS 6115, WK 2 geh; AS 5515, WK 2 geh Spez Blitz.

19. For contacts with dissident politicians, reputedly including Thomas, see: footnote 16. For contacts with Judet, see: footnote 17. AS 5324, AS 5326, zu AS 5326, AS 5511, AS 5975, WK 2 geh Spez Blitz; Scherer, *L'Allemagne*, pp. 204, 206, 229-31. For contact with Caillaux, see footnote 17. For contacts with Duval, see: footnote 17.; Scherer, *L'Allemagne*, pp. 239-40; Wormser, "Sondages,"

pp. 252-53. For efforts to purchase French papers through Lenoir, see: AS 4098, AS 4196, WK 2 geh. For contacts with the ex-Khedive and Bolo, see: A 30042, AS 5420, A 30690, A 31042, A 34081, AS 5898, AS 5941, WK 2 geh. For German efforts through Erzberger to make contacts with French in Switzerland, see: AS 3861, zu AS 3861, AS 4131, WK 2 geh.

Chapter IV

1. *Weltkrieg*, Volume X, pp. 1-3; AS 6077, WK 2 geh.

2. Falkenhayn, *Heeresleitung*, pp. 176-78; *Weltkrieg*, pp. 2-4.

3. Birnbaum, *Moves*, p. 50.

4. Ibid., pp. 45-63.

5. Müller, *Kaiser*, p. 154; AS 537, WK 2 geh.

6. A 537, A 538; zu A 538, AS 72, AS 179, AS 179 I, zu AS 233, AS 482, AS 499, AS 537, WK 2 geh; AS 266, WK 2 geh Spez Blitz; Wormser, "Sondages," p. 260.

7. AS 1069, AS 1100, zu AS 1100, zu AS 1221, zu AS 1269, zu AS 1269 II, AS 1298. AS 1316, zu AS 1679, WK 2 geh; AS 1130, WK 2 geh Spez Blitz; Hanssen, *Diary*, p. 139; Thimme, *Kriegsreden*, pp. 90-91; Fischer, *Griff*, pp. 280-84; Scherer, *L'Allemagne*, pp. 296-300; Wormser, "Sondages," pp. 260-61.

8. 342, AS 1657, WK 2 geh; Birnbaum, *Moves*, pp. 75-87, 95-99; Haussmann, *Schlaglichter*, pp. 61-62.

9. A 9917, AS 1376, AS 1427, zu AS 1427, AS 1436, AS 1509, zu AS 1509/1436, AS 1523, AS 1565, AS 1609, AS 1650, AS 1679, AS 1727, WK 2 geh; AS 1522, zu AS 1522, WK 2 geh Spez Blitz; Haussmann, *Schlaglichter*, pp. 61-62; Cruttwell, *History*, pp. 249-50; Scherer, *L'Allemagne*, pp. 314-34; W. W. Gottlieb, *Studies in Secret Diplomacy during the First World War*, London, 1957, pp. 391-92 (hereafter, Gottlieb, *Studies*).

10. AS 1891, WK 2 geh; AS 1744, AS 1780, AS 1821, WK 2 geh Spez Blitz; Cruttwell, *History*, p. 251; King, *Generals*, p. 110; Scherer, *L'Allemagne*, pp. 344-47.

11. AS 1891, WK 2 geh; AS 1840, WK 2 geh Spez Blitz; AS 1798, WK 18 geh; Müller, *Kaiser*, p. 185; Cruttwell, *History*, p. 250; King, *Generals*, pp. 110-20; Janssen, "Wechsel," pp. 343-44; Scherer, *L'Allemagne*, pp. 354-58; Wormser, "Sondages,", pp. 262-62.

12. Birnbaum, *Moves*, pp. 103-6; Basler, *Annexionspolitik*, p. 47.

13. Zu AS 1891, zu AS 1891 II, WK 2 geh; Scherer, *L'Allemagne*, pp. 363-64.

14. Zu AS 2721, AS 2890, WK 2 geh; AS 2106, AS 2167, WK 2 geh Spez Blitz; Cruttwell, *History*, p. 251; Janssen, "Wechsel," p. 344; Birnbaum, *Moves*, p. 118; Scherer, *L'Allemagne*, pp. 399-401;

King, *Generals*, pp. 110-23; Max von Baden, *Erinnerungen und Dokumente*, Stuttgart, 1927, p. 23 (hereafter, Max, *Erinnerungen*).

15. A 18300, A 18463, A 18609, AS 2304, zu AS 2304/2312, zu AS 2321, AS 2423, AS 2590, AS 2657, AS 2721, WK 2 geh; zu AS 2249, WK 2 geh Spez Blitz; Scherer, *L'Allemagne*, pp. 411-26.

16. AS 2819, AS 2832, AS 2890, WK 2 geh; Birnbaum, *Moves*, pp. 119-21; Max, *Erinnerungen,* p. 24; Scherer, *L'Allemagne*, pp. 431-54.

17. King, *Generals*, p. 123.

Chapter V

1. *Weltkrieg*, Volume X, pp. 1-10; Birnbaum, *Moves*, p. 50; Müller, *Kaiser*, p. 154.

2. Zu AS 4050, WK 2 geh; *Weltkrieg*, Volume X, p. 2.

3. Conze, *Nation*, pp. 138-51; Müller, *Kaiser*, p. 152.

4. Conze, *Nation*, pp. 138-51, AS 5968, AS 5969, WK 2 geh.

5. A 3333, A 3467, WK 2; AS 580, zu AS 580, AS 612, WK 2 geh. Parlamentarischer Untersuchungsausschuss, 2112, Parts XXXII and XXXV (hereafter, 2112).

6. A 1601, A 2400, A 9155, A 15819, A 16689, zu A 16681, A 18976, A 34612, WK 2; AS 761, AS 936, AS 954, zu AS 954, AS 1086, AS 1146, AS 1156, AS 1209, AS 1223, AS 1253, AS 1291, AS 3084, AS 3750, AS 3760, WK 2 geh; 2112, Pt. XXXII; Müller, *Kaiser*, pp. 164-66; *Weltkrieg*, Volume X, p. 426; Fischer, "Kriegsziele," p. 269; Thimme, *Kriegsreden*, p. 90; Erwin Hölzle, "Deutschland und die Wegscheide des ersten Weltkrieges," in *Geschichtliche Kräfte und Entscheidungen, Festschrift für Otto Becker*, Wiesbaden, 1954, passim (hereafter, Hölzle, "Deutschland"); Mattias Erzberger, *Erlebnisse im Weltkrieg*, Stuttgart, 1920, pp. 269-70 (hereafter, Erzberger, *Erlebnisse*).

7. AS 1410, AS 1444, AS 1454, AS 1491, AS 1594, zu AS 1594, AS 1606, AS 1606 II, AS 1621, AS 1622, AS 1626, AS 1630 AS 1657, zu AS 1657 I AS 1776, WK 2 geh; zu A 11096, WK 2; 2112, Pts. XXXII, XXXV.

8. AS 1702, zu AS 1702 II, AS 1704, AS 1710, AS 1712, AS 2254, WK 2 geh; A 20941, WK 2; 2112, Pt. XXXII; Adamov, *Mächte,* Volume II, p. 309.

9. AS 1813, zu AS 1813, AS 1976, WK 2 geh; 2112, Pts. XXXII , XXXV; Conze, *Nation*, pp. 170-71, 176.

10. 2112, Pts. XXXV, XXXVI.

11. Müller, *Kaiser*, p. 185; Janssen, "Wechsel," p. 343-44.

12. Müller, *Kaiser,* p. 200; Janssen, "Wechsel," pp. 344-45; *Weltkrieg,* Volume X, pp. 202, 321, 416, 528; Conze, *Nation,* p. 177; Max, *Erinnerungen,* p. 23; R. Valentini, *Kaiser und Kabinettschef,* Oldenburg, 1931, p. 234 (hereafter, Valentini, *Kaiser*).

13. AS 2309, WK 2 geh; zu AS 2249, WK 2 geh Spez Blitz; *Weltkrieg,* Volume X, pp. 527-32; Müller, *Kaiser,* pp. 181, 203-6; Bethmann, *Betrachtungen,* Volume II, p. 46.

14. AS 1732, AS 1876, AS 2222, AS 2469, AS 2495, AS 2927, WK 2 geh (1916); AS 758, WK 2 geh (1917); zu A 19195, A 19492, A 19537, A 19612, WK 2; 2112, Pts. XXXII, XXXV; Adamov, *Mächte,* Volume II, pp. 331-39; Buchanan, *Mission,* Volume II, p. 18; Paleologue, *Russie,* Volume II, p. 306; Zeman, *Germany,* pp. 184-86; A. V. Nekludoff, *Diplomatic Reminiscences Before and During the War, 1911-1917,* London, 1920, pp. 411-68 (hereafter, Nekludoff, *Reminiscences*).

15. AS 2672, AS 2819, AS 2832, AS 2890, WK 2 geh; Birnbaum, *Moves,* p. 120; Conze, *Nation,* pp. 173-77, 184-86, 195.

16. AS 2819, zu AS 2925, AS 2929, AS 2966, AS 3049, AS 3079, WK 2 geh; 522, 599/5, WK/GHQ; 2112, Pt. XXXV; Müller, *Kaiser,* pp. 213-15; Conze, *Nation,* p. 189; Max, *Erinnerungen,* p. 23; *Weltkrieg,* Volume X, pp. 637-43.

17. Zu AS 3079, AS 3113, zu AS 3120, WK 2 geh. Müller, *Kaiser,* p. 215; *Weltkrieg,* Volume X, pp. 643-44; Janssen, "Wechsel," pp. 369-70; Karl Helfferich, *Der Weltkrieg,* Berlin, 1919, Volume II, p. 352 (hereafter, Helfferich, *Weltkrieg*).

18. Janssen, "Wechsel,", passim.

19. Birnbaum, *Moves,*, pp. 131-32.

20. AS 3120, WK 2 geh; Birnbaum, *Moves,* pp. 151-52.

21. AS 2389, AS 3321, WK 2 geh; Cruttwell, *History,* pp. 294-96; Thimme, *Kriegsreden,* p. 130; W. Patin, *Beiträge zur Geschichte der deutsch-vatikanischen Beziehungen in den letzten Jahrzehnten,* Berlin, 1942, p. 41 (hereafter, Patin, *Beiträge*).

22. AS 2966, zu AS 3503, AS 3516, WK 2 geh; Conze, *Nation,* pp. 153, 189, 194-95.

23. AS 3471, zu AS 3471, AS 3501, AS 3516, AS 3523, AS 3550, AS 3551, AS 3567, zu AS 3567/3569 II, AS 3578, AS 3630, AS 3730, AS 3821, zu AS 3821, zu AS 3855, WK 2 geh; Birnbaum, *Moves,* pp. 178-79; Müller, *Kaiser,* p. 226; Conze, *Nation,* p. 210; Erich Ludendorff, *Meine Kriegserinnerungen, 1914-1918,* Berlin, 1919, p. 181 (hereafter, Ludendorff *Kriegserinnerungen*); Wolfgang Steglich, *Bündissicherung oder Verständigungsfrieden,* Göttingen, 1958, pp. 45, 209 (hereafter, Steglich, *Bündnissicherung*).

24. AS 3523, AS 3630, WK 2 geh; Conze, *Nation*, pp. 210-14;
Steglich, *Bündnissicherung*, pp. 45-47, 147; Müller, *Kaiser*, p. 226;
Birnbaum, *Moves*, pp. 178-79; *Weltkrieg*, Volume XI, pp. 245-58.

25. AS 3810, AS 3816, AS 3832, WK 2 geh.

26. AS 3843, AS 3870, AS 3879, WK 2 geh; Cruttwell, *History*,
pp. 295-96; Steglich, *Bündnissicherung*, pp. 34-35.

27. AS 3832, WK 2 geh; Steglich, *Bündnissicherung*, p. 35; Birnbaum, *Moves*, pp. 182-217. *Weltkrieg*, Volume X, pp. 38-39; Haussmann, *Schlaglichter*, pp. 82-83.

28. Steglich, *Bündnissicherung*, pp. 35-36; Birnbaum, *Moves*, pp.
182-217.

29. AS 4021, WK 2 geh; Birnbaum, *Moves*, pp. 218-34.

30. AS 4021, AS 4034, AS 4091, AS 4156, zu AS 4156, AS 4189,
zu AS 4189, AS 4237, zu AS 4237, AS 4402, WK 2 geh; 2112, Pt.
XXXII; Steglich, *Bündnissicherung*, pp. 197-98; Conze, *Nation*, pp.
235-36, Birnbaum, *Moves*, p. 236, Adamov, *Mächte*, Volume II, pp.
304-5; Schulthess, *Geschichtskalender, 1916*, p. 431.

31. AS 2867, AS 2985, AS 2993, AS 3060, AS 3151, AS 3242,
AS 3355, AS 3389, AS 3401, AS 3633, AS 3770, AS 3795, zu AS
3838, zu AS 3870, AS 3883, zu AS 3907, AS 4055, AS 4062, AS
4064, zu AS 4064, AS 4248, AS 4337, WK 2 geh; A 27660, WK 2.

32. Zu AS 3370, AS 3409, AS 3526, AS 3613, AS 3614, AS
3816, AS 3832, WK 2 geh; *Weltkrieg*, Volume XI, pp. 92-99.

33. AS 4337, WK 2 geh; 2112, Pt. XXVI; Birnbaum, *Moves*, pp.
233-47; Steglich, *Bündnissicherung*, pp. 137-38.

34. AS 3832, AS 4337, AS 4747, WK 2 geh; Steglich *Bündnissicherung*, p. 137; Birnbaum, *Moves*, pp. 236, 256-57, 296; *Weltkrieg*,
Volume XII, pp. 1-2.

35. AS 4399, AS 4416, AS 4447, AS 4452, AS 4512, zu AS 4512,
AS 4517, AS 4518, zu AS 4517/4518, AS 4539, AS 4556, AS 4572,
AS 4591, AS 4599, zu AS 4599, AS 4607, AS 4614, AS 4642, AS
4646, zu AS 4646, AS 4660, AS 4662, AS 4685, AS 4711, zu AS
4711, AS 4746, AS 4764, AS 4813, AS 4815, AS 4816, AS 4817,
AS 4852, zu AS 4852, WK 2 geh (1916); AS 121, AS 163, AS 380,
AS 816, WK 2 geh (1917); A 34832, A 35428, WK 2; Birnbaum,
Moves, pp. 247-50, 255, 315-17; Steglich, *Bündnissicherung*, p. 170;
Forster, *Failures*, pp. 50-52.

36. Birnbaum, *Moves*, pp. 315-17.

Chapter VI

1. Birnbaum,*Moves*; Ritter, *Staatskunst*; Fischer, *Griff*; Konrad H. Jarausch, *The Enigmatic Chancellor: Bethmann Hollweg and the Hubris of Imperial Germany*, New Haven, 1972 (hereafter, Jarausch, *Chancellor*); Ernest May, *The World War and American Isolation, 1914-1918*, Cambridge (Mass.), 1959 (hereafter, May, *War*).

2. *Weltkrieg*, Volume XI, pp. 422, 477, 496, Volume XII, p. 138; Müller, *Kaiser*, p. 264; Schulthess, *Geschichtskalender*, p. 371; Birnbaum, *Moves*, p. 259; zu AS 4820, AS 4846, AS 4847, WK 2 geh (1916); AS 146, AS 343, AS 627, AS 680, AS 718, AS 798, zu AS 798, zu AS 825, AS 1057, AS 1732, WK 2 geh (1917); A 694, A 2697, WK 2 (1917).

3. Forster, *Failures*, pp. 91-105; Ludendorff, *Kriegserinnerungen*, Volume II, pp. 417-31; Bethmann, *Betrachtungen*, Volume II, p. 202; 2112, Parts VII, X, XXVIII and 2118, Parts I and XVIII; AS 1190, AS 1250, AS 1254, AS 1255, AS 1268, AS 1384, zu AS 1384, AS 1453, zu AS 1453/1531, zu AS 1483/1531 II, WK 2 geh.

4. AS 770, zu AS 770, AS 1072, AS 1073, AS 1138, zu AS 1138, AS 1190, zu AS 1384, WK 2 geh; 2112, Parts X, XXVIII and XXIX; Schulthess, *Geschichtskalender, 1917*, p. 369; Forster, *Failures*, pp. 106-112; Müller, *Kaiser*, p. 270; Philipp Scheidemann, *Memoiren eines Sozialdemokraten*, Dresden, 1928, Volume I, p. 299 (hereafter, Scheidemann, *Memoiren*); Lancken, *Dienstjahre*, pp. 252-53; Georges Suarez, *Briand, Sa Vie, son oeuvre avec son journal*, Paris, 1940, Volume IV, pp. 237-40 (hereafter, Suarez, *Briand*); A. Chatelle, *La Paix manquée*, Paris, 1936, passim (hereafter, Chatelle, *Paix*).

5. Zeman, *Germany*, pp. 24, 32; Hahlweg, *Rückkehr*, p. 10; Fischer, "Kriegsziele," pp. 260, 288-99; AS 791, WK 11c secr; AS 4640, WK 2 geh (1916); AS 345, AS 1311, WK 2 geh (1917).

6. Epstein, *Erzberger*, pp. 164-81; Klaus Epstein, "The Development of German-Austrian War Aims in the Spring of 1917," *The Journal of Central European Affairs*, April, 1957, pp. 24-47 (hereafter, Epstein, "Development"); Adamov, *Mächte*, Volume II, pp. 306-9;Schulthess, *Geschichtskalender, 1917*, pp. 379-70; Max Hoffmann, *Die Aufzeichnungen des Generalmajors Max Hoffmann*, Berlin, 1929, Volume I, pp. 161-62 (hereafter, Hoffmann, *Aufzeichnungen*); AS 685, zu AS 685, zu AS 782, AS 806, AS 807, AS 943, AS 974, AS 1254, WK 2 geh.

7. Schulthess, *Geschichtskalender, 1917*, pp. 406, 672; Epstein, *Erzberger*, pp. 168-73; Zeman, *Germany*, pp. 46-49; 2112, Part VIII, AS 1456, WK 2 geh.

8. Hahlweg, *Rückkehr*, pp. 11, 28, 53; Zeman, *Germany*, pp. 46-49; Schulthess, *Geschichtskalender, 1917*, p. 403; Conze, *Nation*, p. 87; AS 1346, AS 1456, WK 2 geh.

9. Zeman, *Germany*, p. 25; Müller, *Kaiser*, p. 274; Epstein, "Development," pp. 36-39; Schulthess, *Geschichtskalender, 1917*, pp. 398-99; 2112, Part VIII; 2118, Part X, AS 1125, AS 1346, AS 1487, AS 1916, WK 2 geh.

10. Ludendorff, *Kriegserinnerungen*, Volume II, pp. 421-25. Müller, *Kaiser*, pp. 273-76; *Weltkrieg*, Volume XII, pp. 138, 209ff; Epstein, "Development," pp. 30ff; AS 4762, AS 4771, WK 2 geh (1916); AS 1453, zu AS 1453, WK 2 geh (1917); AS 1346, WK 15 geh; 2112, Part XVIII.

11. Müller, *Kaiser*, p. 277; Epstein, *Erzberger*, p. 168; zu AS 1487, WK 2 geh; AS 1545, WK 15 geh.

12. Müller, *Kaiser*, pp. 279-90; *Weltkrieg*, Volume XII, p. 539; Epstein, "Development," pp. 31-32; Epstein, *Erzberger*, pp. 191-99; Volkmann, *Annexionsfragen*, pp. 200ff; Kuno Westarp, *Konservative Politik im letzten Jahrzehnt des Kaiserreiches*, Berlin, 1936, Volume II, p. 85 (hereafter, Westarp, *Politik*); AS 1600, AS 1669, WK geh; 2112, Parts VIII and XI.

13. Epstein, "Development," pp. 33-51; Müller, *Kaiser*, p. 279; Volkmann, *Annexionsfragen*, pp. 202-4; *Weltkrieg*, XIII, pp. 209-56, 307-76, 513; zu AS 1600II, AS 1968, AS 2047, WK 15 geh; AS 1659, AS 1664, AS 1708, zu AS 1708, zu AS 1453/1531 II, zu AS 1753, I, WK 2 geh; 2112, Part VIII.

14. Epstein, "Development," pp. 36-37; Epstein, *Erzberger*, pp. 170-71; AS 1688, AS 1805, AS 1872, AS 1883, WK 2 geh; 2112, Part VIII.

15. Zeman, *Germany*, pp. 25, 30, 43, 46-48, 54-56; Hahlweg, *Rückkehr*, p. 44; Friedrich Ebert, *Schriften, Aufzeichnungen, Reden*, Dresden, 1926, pp. 353-54 (hereafter, Ebert, *Schriften*); AS 938, AS 1125, AS 1258, AS 1273, AS 1363, AS 1456, AS 1494, AS 1579, WK 2 geh; A 14175, A 14332, WK 2; 2112, Part VIII; 2118, Part I.

16. Zeman, *Germany*, pp. 53-54; Epstein, "Development," pp. 42-43; Epstein, *Erzberger*, p. 194; Müller, *Kaiser*, p. 287; Schulthess, *Geschichtskalender, 1917*, p. 568; zu AS 1453/1531 II, WK 2 geh; A 14550, A 15477, WK 2; AS 1866, WK 15 geh; 2112, Part VIII.

17. *Weltkrieg*, XII, pp. 499-506; Zeman, *Germany*, pp. 60-61, 64-65; Schulthess, *Geschichtskalender, 1917*, pp. 640, 697, 891; O. H. Gankin and H. H. Fisher (eds.), *The Bolsheviks and the World War*, Stanford, 1940, pp. 613-17, 663 (hereafter, Gankin, *Bolsheviks*); AS 1886, AS 1933, AS 2186, AS 2198, AS 2433, WK 2 geh; A 14917, A 15043, A 15509, A 15735, A 15944, A 16010, A 16032, A 16529, A 17135, A 17775, A 23125, WK 2; 2112, Part VIII.

18 Cruttwell, *History*, p. 402; Lancken, *Dienstjahre*, p. 258; Epstein, "Development," p. 31; Ludendorff, *Erinnerungen*, Volume II, pp. 210, 204; Müller, *Kaiser*, p. 290; Schulthess, *Geschichtskalender, 1917*, pp. 565-69; AS 1343, AS 1473, AS 1675, AS 1700, AS 1882, AS 1884, AS 1926, AS 2101, AS 2148, WK 2 geh; A 16057, zu A 17581, WK 2; zu AS 1346, zu AS 1453/1531 II, WK 15 geh; 2112, Part XXIX; 2118, Parts I and V.

19. Birnbaum, *Moves*, pp. 315ff; Müller, *Kaiser*, p. 295; 2112, Part XI.

20. Epstein, *Erzberger*, p. 187; Müller, *Kaiser,* p. 292; 2112, Parts XI and XII.

21. Epstein, *Erzberger*, pp. 187, 200-1; Müller, *Kaiser*, pp. 293-96; Ludendorff, *Kriegserinnerungen*, II, pp. 478ff; *Weltkrieg*, XII, pp. 376-84, 463-67; Theobald von Bethmann Hollweg, "Die Friedensmöglichkeiten im Frühsommer 1917,"*Deutsche Allgemeine Zeitung*, 29 February 1920 (hereafter, Bethmann, "Friedensmöglichkeiten"); zu AS 2542 I, zu AS 2542 II, AS 2575, zu AS 2575, WK 2 geh; 2112, Parts VIII and XI; 2118, Parts XVIII and XX.

22. Müller, *Kaiser*, pp. 298-99; Schulthess, *Geschichtskalender, 1917*, pp. 304-5; Ebert, *Schriften*, pp. 376ff; 2118, Part XVIII.

23. Müller, *Kaiser*, pp. 295, 298-99; 2112, Part XI; 2118, Part XXI.

24. Epstein, *Erzberger*, p. 200; 2118, Part XVIII.

25. Epstein, *Erzberger*, pp. 194, 199; Victor Bredt (ed.), *Der Reichstag im Weltkrieg*, Berlin, 1926, pp. 69-131 (hereafter, Bredt, *Reichstag*); Arthur Rosenberg, *The Birth of the German Republic, 1871-1918*, London, 1931 (hereafter, Rosenberg, *Birth*).

Chapter VII

1. See pp. 5-6.

2. See pp. 5-6.

3. See pp. 49-51, 63-65, 72-73.

4. Epstein, *Erzberger*, pp. 182-204; Bredt, *Reichstag*; Rosenberg, *Birth*; Ludendorff, *Kreigserinnerungen*, Volume II, pp. 468-75; 2112, Part XII; Erzberger, *Erlebnisse*, pp. 264ff; Philipp Scheidemann, *Zusammenbruch*, Berlin, 1921, pp. 92-94 (hereafter, Scheidemann, *Zusammenbruch*).

5. See pp. 65-67, 72-75.

6. Scheidemann, *Zusammenbruch*, p. 100; Georg Michaelis, *Für Staat und Volk*, Berlin, 1922, p. 321 (hereafter, Michaelis, *Staat*); E. Hoop, "Die Innenpolitik der Reichskanzler Michaelis und Graf Hertling," Unpublished PhD dissertation, Kiel University, 1951, p. 169; 2118, Part XXI; Kameke to W. Michaelis (Chancellor Michaelis' son), Michaelis Papers.

7. Müller, *Kaiser*, p. 303; Epstein, *Erzberger*, p. 217; Forster, *Failures*, p. 134; J. W. Wheeler-Bennett, *Brest-Litovsk: The Forgotten Peace*, London, 1938, pp. 102-3 (hereafter, Wheeler-Bennett, *Brest-Litovsk*); Lewis B. Namier, *Avenues of History*, London, 1948, pp. 74-91 (hereafter, Namier, *Avenues*); Gatzke, *Drive*, p. 224; Friedrich Meinecke, "Kühlmann und die päpstliche Friedensaktion von 1917," *Preussische Akademie der Wissensschaften*, 1928. p. 205 (hereafter, Meinecke, "Kühlmann"); Wolfgang Steglich, *Die Friedenpolitik der Mittelmächte 1917/18*, Wiesbaden, 1964, Volume I (hereafter, Steglich, *Friedenspolitik*); Ahlswede, "Friedensbemühungen"; 2112, Part XVIII.

8. Meinecke, "Kühlmann," pp. 191-92, 207-8; Richard Kühlmann, *Erinnerungen*, Heidelberg, 1948, p. 471 (hereafter, Kühlmann, *Erinnerungen*); AS 3052, AS 3071, zu AS 3117, WK 2 geh; 2112, Parts XV, XXIX, XXX; 2118, Part XX.

9. Epstein, *Erzberger*, pp. 216ff; 2112, Parts XV and XXIII; 2118, Parts II and XVIII.

10. Kühlmann to Kameke, Kameke to W. Michaelis, Michaelis Papers; 2118, Parts II and XV.

11. Müller, *Kaiser*, p. 315; Ernst Deuerlein, "Zur Friedensaktion Papst Benedikts XV (1917)," *Stimmen der Zeit*, January, 1955, p. 248 (hereafter, Deuerlein, "Friedensaktion"); Max, *Erinnerungen*, pp. 135, 143; 2118, Parts XVIII and XXI; AS 3166, WK 15 geh; Scherer, *L'Allemagne*, Volume II; *anon.*, "À propos de l'offre de paix du Saint-Siège en 1917," *Revue historique de la guerre mondiale*, 1926, pp. 131-40 (hereafter, *anon.*, "L'offre"); Karl Dietrich Erdmann, "Schlussbemerkungen zur Diskussion um den Kanzler Michaelis und die päpstliche Friedensktion," *Geschichte in Wissenschaft und Unterricht*, 1956, pp. 304-7 (hereafter, Erdmann, "Schlussbemerkungen"); Friedrich Lama, *Der vereitelte Friede*, Augsburg, 1926 (hereafter, Lama, *Friede*); Friedrich Lama, *Die Friedensvermittlung Papst Benedikt XV, und ihre Vereitlung durch den deutschen Reichskanzler Michaelis (August-September 1917)*, Munich, 1932 (hereafter, Lama, *Friedensvermittlung*); Robert Leiber, "Die Friedenstätigkeit Benedikts XV," *Stimmen der Zeit* 1921-2, pp. 267-80 (hereafter, Leiber, "Friedenstätigkeit"); Wilhelm Michaelis, "Der Reichskanzler Michaelis und die päpstliche Friedensaktion von 1917," *Geschichte in Wissenschaft und Unterricht*, 1956, pp. 14-24, 128-38 (hereafter, Michaelis, "Michaelis," 1956), 1961, pp. 418-34 (hereafter, Michaelis, "Michaelis," 1961); "Stellungnahme zu dem Aufsatz von Ernst Schütte," 1956, pp. 297-307 (hereafter, Michaelis, "Stellungnahme"); Ernst Schütte,

"Noch einmal: Der Reichskanzler Michaelis und die päpstliche Friedensaktion von 1917," *Geschichte in Wissenschaft und Unterricht*, 1956, pp. 293-97 (hereafter, Schütte, "Michaelis"); John Snell, "Benedict XV, Wilson, Michaelis and German Socialism," *Catholic Historical Review*, July, 1951, pp. 151-78 (hereafter, Snell, "Benedict").

12. Deuerlein, "Friedensaktion," p. 247; Hanssen, *Diary*, p. 234; Erich Matthias and Rudolph Morsey (eds.), *Der Interfraktionelle Ausschuss, 1917/18*, Düsseldorf, 1959, Volume I/1, pp. 168-74 (hereafter, Matthias, *Ausschuss*); 2118, Part II.

13. Forster, *Failures*, pp. 102-3; Scherer, *L'Allemagne*, Volume II; Robert F. Hopwood, "Interalliance Diplomacy: Count Czernin and Germany, 1916-1918," Unpublished PhD dissertation, Stanford University, 1965 (hereafter, Hopwood, "Diplomacy"); Arthur J. May, *The Passing of the Habsburg Monarchy, 1914-1918*, Philadelphia, 1966, Volume II (hereafter, May, *Passing*); zu AS 3289 I, AS 3345, AS 3346, WK 2 geh.

14. AS 3200, AS 3252, AS 3256, zu AS 3252, WK 15 geh; 2112, Part XXIII; 2118, Parts XVIII, XIX and XXIII.

15. Michaelis, *Staat*, pp. 342-43; H. J. T. Johnson, *Vatican Diplomacy in the World War*, Oxford, 1933 (hereafter, Johnson, *Diplomacy*); R. Fester, *Die politischen Kämpfe und den Frieden (1916-1918) und das Deutschtum*, Munich, 1938, pp. 131ff (hereafter, Fester, *Kämpfe*); G. D. L. Dickinsen (ed.), *Documents and Statements relating to Peace Proposals and War Aims*, London, 1919 (hereafter, Dickensen, *Documents*); Poincaré, *Service*, Volume IX; Alexandre Ribot, *Journal et correspondence inedité*, Paris, 1936, pp. 64, 90-91 (hereafter, Ribot, *Journal*); 2112, Part XVII.

16. Kühlmann memorandum, Michaelis Papers; AS 3345, WK 2 geh; 2112, Parts XVII and XXII.

17. Epstein, *Erzberger*, p. 218; Matthias, *Ausschuss*, pp. 181ff; Kühlmann, *Erinnerungen*, pp. 478-79; Scheidemann, *Memoiren*, Volume II, pp. 81ff; Westarp, *Politik*, Volume II, pp. 536-37; 2112, Part XXVI; 211k, Part II.

18. Gatzke, *Drive*, pp. 206ff. Michaelis, *Staat*, pp. 345-46; Kühlmann, *Erinnerungen*, p. 480; 2112, Part XV.

19. Michaelis, *Staat*, pp. 345-46; Ludendorff, *Kriegserinnerungen*, Volume II, pp. 514-15; AS 3441, WK 2 geh; 2112, Parts XVII and XXIII; Michaelis Papers.

20. Michaelis, *Staat*, pp. 352-53; Ludendorff, *Kriegserinnerungen*, Volume II, pp. 491-500; Kühlmann, *Erinnerungen*, p. 483; Gatzke, *Drive*, pp. 226-27; AS 3487, WK 15 geh; 2112, Parts XV and XVII.

21. Scherer, *L'Allemagne*, Volume II; Kühlmann, *Erinnerungen*, p. 472; Lancken, *Dienstjahre*, pp. 164-65; Friedrich Meinecke, *Strassburg, Freiburg, Berlin, 1901-1919: Erinnerungen*, Stuttgart, 1949, p. 205 (hereafter, Meinecke, *Strassburg*); AS 2423, AS 2877, AS 3444, WK 2 geh; 2112, Part XV; 2118, Part XIX.

22. Schulthess, *Geschichtskalender, 1917*, pp. 821-23; 2112, Part XXII; 2118, Part II.

23. Scherer, *L'Allemagne*, Volume II; Lancken, *Dienstjahre*, p. 260; Suarez, *Briand*, pp. 254-57, 277; AS 3493, WK 2 geh; 2112, Parts XXVIII and XXIX.

24. David Lloyd George, *War Memoirs*, London, 1938, Volume II, pp. 1232-45 (hereafter, Lloyd George, *Memoirs*); AS 3593, WK 2 geh.

25. AS 3593, zu AS 3593, WK 2 geh; 2112, Parts XV and XXII.

26. Lloyd George, *Memoirs*, Volume II, pp. 1237-45; *Vorwärts*, 21 September 1917, Schulthess, *Geschichtskalender, 1917*, pp. 339-40; C. Nabokoff, *The Ordeals of a Diplomat*, London, 1921, pp. 167-68 (hereafter, Nabokoff, *Ordeals*); Max Montgelas, "War im Sommer 1917 ein Verständigungsfriede möglich?" *Berliner Monatshefte*, July, 1932, p. 647 (hereafter, Mongelas, "Sommer"); Milner Papers; AS 3644, AS 3788, A 34407, AS 5024, WK 2 geh; 2112, Parts XV and XXII.

27. Montgelas, "Sommer," pp. 653-54; Lloyd George, *Memoirs*, Volume II, pp. 1244-45; Schulthess, *Geschichtskalender, 1917*, pp. 878-81; AS 3584, WK 2 geh; 2112, Part II.

28 Guinn, *Strategy*; C. J. Lowe and M. L. Dockrill, *The Mirage of Power*, London, 1972, Volume II (hereafter, Lowe, *Mirage*); V. H. Rothwell, *British War Aims and Peace Diplomacy 1914-1918*, Oxford, 1971 (hereafter, Rothwell, *Aims*); Scherer, *L'Allemagne*, Volume II; AS 4946, WK 2 geh; 2112, Part XXX.

Chapter VIII

1. Meinecke, "Kühlmann," p. 192; Deuerlein, "Friedensaktion," p. 247; Matthias, *Ausschuss*, pp. 168-80; Hanssen, *Diary*, p. 234; Zeman, *Germany*, pp. 70-71; AS 2936, AS 3640, WK 2 geh.

2. Zeman, *Germany*, pp. 94-95; Wheeler-Bennett, *Brest-Litovsk*, pp. 75-77, 99; Werner Hahlweg, *Der Diktatfrieden von Brest-Litovsk*, Münster, 1960 (hereafter Hahlweg, *Diktatfrieden*); Erhard Walz, *Reichsleitung und Heeresleitung in der Periode des Friedens von Brest-Litovsk. Der Konflikt über Ostannexionen*, Düsseldorf, 1936 (hereafter, Walz, *Reichsleitung*); Robert D. Warth, *The Allies and the Russian Revolution. From the Fall of the Monarchy to the Peace of*

Brest-Litovsk, Durham, 1954 (hereafter, Warth, *Allies*; AS 4486, WK 2 geh; 2112, Part XXX.

3. Kühlmann, *Erinnerungen*, p. 285; Wheeler-Bennet, *Brest-Litovsk*, p. 107; Zeman, *Germany*, ,pp. 72-79, 91-93, 105-8; Matthias, *Ausschuss*, pp. 614-22; Scheidemann, *Memoiren*, Volume II, pp. 119-25; Epstein, *Erzbgerger*, pp. 233ff; Ottokar Czernin, *Im Weltkriege*, Berlin/Vienna, 1919, p. 217 (hereafter, Czernin, *Weltkriege*); AS 4266, AS 4344, WK 2 geh; AS 4240, WK 2f, Nr. 1; AS 4486, WK 131 geh.

4. Müller, *Kaiser*, pp. 337-38; Wheeler-Bennett, *Brest-Litovsk*, pp. 83ff.; Zeman, *Germany*, pp. 94-95; AS 4231, AS 4352, AS 4571, WK 2 geh; AS 4486, WK 131 geh; 2112, Part XXXI.

5. Wheeler-Bennett, *Brest-Litovsk*, p. 82; AS 4231, WK 2 geh; 2112, Parts XV and XXXI.

6. AS 4803, AS 64 (1918), WK 2 geh; 2112, Parts XXV and XXXI; 2118, Part XXI.

7. Wheeler-Bennett, *Brest-Litovsk*, pp. 107-11; Müller, *Kaiser*, p. 342.

8. Müller, *Kaiser,* pp. 341-45; Fischer, "Kriegsziele," p. 282.

9. Wheeler-Bennett, *Brest-Litovsk*, p. 243; Gerald Freund, *Unholy Alliance*, London, 1957 (hereafter, Freund, *Alliance*).

10. Freund, *Alliance*, pp. 13-19; Haussmann, *Schlaglichter*, pp. 189ff; Forster, *Failures*, p. 144; Fischer, *Griff*; Ritter, *Staatskunst*, Volume IV; Winfried Baumgart, *Deutsche Ostpolitik 1918. Von Brest-Litovsk bis zum Ende des Ersten Weltkrieges*, Vienna, 1966; K. Raumer, *Zwischen Brest-Litovsk und Compiègne: Die deutsche Ostpolitik vom Sommer 1918*, Berlin, 1939; Bernhard Schwertfeger, *Die politischen und militärischen Verantwortlichkeiten im Verlaufe der Offensive von 1918*, Das Werk des Untersuchungsausschusses, Series 4, Volume II, Berlin, 1925.

11. Grey, *Years*, Volume II, pp. 161ff.

12. Haussmann, *Schlaglichter*, pp. 183ff.

13. Forster, *Failures*, pp. 142ff.

Conclusion

1. For further details on the author's view of the debate over war aims, see: *Illusion*, pp. 33-37; Introduction to Fritz Fischer, *World Power or Decline*, New York, 1974, pp. xiii-xxi (hereafter, Fischer, *Power*). For the views of the major participants, see: Fischer, *Power*; Fischer, *Griff*; Ritter, *Staatskunst*, Volumes II-IV; Zechlin, "Friedensbestrebungen;" Zechlin, "Deutschland;" Hans Herzfeld, "Zur deutschen Politik im ersten Weltkriege: Kontinuität oder permanente

Kriese?" *Historische Zeitschrift*, 191, pp. 67-82; Hans Herzfeld, "Die deutsche Kriegspolitik im ersten Weltkriege," *Vierteljahreshefte für Zeitgeschichte*, July, 1963, pp. 224-45. Among many aritcles and collections on the debate, see: James Joll, "The Debate Continues," *Past and Present*, July, 1966, pp. 100-13; Ernst W. Graf Lynar (ed.), *Deutsche Kriegsziele 1914-1918*, Frankfurt/Berlin, 1964; John A. Moses (ed.), *The War Aims of Imperial Germany: Professor Fritz Fischer and His Critics*, St. Lucia (Queensland, Australia), 1968.

2. AS 3904, WK 2 geh.

3. Lerchenfeld Documents, p. 196.

4. AS 3042, WK 2 geh.

5. AS 2832 (1916), WK 2 geh.

6. Zu AS 1346, WK 15 geh.

7. AS 1535, WK 2 geh.

8. Zu AS 1427, WK 2 geh.

9. Zu AS 1021, WK 2 geh.

10. AS 1891 (1916), WK 2 geh.

11. AS 3345, WK 2 geh.

12. AS 4486, Deutschland 131 geh.

13. AS 2769, WK 2 geh.

14. 2112, Pt. XXIII; Michaelis Papers.

15. 2112, Pt. XXX.

16. E.g., Ritter, *Staatskunst*, Volume III (subtitle: "The Tragedy of Statecraft—Bethmann Hollweg as War Chancellor"); Janssen, *Kanzler* (full title: "The Chancellor and the General: The Leadership Crisis involving Bethmann Hollweg and Falkenhayn, 1914-1916"); Jarausch, *Chancellor*.

17. 2118, Pt. XXI.

18. Ritter, *Staatskunst*, Volume III, p. 586; Craig, *Politics*, p. 300.

19. *Weltkrieg*, Volume III, p. 622.

20. Zu As 2769, WK 2 geh.

BIBLIOGRAPHY

Abbreviations for Periodicals and Newspapers

AHR   *American Historical Review*
AOA   *Anzeiger der österreichen Akademie*
ASEER *American Slavic and East European Review*
BMH   *Berliner Monatshefte*
CEH   *Central European History*
CH   *Current History*
CHR   *Catholic Historical Review*
CJH   *Canadian Journal of History*
CR   *Contemporary Review*
CW   *Christ und Welt*
DOB   *Deutsche Offizier Bund*
DP   *Deutsche Politik*
DR   *Deutsche Revue*
EHR   *Economic History Review*
       Encounter
       Esquire
FAZ   *Frankfurter Allgemeine Zeitung*
FG   *Forschung zur osteuropäischen Geschichte*
GWU   *Geschichte in Wissenschaft und Unterricht*
       History
HJ   *Historisches Jahrbuch*
HPBKD *Historisch-politische Blätter für das katholische Deutschland*
HS   *Historical Studies*
HV   *Historische Vierteljahresschrift*
HZ   *Historische Zeitschrift*
IA   *International Affairs*
IRHPS *International Review of History and Political Science*
IRSH   *International Review of Social History*
JCEA   *Journal of Central European Affairs*
JCH   *Journal of Contemporary History*
JCR   *Journal of Conflict Resolution*
JfG   *Jahrbuch für Geschichte*
JGO   *Jahrbücher für die Geschichte Osteuropas*
JGUdSSRVLE *Jahrbuch fur Geschichte der UdSSR und der Volks-demokratischer Lander Europas*
JIR   *Jahrbuch für internationalen Recht*
JMH   *Journal of Modern History*
KSF   *Kriegsschuldfrage*

LA   *Living Age*
MGM   *Militärgeschichtliche Mitteilungen*
          Der Monat
MOS   *Mitteilungen des österreichischen Staatsarchivs*
MVHR   *Mississippi Valley Historical Review*
MWB   *Militär-Wochenblatt*
MWM   *Militärwissenschaftliche Mitteilungen*
NAWG   *Nachrichten der Akademie der Wissenschaften Göttingen*
NCA   *Nineteenth Century and After*
          Neue Welt
NPL   *Neue Politische Literatur*
NYRB   *New York Review of Books*
NZZ   *Neue Zürcher Zeitung*
OGL   *Österreich in Geschichte und Literatur*
          L'Opinion
OW   *Ostdeutsche Wissenschaft*
PAPZ   *Das Parlament, Aus Politik und Zeitgeschichte*
PAW   *Preussische Akademie der Wissenschaften*
PJ   *Preussische Jahrbücher*
PP   *Past and Present*
PV   *Politische Vierteljahresschrift*
QFAB   *Quellen und Forschungen aus italienischen Archiven und*
          Bibliotheken
Rdm   *Revue des deux mondes*
Rh   *Revue d'histoire diplomatique*
Rhes   *Revue d'histoire economique et social*
Rhgm   *Revue d'histoire de la guerre mondiale*
Rihm   *Revue internationale d'histoire militaire*
RP   *Review of Politics*
RdP   *La Revue de Paris*
Rtasmp   *Revue des travaux de l'academie des sciences morales et*
          politiques
SBAW   *Sitzungberichte der Bayerischen Akademie der Wissenschaften*
SM   *Süddeutsche Monatshefte*
SMH   *Schweizer Monatshefte*
SPSSQ   *Southwestern Political and Social Science Quarterly*
SnR   *Slavonic Review*
SR   *Slavic Review*
          Der Staat
SZ   *Stimmen der Zeit*
VfZ   *Vierteljahrshefte für Zeitgeschichte*
VfSWG   *Vierteljahrsschrift für Sozial- und Wirtschaftsgeschichte*

	Vorwärts
WG	*Welt als Geschichte*
WI	*Welt des Islams*
WP	*World Politics*
WW	*Wissen und Wehr*
WZKMU	*Wissenschaftliche Zeitschrift der Karl-Marx-Universität* (Leipzig)
	Die Zeit
ZfG	*Zeitschrift für Geschichtswissenschaft*
ZO	*Zeitschrift für Ostforschung*

Published and Unpublished Documents
Official Histories and Chronologies

(Arranged Alphabetically by Title)

L'Allemagne et les problèmes de la paix pendant la première guerre mondiale, Volumes I-II. André Scherer and Jacques Grunewald (eds.). Paris, 1962 and 1966.

Les Armées françaises dans la grande guerre, Ministère de la Guerre, État-Major de l'Armée, Service Historique. Paris, 1922-5.

Von Brest-Litovsk zur deutschen November-Revolution. Winfried Baumgart (ed.), Göttingen, 1971.

The Causes of Germany's Collapse in 1918. Ralph H. Lutz (ed.), Stanford, 1934.

Die deutschen Dokumente zum Kriegsausbruch 1914. Karl Kautsky (ed.), Berlin, 1924. 4 Volumes.

Die Deutsche Nationalversammlung 1919/1920, Volumes I-II. Stenographische Berichte über die öffentlichen Verhandlungen des 15. Untersuchungsausschusses der Verfassunggebenden Nationalversammlung. Berlin, 1920.

Deutsch-sowjetische Beziehungen von den Verhandlungen in Brest-Litovsk bis zum Abschluss des Rapallo-vertrages, Volume I, Berlin, 1967.

"Dokumentation zu den deutsch-russischen Beziehungen 1918," Hans W. Gatzke (ed.), VfZ, 1955, pp. 67-98.

Documents and Statements Relating to Peace Proposals and War Aims. G. D. L. Dickenson (ed.), New York, 1919.

Die Europäischen Mächte und die Türkei während des Weltkrieges: Konstantinopel und die Meerengen, Volume I. Nach den Geheimdokumenten des ehemaligen Ministeriums für Auswärtige Angelegenheiten, E. A. Adamov (ed.), Dresden, 1930.

Europäischer Geschichtskalender, 1914-1918. Schulthess, Munich, 1917-1921.

The Fall of the German Empire, 1914-1918, Volumes I-II. Ralph H. Lutz (ed.), Stanford, 1932.

Der Friede von Brest-Litovsk. Werner Hahlweg (ed.), Düsseldorf, 1971.

Der Friedensappell Papst Benedikts XV vom 1. August 1917 und die Mittelmächte. Wolfgang Steglich (ed.), Wiesbaden, 1970.

German Foreign Office Archives. File Numbers: WK 1, WK 2, WK 2 geh, WK 2 geh Spez Blitz, WK 2f Nr. 1, WK 11, WK 11adh 1, WK a geh, WK b geh, WK c geh, WK 15, WK 15 geh, WK 15 Adh, WK 16, WK 20 c geh, WK 21, WK 131 geh, WK/GHQ, Deutschland 131, Deutschland 180 geh, Russland 61, Russland 63 Nr. 1 geh, Russland Politisches Nr. 1.

Germany and the Revolution in Russia, 1915-1918. Z. A. B. Zeman (ed.), London, 1958.

History of the Great War. Historical Section of the Committee of Imperial Defence, J. E. Edmonds (ed.), London, 1922-7.

Der Interfraktionelle Ausschuss 1917/18. Erich Matthias and Rudolf Morsey (eds.), Düsseldorf, 1959.

Die Internationalen Beziehungen im Zeitalter des Imperialismus. Dokumente aus den Archiven der Zarischen und Provisorischen Regierung, M. N. Prokowski (ed.). Otto Hoetzsch (ed. German edition), Series II, 1, 2, Berlin, 1933-43.

Iswolski im Weltkriege. Der diplomatische Schriftwechsel Iswolskis aus den Jahren 1914-1917, Volumes I-II. Friedrich Stieve (ed.), Berlin, 1925.

Kriegsreden Bethmann Hollwegs. Friedrich Thimme (ed.), Berlin, 1919.

Der Krieg zur See 1914-1918, Marine-Archiv und Kriegswissenschaftliche Abteilung der Marine. Berlin, 1928-38.

Lerchenfeld Documents (unpublished). Collected and edited by Ernst Deuerlein. Munich.

Lenins Rückkehr nach Russland, 1917. Werner Hahlweg (ed.), Leiden, 1957.

Official Statements of War Aims and Peace Proposals, December, 1916-November, 1918. J. B. Scott (ed.), Washington, D. C., 1919.

Österreich-Ungarns letzter Krieg 1914-1918, Österreiches Bundesministerium für Heerwesen und von Kriegsarchiv. E. von Glaise-Horstenau (ed.), Vienna, 1931-8.

Out of Their Own Mouths: Utterances of German Rulers, Statesmen... W. R. Thayer (ed.), New York, 1917.

Michaelis Papers (unpublished). Possession of Wilhelm Michaelis, Rechlinghausen, Germany.

Milner Papers (unpublished). Possession of New College, Oxford, England.

Papers Relating to the Foreign Relations of the United States. Washington, D. C., 1927.

Parlamentarischer Untersuchungsausschuss (unpublished), File Numbers: 2112 and 2118.

The Peace Proposals Made by His Holiness the Pope to the Belligerent Powers on August 1, 1917. London, 1919.

Politische Dokumente, Volumes I-II. Alfred von Tirpitz (ed.), Berlin, 1924 and 1926.

Die Regierung des Prinzen Max von Baden. Erich Matthias and Rudolf Morsey (eds.), Düsseldorff, 1962.

The Russian Provisional Government 1917, Volumes I-III. R. P. Browder and A. F. Kerensky (eds.), Stanford, 1961.

Secret Treaties and Understandings. F. S. Cocks (ed.), London, 1918.

Der Weltkrieg 1914-1918, Volumes I-XII. Reichsarchiv, Berlin, 1925-39.

Das Werk des Untersuchungsausschusses der Verfassunggebenden Nationalversammlung und des Deutschen Reichstags 1919 bis 1928, Third Series, Völkerrecht im Weltkrieg, 1914-1918, Volume I; Fourth Series, Die Ursachen des Deutschen Zusammenbruchs im Jahre 1918, Volume II, Die politischen und militärischen Verantwortlichkeiten im Verlaufe der Offensive von 1918; Volume VII, Der deutsche Reichstag im Weltkriege; Volume XII, Part I, Die Annexionsfragen des Weltkrieges. Berlin, 1926-9.

Other Works

(anon.), "La Paix des empires centraux," Rdm, 1929, pp. 42-80, 304-42.

(anon.), "À propos de l'offre de paix du Saint-Siège en 1917," Rhgm, 1926. pp. 131-40.

(anon.), "Die Friedensgespräche der Grafen Mensdorff und Revertera im Dezember 1917 und Februar 1918 nach ihren Berichten an den Grafen Czernin," BMH, 1937, pp. 401-19.

(anon.), "Der Friedensvermittlungsversuch des Grafen Revertera," BMH, 1938, pp. 64-67.

(anon.), "Les Négotiations Armand-Revertera," *L'Opinion*, 1920, pp. 31-37, 87-94, 115-21.

Abbott, G. F., *Greece and the Allies 1914-1922*, London, 1922.

Adams, G., *Treason and Tragedy: An Account of French War Trials*, London, 1929.

Ahlswede, Dieter, "Friedensbemühungen zwischen dem Deutschen Reich und Grossbritanien, 1914-1918," University of Bonn PhD dissertation, 1959.

————, "Deutsch-britische Friedensgespräche im Haag 1918?" WG, 1960, pp. 187-97, 260-62.

(Anderson, H. C.) Obituary. *Berliner Monatshefte*, February, 1938.

Andrassy, J., *Diplomacy and the World War*. London, 1921.

Albert Ier, *Les Carnets de guerre d'Albert Ier, Roi des Belges*, ed. R. van Overstraeten, Brussels, 1953.

Alberti, Adriano, *General Falkenhayn: Die Beziehungen zwischen den Generalstabschefs des Dreibundes*. Berlin, 1924.

Albertini, Luigi, *The Origins of the War of 1914*, Volume I. London, 1957.

Alexandra, *Lettres de l'Impératrice Alexandra Feodorovna à l'Empereur Nicolas II*, Paris, 1924.

Amiguet, P. H., *La Vie du Prince Sixte de Bourbon*, Paris, 1934.

Appuhn, Charles, *La Politique allemande pendant la guerre*, Paris, 1926.

————, "Les Négotiations austro-allemandes du printemps de 1917 et la mission du prince Sixte," Rhgm, 1935, pp. 209-23.

Arz, Artur, *Zur Geschichte des Grossen Krieges*, Vienna/Leipzig/Munich, 1924.

Asquith, Herbert Henry, *Memories and Reflections, 1852-1927*, Boston, 1928, Volumes I-II.

Auerbach, Bertrand, *L'Autriche et la Hongrie pendant la guerre*, Paris, 1925.

Auffenberg-Komaròw, Moritz, *Aus Österreich-Ungarns Teilnahme am Weltkriege*, Berlin, 1920.

F. B., "Die militärischen Durchgangsfrachten zwischen Deutschland und der Türkei während des Weltkrieges," WW, 1926, pp. 346-55.

Bachmann, G., "Admiral v. Müller gegen Grossadmiral v. Tirpitz," DP, 1920, 1, pp. 52ff.

Barnett, Corelli, *Anatomy of a War*, London, 1963.

Barthels, Walter, *Die Linken in der Sozialdemokratie im Kampf gegen Militarismus und Krieg*, Berlin, 1958.

Basilesco, Nicholas, *La Roumanie dans la guerre et dans la paix*, Paris, 1919.

Basler, Werner, "Die Politik des deutschen Imperialismus gegenüber Litauen, 1914-1918," JGUdSSRVLE, IV, Berlin, 1960.

————, *Deutschlands Annexionspolitik in Polen und Baltikum*, Berlin, 1962.

Bauer, Hermann, *Reichleitung und U-Booteinsatz 1914-1918*, Lippoldsberg, 1956.

Bauer, Ludwig, *Der Kampf um der Frieden.*

Bauer, Max, *Der grosse Krieg in Feld und Heimat. Erinnerungen und Betrachtungen aus der Zeit des Weltkrieges*, Tübingen, 1921.

Baumgart, Winfried, "Ludendorff und das Auswärtige Amt zur Besetzung der Krim 1918," JGO, 1966.

————, *Deutsche Ostpolitik 1918. Von Brest-Litovsk bis zum Ende des Ersten Weltkrieges*, Vienna, 1966.

————, "Dokumentation: Die militär-politische Berichte des Freiherrn von Keyserlingk aus Petersburg, Januar-February 1918," VfZ, 1967, pp. 87ff.

Beaverbrook, Lord, *Politicians and the War, 1914-1916*, London, 1928.

————, *Men and Power, 1917-1918*, London, 1956.

Beck, Ludwig, *Studien*, Stuttgart, 1955.

Becker, Otto, *Der Ferne Osten und das Schicksal Europas, 1907-1918*, Leipzig, 1940.

Bell, Archibald C., *A History of the Blockade of Germany and of the Countries Associated with her in the Great War, 1914-1918*, London, 1961.

Beloff, Max, *Imperial Sunset*, Volume I: *Britain's Liberal Empire 1897-1971*, New York, 1970.

Benedikt, Heinrich, *Die Friedensaktion der Meinl-Gruppe 1917/18*, Graz/Cologne, 1962.

Berghahn, Volker R., "Zu den Zielen des deutschen Flottenbaus unter Wilhelm II," HZ, 1970, pp. 34-54.

Bergsträsser, Ludwig, *Die preussische Wahlrechtsfrage im Kriege und die Entstehung der Osterbotschaft 1917*, Tübingen, 1924.

————, *Das Alte System über sich selbst*, Tübingen, 1930.

Berlau, Joseph, *The German Social Democratic Party, 1914-1921*, New York, 1949.

Bermbach, Udo, "Aspekte der Palamentarismus-Diskussion im kaiserlichen Reichstag. Die Erörterungen im Interfraktionellen Ausschuss, 1917-1918," PV, 1967, pp. 51-70.

Bernstorff, Johann H., *My Three Years in America*, London, 1920.

————, *Erinnerungen und Briefe*, Zurich, 1936.

Bertie, Lord, *Diary of Lord Bertie of Thame, 1914-1918*, ed. Lady Algernon Gordon Lennox, London, 1924.

Bethmann Hollweg, Theobald, *Betrachtungen zum Weltkriege*, Berlin, Volume I, 1919, Volume II, 1922.

————, "Das Friedensangebot vom 1915," PJB, 1919.

————, "Die Friedensmöglichkeiten im Frühsommer, 1917," DAZ, 19, February 1920.

156   Bibliography

Beyens, Baron, L'Allemagne avant la guerre, Brussels/Paris, 1915.
Beyer, Hans, Die Mittelmächte und die Ukraine, Munich, 1956.
————, "Die Mittelmächte und die Ukraine, 1918," JGO, 1956.
Beyerhaus, Gisbert, Einheitlicher Oberbefehl, Munich, 1938.
Bihl, Wolfdieter, "Zu den österreichische-ungarischen Kriegszielen
    1914," JGO, 1968, pp. 505-30.
Birke, Ernst, "Die französische Osteuropapolitik 1914-1918," ZO,
    1954, pp. 321ff.
Birnbaum, Karl E., Peace Moves and U-boat Warfare: A Study of
    Imperial Germany's Policy towards the United States, April 18,
    1916 January 9, 1917, Stockholm, 1958.
Blücher, Princess Evelyn, An English Wife in Berlin, London, 1920.
Boelcke, Willi, Krupp und die Hohenzollern. Aus der Korrespondenz
    der Familie Krupp 1850-1916, Berlin, 1956.
Bompard, Maurice, "L'Entre en guerre de la Turquie," RdP, 1 July
    1921, pp. 61-85, 15 July 1921, pp. 261-88.
Bonhard, O., Geschichte des alldeutschen Verbands, 1920
Bonnefous, Georges, Histoire politique de la troisième republique ,
    Paris, 1957, Volume II.
Borowsky, P., "Deutsche Ukrainepolitik 1918 und der besonderer
    Berücksichtigung der wirtschaftlichen Ziele," University of
    Hamburg PhD dissertation, 1968.
Botkin, Gleb, The Real Romanovs, New York, 1931.
Böttchev, H. M., Rathenau: Persönlichkeit und Werke, Bonn, 1958.
Bourbon, Prince Sixte de, L'offre de paix séparée de l'Autriche, Paris,
    1934.
Bracher, Karl Dietrich, review of Fischer's Griff nach der Weltmacht,
    NPL, 1962, pp. 471-82.
Brecht, Arnold, Aus nächster Nähe. Lebenserinnerungen, Berlin, 1966.
Bredt, Victor, "Reichskanzler Michaelis und die päpstliche Friedens-
    aktion," PJ, October-December, 1926, pp. 180-203.
Briand, Aristide, Souvenirs parlés de Briand, ed. R. Escholier, Paris,
    1932.
Briggs, Mitchell P., George D. Herron and the European Settlement,
    Stanford, 1932.
Brussilov, A. A., A Soldier's Notebook, 1914-1918, London, 1930.
Buchanan, George, My Mission to Russia and Other Diplomatic
    Memories, Boston, 1923, Volumes I-II.
Buehrig, E. H., Woodrow Wilson and the Balance of Power, Bloom-
    ington, 1955.
Bülow, B. H. M. K., Denkwürdigkeiten, Berlin, 1931, Volume III.
Bülter, Horst, "Zur Geschichte Deutschlands im ersten Weltkrieg
    1914-1915)," ZfGW, III, 1955, pp. 835-55.

Bülter, Horst, "Zur Geschichte Deutschlands im ersten Weltkrieg (1914-1915)," ZfGW, III, 1955, pp. 835-55.

Burian, Stephen Graf, *Drei Jahre aus der Zeit meiner Amtsführung im Kriege*, Berlin, 1923.

Bury, J. P. T., *France, 1814-1940*, New York, 1962.

Buse, D. K., "Ebert and the German Crisis, 1917-1920," CEH, September, 1972, pp. 234-55.

Caillaux, J., *Mes Memoires*, Paris, 1941.

Callwell, C. E., *Field Marshall Sir Henry Wilson: His Life and Diaries*, London, 1927, Volume I.

Cambon, Paul, *Correspondance, 1870-1924*, Paris, 1946, Volume III.

Carlgren, W. M., *Neutralität oder Allianz: Deutschlands Beziehungen zu Schweden in den Anfangsjahren des ersten Weltkrieges*, Stockholm/ Göteborg/Uppsala, 1962.

Carr, Edward H., *The Bolshevik Revolution 1917-1923*.

Carroll, E. M., *Germany and the Great Powers. A Study in Public Opinion and Foreign Policy*, New York, 1938.

Carsten, F. L., "Living with the Past: What German Historians are Saying," *Encounter*, 127, April, 1964, pp. 100-10.

Cassar, Gaston, *L'Entremise pontificale de 1917 pour la paix*, Fribourg, 1945.

Caukin, E., "Peace Proposals of Germany and Austria-Hungary, 1914-1918," Unpublished PhD dissertation, Stanford University, 1927.

Cecil, Lamar, *Albert Ballin: Business and Politics in Imperial Germany, 1888-1918*, Princeton, 1967.

Chambers, F., *The War Behind the War*, London, 1939.

Charles-Roux, F., *La Paix des empire centraux*, 1947.

Chatelle, A., *La Paix manquée*, Paris, 1936.

Child, C. J., "German-American Attempts to Prevent the Exportation of Munitions of War, 1914-1915," MVHR, 1938, pp. 351-68.

Churchill, Winston S., *The World Crisis*, London, 1923-7.

Class, Heinrich, *Wenn ich der Kaiser wär*, Berlin, 1912.

—————, *Wider den Strom: Vom Werden und Wachsen der nationalen Oppostion im alten Reich*, Leipzig, 1932.

Clemenceau, Georges, *Grandeur and Misery of Victory*, London, 1930.

Colliander, Borje, *Die Beziehungen zwischen Litauen und Deutschland während der Okkupation 1915-1918*, Turku, 1935.

Conrad von Hötzendorf, Franz, *Aus meiner Dienstzeit*, Vienna/ Leipzig/Munich, 1922-5, Volumes III-V.

Conze, *Polnische Nation und deutsche Politik*, Cologne, 1958.

—————, "Nationalstaat oder Mitteleuropa: Die Deutschen des Reiches und die Nationalitätenfragen Ostmitteleuropas im ersten

Weltkrieges," *Deutschland und Europa: Historische Studien zur Völker- und Staatenordnung des Abendlandes*, Düsseldorf, 1951, pp. 201-32.

Cooper, John M., Jr., *The Vanity of Power: American Isolationism and the First World War, 1914-1917*, Westport (Conn.), 1972.

Craig, Gordon A., *The Politics of the Prussian Army 1640-1945*, Oxford, 1955.

————, "The World War I Alliance of the Central Powers in Retrospect: The Military Cohesion of the Alliance," JMH, September, 1965, pp. 336-45.

————, "Relations between Civil and Military Authorities in the Second German Empire: Chancellor and Chief of Staff, 1871-1918," in *War, Politics and Diplomacy*, New York, 1968, pp. 121-33.

Cramon, A., *Unser österreichisch-ungarischer Bundesgenosse im Weltkriege*, Berlin, 1920.

———— and Fleck, P., *Deutschlands Schicksalsbund mit Österreich-Ungarn. Von Conrad von Hötzendorf zu Kaiser Karl*, Berlin, 1932.

Cruttwell, C. R. M. F., *A History of the Great War 1914-1918*, Oxford, 1934.

Czernin, Ottokar, *Im Weltkriege*, Berlin/Vienna, 1919.

————, *Über die Politik während des Weltkrieges. Rede gehalten den 11. Dezember 1918*, Vienna, 1919.

Dahlin, E., *French and German Public Opinion on Declared War Aims*, Stanford, 1933.

Dallin, Alexander, *Russian Diplomacy and Eastern Europe, 1914-1919*, New York, 1963.

Danilov, Youri, *La Russie dans la guerre mondiale (1914-1917)*, Paris, 1927.

David, Eduard, *Das Kriegstagebuch des Reichstagsabgeordneten Eduard David, 1914-1918*, Düsseldorf, 1966.

Dehio, Ludwig, *The Precarious Balance*, New York, 1962.

————, *Germany and World Problems in the Twentieth Century*, London, 1959.

Deist, Wilhelm, *Militär und Innenpolitik im Weltkrieg*, Düsseldorf, 1970, Volumes I-II.

Delbrück, Clemens, *Die wirtschaftliche Mobilmachung in Deutschland 1914*, Munich, 1924.

Delbrück, Hans, "Die Erklärung über Belgien. Staatssekretär von Hintze. Das Eingreifen der Amerikaner," PJ, July-September, 1918, pp. 270-78.

Demblin, A., *Czernin und die Sixtus-Affaire*, Munich, 1920.

Dennis, Alfred L. P., *The Anglo-Japanese Alliance*, Berkeley, 1923.

Deuerlein, Ernst, *Der Bundesratsausschuss für auswärtige Angelegenheiten 1870 bis 1918*, Regensburg, 1955.

————, "Eine unbekannte Kontroverse zwischen Staatsminister Graf Hertling und der Oberste Heeresleitung im February/März 1917," HJ, 1950, pp. 260-95.

————, "Zur Friedensaktion Papst Benedikts XV," SZ, 1954-5, pp. 241-56.

————, *Deutsche Kanzler von Bismarck bis Hitler*, Munich, 1968.

Diamandy, Constantin, "Ma Mission en Russie, octobre 1914-mai 1915," Rdm, November-December 1930, pp. 421-32.

Dix, Arthur, *Wirtschaftskrieg und Kriegswirtschaft: zur Geschichte des deutschen Zusammenbruchs*, Berlin, 1925.

Dumba, Constantin, *Dreibund und Ententepolitik*, Vienna, 1931.

Ebert, Friedrich, *Schriften, Aufzeichnungen, Reden*, Dresden, 1926.

Edwards, Marvin L., *Stresemann and the Greater Germany, 1914-1918*, New York, 1963.

Eggert, S., "Die deutschen Eroberungspläne im ersten Weltkrieg," *Neue Welt*, II (1947), pp. 45-47.

Engel-Janosi, Friedrich, *Österreich und der Vatikan 1845-1918*, Graz/Vienna, 1960, Volume II.

————, "Die Friedensbemühungen Kaiser Karls mit besonderer Berücksichtigung der Besprechungen des Graf Revertera mit Comte Armand," in *Comité International des Sciences Historiques*, XII Congrès International des Sciences Historiques, Vienna, 29 août-5 septembre, Vienna, 1965, IV, Actes, pp. 323-40.

————, "Die Friedensgespräche N. Graf Reverteras mit Comte A. Armand 1917/18," AOA, 1965, pp. 40-57.

Epstein, Fritz T., "Ost-Mitteleuropa als Spannungsfeld zwischen Ost und West um die Jahrhundertwende bis Ende des ersten Weltkrieges," WG, 1956, pp. 64-123.

————, "Die deutsche Ostpolitik im Ersten Weltkrieg," JGO, 1962, pp. 381-94.

Epstein, Klaus, *Matthias Erzberger and the Dilemma of German Democracy*, Princeton, 1959.

————. "The Development of German-Austrian War Aims in the Spring of 1917," JCEA, April, 1957, pp. 24-47.

————, review of Matthias and Morsey, *Der Interfraktionelle Ausschuss*, HZ, 1960, 562-84.

————, "German War Aims in the First World War," WP, 1962, pp. 163-68.

Erdmann, Karl Dietrich, *Die Zeit der Weltkriege*, Stuttgart, 1961.

————, "Schlussbermerkungen zur Diskussion um den Kanzler Michaelis und die päpstliche Friedensaktion," GWU, 1956, pp. 304-7.

————, "Zur Beurteilung Bethmann Hollwegs," GWU, September, 1964, pp. 525-40.

Ernst, Fritz, *The Germans and their Modern History*, New York, 1966.

Erzberger, Matthias, *Erlebniss im Weltkrieg*, Stuttgart, 1920.

————, *Der Verständigungsfriede. Rede des Reichstagsabgeordneten M. Erzberger gehalten auf einer Versammlung der württembergischen Zentrumspartei im Saalbau zu Ulm am 23. September 1917*, Stuttgart, 1917.

————, *Papst, Kurie und Weltkrieg*, Berlin, 1918.

Esher, Reginald Viscount, *Journals and Letters*, ed. M. V. Brett, London, 1934, Volume III

Essame, H., *The Battle for Europe 1918*, London, 1972.

Eubank, Keith, *Paul Cambon: Master Diplomatist*, Norman, Oklahoma, 1960.

Eulenburg-Hertefeld, P., *Aus 50 Jahren: Erinnerungen, Tagebücher und Briefe*, Berlin, 1925.

Eyck, Erich, *Das persönliche Regiment Wilhelms II*, Zurich, 1948.

Eynern, M. (ed.), *Walther Rathenau—ein preussischer Europäer*, Berlin, 1955.

Fainsod, Merle, *International Socialism and the World War*, Cambridge, 1935.

Falkenhayn, Erich, *Die Oberste Heeresleitung 1914-16 in ihren wichtigsten Entschliessungen*, Berlin, 1920.

Falls, Cyril, *Armageddon: 1918*, Philadelphia, 1964.

Farrar, L. L., Jr., "Impotence of Omnipotence: The Paralysis of the European Great Power System, 1871-1914," IRHPS, February, 1972, pp. 13-44.

————, "The Limits of Choice: July 1914 Reconsidered," JCR, March, 1972, pp. 1-23.

————, "The Short-War Illusion: The Dilemma of German Military Strategy, August-December, 1914," MGM, October, 1972, pp. 39-52.

————, "Ends and Means," IRHPS, November, 1973, pp. 34-58.

————, *The Short-War Illusion: An Analysis of German Policy, Strategy and Domestic Affairs, August-December, 1914*, Santa Barbara/Oxford, 1973.

————. Translation and Introduction to Fischer, *World Power or Decline*, New York, 1974, pp. xiii-xxi.

Farrar, L. L., Jr., "Peace Through Exhaustion: German Diplomatic Motivations for the Verdun Campaign," RiHm, 32, 1972-5, pp. 477-94.

————, "Opening to the West: German Efforts to Conclude a Separate Peace with England, July 1917-March 1918," CJH, April, 1975, pp. 73-90.

Feldman, Gerald D., *Army, Industry and Labor in Germany, 1914-1918*, Princeton, 1966.

————, (ed.) *German Imperialism, 1914-1918: The Development of a Historical Debate*, New York, 1972.

Fellner, F., Comment on statements by Ritter and Fischer, in *Comité International des Sciences Historiques*, XII Congrès International des Sciences Historiques, Vienna, 29 août-5 septembre 1965, Vienna, 1965, V, Actes, pp. 746-48.

————, *Der Dreibund. Europäische Diplomatie vor dem Ersten Weltkrieg*, Munich, 1960.

Fester, R., *Die Politik Kaiser Karls und der Wendepunkt des Weltkrieges*, Munich, 1925.

————, *Die politischen Kämpfe um den Frieden (1916-1918) und das Deutschtum*, Munich, 1938.

Fischer, Fritz, *Griff nach der Weltmacht. Die Kriegszielpolitik des kaiserlichen Deutschland 1914/18*, Düsseldorf, 1964.

————, "Deutsche Kriegziele, Revolutionierung und Separatfrieden im Osten, 1914-1918," HZ, 188, pp. 249-310.

————, "Kontinuität des Irrtums: Zum Problem der deutschen Kriegszielpolitik im ersten Weltkrieg," HZ, 191, pp. 83-100.

————, "Weltpolitik, Weltmachtstreben und deutsche Kriegsziele, "HZ, 199, pp. 265-346.

————, *World Power or Decline*, New York, 1974.

———— Reply to Ritter, in *Comité International des Sciences Historiques*, XII Congrès International des Sciences Historiques, Vienna, 29 août-5 septembre, Vienna, 1965, V, Actes, pp. 721-25.

————, *Der Zeit*, 3 September 1965.

Foch, Ferdinand, *Mémoires pour servir à l'histoire de la guerre de 1914/1918*, Paris, 1931, Volumes I-II.

Foerster, Friedrich Wilhelm, *Mein Kampf gegen das militaristische und nationalistische Deutschland*, Stuttgart, 1920.

————, (ed.), *Mackensen: Briefe und Aufzeichnungen*, Leipzig, 1938.

Forster, Kent, *The Failures of Peace*, Washington, D. C., 1941.

Franek, Fritz, *Die Entwicklung des Österreich-Ungarns Wehrmacht in den ersten zwei Kriegsjahren*, Vienna, 1933.

Franek, Fritz, "Probleme des Organisation im ersten Kriegsjahre," MWM, 1930, pp. 977-90.

Frantz, G., *Russland auf dem Wege zur Katastrophe*, Berlin, 1926.

————, "Friedensfühler bis Ende 1915: ein Beitrag nach russischen Quellen," BMH, XI, 1933, pp. 581-601.

Frauendienst, W., "Deutsche Weltpolitik. Zur Problematik des Wilhelminischen Reichs," WG, 1959, pp. 1-39.

French, Field Marshal, *1914*, London, 1957.

Freund, Gerald, *Unholy Alliance*, London, 1957.

Freund, Michael, "Bethmann-Hollweg, der Hitler des Jahres 1914?" FAZ, 28 March 1964.

Freytag-Loringhoven, Freiherr von, *Menschen und Dinge wie ich sie in meinem Leben sah*, Berlin, 1923.

Fuchs, Gustav, *Der deutsche Pazifismus im Weltkrieg*, Stuttgart, 1928.

Galántai, Joszef, "Stefan Tisza und der Erste Weltkrieg," OGL, 1964, Nr. 10, pp. 55-70.

————, "Die Kriegszielpolitik der Tisza-Regierung 1913-1917," in *Nouvelles études historiques*, Budapest, 1965, Volume II, pp. 201-21.

Gallieni, Joseph S., *Mémoires du Général Gallieni: défense de Paris 25 août—11 septembre 1914*, Paris, 1920.

Gallwitz, Max, *Meine Führertätigkeit im Weltkriege, 1914-1916*, Berlin, 1929.

Gatzke, Hans W., *Germany's Drive to the West: A Study of Germany's Western War Aims during the First World War*, Baltimore, 1950.

Gehrke, U., "Persien in der deutschen Orientpolitik während des ersten Weltkrieges," Berlin, 1960, 2 volumes.

Geiss, Imanuel, *Der polnische Grenzestreifen 1914-1918*, Lübeck/Hamburg, 1960.

Gerard, James W., *My Four Years in Germany*, New York, 1917.

————, *Face to Face with Kaiserism*, New York, 1917.

Gerson, Louis L., *Woodrow Wilson and the Rebirth of Poland 1914-1920*, New Haven, 1953.

Geyer, Dietrich, "Wilson und Lenin. Ideologie und Friedenssicherung in Osteuropa 1917-1919," JGO, 1955, pp. 430-41.

————, "Die Ukraine im Jahre 1917. Russische Revolution und nationale Bewegung," GWU, 1957, pp. 670-87.

————, "Die russischen Râte und die Friedensfrage im Frühjahr und Sommer 1917," VfZ, 1957, pp. 220-40.

Gilbert, Charles, *American Financing of World War I*, Westport (Conn.), 1972.

Gilbert, Martin, *Winston S. Churchill*, Volume III: 1914-1916, London, 1971.

Giovanetti, Alberto, *Der Vatikan und der Krieg*, Cologne, 1961.

Goerlitz, Walter, *History of the German General Staff, 1657-1945*, New York, 1953.

Goetz, Walter, "Die Erinnerung des Staatssekretärs Richard von Kuhlmann," SBAW, 1952, III, pp. 25-45.

Golovine, Nicholas N., *The Russian Campaign of 1914*, London, 1933.

————, *The Russian Army in the World War*, New Haven, 1931.

Gooch, G. P., *Germany*, London, 1926.

————, *Recent Revelations in European Diplomacy*, London, 1927.

Gottlieb, W. W., *Studies in Secret Diplomacy during the First World War*, London, 1957.

Gourko, Vasili, *War and Revolution in Russia, 1914-1917*, New York, 1919.

Gratz, G. and Schüller, R., *The Economic Policy of Austria-Hungary during the War*, New Haven, 1929.

Grebing, Helga, "Osterreich-Ungarn und die 'Ukrainische Aktion' 1914-18," JGO, Volume VII, pp. 270-91.

Grebler, Leo, and Winkler, Wilhelm, *The Cost of the War to Germany and Austria-Hungary*, New Haven, 1940.

Gregor, R., "Lenin's Foreign Policy 1917-1922," Unpublished PhD dissertation, University of London, 1966.

Grelling, Richard, *J'accuse*, New York, 1915.

Grey, Edward, *Twenty-Five Years, 1892-1916*, New York, 1925, Volumes I-II.

Grimm, Claus, *Jahre deutscher Entscheidung im Baltikum 1918/1919*, Essen, 1939.

Groener, Wilhelm, *Lebenserinnerungen*, Göttingen, 1957.

————, "Politik und Kriegsführung. Ein Rückblick auf den Weltkrieg," DR, 1920, pp. 120-45.

Groener-Geyer, Dorothea, *General Groener: Soldat und Staatsman*, Frankfurt am Main, 1953.

Groh, Dieter, "The 'Unpatriotic Socialists' and the State," JCH, 1966, I, pp. 151-71.

Grumbach, Salomon, *Das annexionistische Deutschland*, Lausanne, 1917.

Grünberg, Carl, *Die Internationale und der Weltkrieg*, Leipzig, 1916, Volume I.

Guinn, Paul, *British Strategy and Politics, 1914-1918*, Oxford, 1965.

Gutsche, Willibald, "Erst Europa—und dann die Welt," ZfG, 1964, pp. 745-67.

Gutsche, Willibald, "Bethmann Hollweg und die Politik der 'Neuorientierung': Zur innenpolitischen Strategie und Taktik der deutschen Reichsregierung während des ersten Weltkrieges," *ZfGW* 1965, pp. 209-34.

————, "Zu einigen Fragen der staatsmonopolistischen Verflechtung in den ersten Kriegsjahren am Beispiel der Ausplünderung der belgischen Industrie und der Zwangsdeportation von Belgiern," *Politik im Krieg*, Berlin, 1964, pp. 66-89.

————, F. Klein, H. Kral, and J. Petzold, "Neue Forschungen zur Geschichte Deutschlands im ersten Weltkrieg," *JfG*, Berlin, 1967, I, pp. 282-306.

————, "Die Beziehungen zwischen der Regierung Bethmann Hollweg und dem Monopolkapital in den ersten Monaten des ersten Weltkrieges," Unpublished Habilitationsscrift, University of Berlin, 1967.

Hallays, André, *L'opinion allemande pendant la guerre 1914-1918*, Paris, 1919.

Hammann, Otto, *Bilder aus der letzten Kaiserzeit*, Berlin, 1922.

Hanak, Harry, *Great Britain and Austria-Hungary during the First World War — A Study in the Formation of Public Opinion*, Oxford, 1960.

————, "The Government, the Foreign Office and Austria-Hungary, 1914-1918," *SEER*, 1969, 162-81.

Hanssen, H. P., *Diary of a Dying Empire*, ed. R. H. Lutz, Bloomington, 1955.

Hantsch, Hugo, *Leopold Graf Berchtold: Grandseigneur und Staatsmann*, Graz, 1963, Volume II.

Haussmann, Conrad, *Schlaglichter: Reichstagsbriefe und Aufzeichnungen*, ed. U. Zeller, Frankfurt am Main, 1924.

Hazlehurst, Cameron, *Politicians at War: July 1914 to May 1915. A Prologue to the Triumph of Lloyd George*, New York, 1970.

Hegemann, Margot, "Zum Plan der Abdankung Carols I von Rumänien im September 1914," *ZfG*, 1957, pp. 823-26.

Heininger, Horst, "Die ökonomische Stellung des deutschen Imperialismus vor dem ersten Weltkrieg und seine bedeutende ökonomische Schwächung im Ergebnis des Krieges," in Heininger, *König*, and Tuchscherer, *Ökonomisch-historische Aufsätze zur Novemberrevolution in Deutschland und zur Gründung der KPD*, Berlin, 1958.

Helfferich, Karl, *Der Weltkrieg*, Berlin, 1919, Volumes I-II.

————, *Die Friedensbemühungen im Weltkrieg. Vortrag gehalten in der Deutschen Gesellschaft 1914 am 1. September 1919*, Berlin, 1919.

Henning, Heinz, "Die Situation der deutschen Kriegswirschaft im Sommer 1918 und ihre Beurteilung durch Heeresleitung, Reichsführung und Bevölkerung," Unpublished PhD dissertation, University of Hamburg, 1957.

Hentig, Hans, *Friedensschluss. Geist und Technik einer verlorenen Kunst*, Stuttgart, 1952.

Herre, Paul, *Kronprinz Wilhelm: Seine Rolle in der Politik*, Munich, 1954.

Hertling, Georg, *Erinnerungen aus meinem Leben*, Volume II, Kempten/Munich, 1920.

Hertling, Karl, *Ein Jahr in der Reichskanzlei*, Freiburg, 1919.

Herwig, Holger H., "Admirals versus Generals: The War Aims of the Imperial German Navy, 1914-1918," CEH, September, 1972, pp. 208-33.

Herzfeld, Hans, *Die deutsche Sozialdemokratie und die Auflösung der nationalen Einheitsfront im Weltkriege*, Leipzig, 1928.

————, "Zur deutschen Politk im ersten Weltkriege: Kontinuität oder permanente Kriese?" HZ, 191, pp. 67-82.

————, "Die deutsche Kriegspolitik im ersten Weltkrieg," VfZ, July, 1963, pp. 224-45.

————, and Loock, H.-D., "Der Weltkrieg und Versailles 1914-1919," in Dahlmann-Waitz, *Quellenkunde der Deutschen Geschichte*, Stuttgart, 1965.

————, *Der Erste Weltkrieg*, Munich, 1968.

Heuss, Theodor, "Der Führerproblem," DP. 1919, pp. 648-68.

Higgins, Trumbull, *Winston Churchill and the Dardanelles: A Dialogue in Ends and Means*, New York, 1963.

Hildebrand, R., *Bethmann Hollweg: Der Kanzler ohne Eigenschaften? Urteile der Geschichtsschreibung. Eine kritische Bibliographie*, Düsseldorf, 1970.

Hindenburg, Paul, *Aus meinem Leben*, Leipzig, 1920.

Hoffmann, Max, *Die Aufzeichnungen des Generalmajors Max Hoffmann*, ed. K. F. Nowak, Berlin, 1929, Volumes I-II.

Hohlfeld, Johannes, *Der Kampf um den Frieden 1914-1918*, Leipzig, 1919.

Hölzle, Erwin, *Der Osten im ersten Weltkrieg*, Leipzig, 1944.

————. "Lloyd George im Weltkrieg," HZ, 1937, pp. 40-70.

————, "Deutschland und die Wegscheide des ersten Weltkrieges," in Festschrift für D. Becker, *Geschichte Kräfte und Entscheidungen*, Wiesbaden, 1954.

————, *Lenin 1917. Die Geburt der Revolution aus dem Kriege*, Munich, 1954.

Hölzle, Erwin, "Das Experiment des Friedens im ersten Weltkrieg, 1914-1917," GWU, September, 1962, pp. 465-522.

Hoop, E., "Die Innenpolitik der Reichskanzlers Michaelis und Hertling," Unpublished PhD dissertation, University of Kiel, 1951.

Hopwood, Robert F., "Interalliance Diplomacy: Count Czernin and Germany, 1916-1918," Stanford University PhD dissertation, 1965.

Horak, Stefan, "Der Brest-Litovsker Friede zwischen der Ukraine und den Mittelmachten vom 9. Februar 1918 in seinen Auswirkungen auf die politische Entwicklung der Ukraine," University of Erlangen PhD dissertation, 1949.

Horne, Alistair, *The Price of Glory: Verdun 1916*, New York, 1962.

House, Edward, *The Intimate Papers of Colonel House*, ed. C. Seymour, London, 1926, Volumes I-II.

Howard, Christopher, "The Treaty of London 1915," *History*, 1941.

Hubatsch, Walther, *Der Weltkrieg, 1914-1918*, Constance, 1955.

————, *Die Ära Tirpitz. Studien zur deutschen Marinepolitik 1890-1918*, Göttingen/Berlin/Frankfurt, 1955.

————, *Der Admiralstab und die obersten Marinebehörden in Deutschland 1848-1945*, Frankfurt, 1958.

————, "Finnland in der deutschen Ostseepolitik 1917/18," OW, II, 1955, pp. 105-25.

Hubrich, Erich-Wolfgang, "Neutralität und Intervention der Vereinigten Staaten von Nordamerika 1914-1917," Unpublished PhD dissertation, University of Kiel, 1956.

Huldermann. Bernhard, *Albert Ballin*, Oldenburg/Berlin, 1922.

Hütten-Csapski, Graff Bogdan, *Sechzig Jahre Politik und Gesellschaft*, Berlin, 1936, 2 Volumes.

Jäckh, E., *Der Goldene Pflug: Lebensernte eines Weltbürgers*, Stuttgart, 1954.

Janssen, Karl Heinz, *Macht und Verblendung: Kriegszielpolitik der deutschen Bundesstaaten 1914-1918*, Göttingen, 1963.

————, "Der Wechsel in der Obersten Heeresleitung im Jahre 1916," VfZ, October, 1959, pp. 337-71.

————, *Der Kanzler und der General: Die Führungskrise um Bethmann Hollwegs und Falkenhayn, 1914-1916*, Göttingen, 1967.

————, (ed.), *Die graue Exzellenz. Aus den Papieren des Kaiserlichen Gesandten Karl Georg von Treutler*, Berlin, 1972.

Japikse, Nicolaus, *Die Stellung Hollands im Weltkrieg*, Gotha, 1921.

Jarausch, Konrad H., *The Enigmatic Chancellor: Bethmann Hollweg and the Hubris of Imperial Germany*, New Haven, 1972.

Jäschke, Gotthard, "Mitteilungen: Zum Eintritt der Türkei in den Ersten Weltkrieg," WI, 1955, pp. 51-61.

Joffre, Joseph J. C. *Memoirs*, New York, 1932, Volumes I-II.

Johann, Ernst, *Innensicht eines Krieges: Bilder-Briefe-Dokumente 1914-1918*, Frankfurt, 1968.

John, Volkwart, *Brest-Litovsk. Verhandlungen und Friedensverträge im Osten 1917-1918*, Würzburg, 1937.

Jusserand, J. J., *Le sentiment américaine pendant la guerre*, Paris, 1931.

Johnson, H. J. T., *Vatican Diplomacy in the World War*, Oxford, 1933.

Joll, James, *Britain and Europe: Pitt to Churchill, 1793-1950*, London, 1950.

————, "The 1914 Debate Continues," PP, July, 1966, pp. 100-13.

Kabisch, E. *Was Wir vom Weltkrieg nicht Wissen*, Leipzig, 1936.

Kaehler, Siegfried A., "Zur Beurteilung Ludendorffs im Sommer 1918," NAWG, I, 1953, pp. 101-20.

————, (ed.), *Generalstabsdienst an der Front und in der OHL. Briefe und Tagebuchaufzeichnungen 1915-19*, Göttingen, 1958.

Kann, Robert A., "J. M. Baernreither und Graf Czernins fragmentarische Darstellung der Sixtus affäre," MOS, XVI, 1963, pp. 25-40.

————, *Das Nationalitätenproblem der Habsburg Monarchie*, Vienna/Graz/Cologne, 1964.

————, *Die Sixtusaffäre und die geheimen Friedensverhandlungen Oesterreich-Ungarns im ersten Weltkrieg*, Munich, 1966.

Karolyi, Michael Graf, *Gegen eine ganze Welt. Mein Kampf um den Frieden*, Munich, 1924.

Katkov, George, "German Foreign Office Documents on Financial Support to the Bolsheviks in 1917," IA, 1956

————, "The Assassination of Count Mirbach," *St. Anthony's Papers*, XII, Soviet Affairs, III, London, 1962, pp. 53-70.

Kautsky, Karl, *Sozialisten und Krieg*, Prague, 1937.

Kennan, George F., *Soviet-American Relations, 1917-1920*, Princeton, 1956, Volume I.

Kerensky, Alexander, *Erinnerungen. Vom Sturz des Zarentums bis zu Lenins Staatsstreich*, Dresden, 1928.

Kerner, Robert J., 'Russia, the Straits and Constantinople, 1914-15," JMH, I, 1929, pp. 400-15.

Kersten, Dietrich, "Die Kriegsziele der Hamburger Kaufmannschaft im Ersten Weltkrieg. Ein Beitrag zur Frage der Kriegszielpolitik im kaiserlichen Deutschland 1914-1918," University of Hamburg PhD dissertation, 1963.

Kielmansegg, Peter Graff, *Deutschland und der Erste Weltkrieg*, Frankfurt, 1963.

King, Jere, *Generals and Politicians: Conflict between France's High Command, Parliament and Government, 1914-1918*, Berkeley, 1951.

————, *The First World War*, New York, 1971.

Klein, A., "Der Einfluss des Grafen Witte auf die deutsch-russischen Beziehungen," University of Münster PhD dissertation, 1933.

Klein, Fritz, *Deutschland von 1897/98 bis 1917*, Berlin, 1961.

————, (ed.), *Politik im Krieg 1914-1918: Studien zur Politik der deutschen herrschenden Klassen im Ersten Weltkrieg*, Berlin, 1964.

————, (ed.), *Deutschland im Ersten Weltkrieg*, Volume I, *Vorbereitung, Entfesselung und Verlauf des Krieges bis Ende 1914*, Berlin, 1970.

Knesebeck, Ludolf Gottschalk von dem, *Die Wahrheit über den Propagandafeldzug und Deutschlands Zusammenbruch. Der Kampf der Publizistik im Weltkriege*, Berlin, 1927.

Koehl, Robert L., "A Prelude to Hitler's Greater Germany," AHR, October, 1953, pp. 43-65.

Kollman, E. C., "Walter Rathenau and German Foreign Policy," JMH, 1952, pp. 55-70.

Komarnicki, Titus, *Rebirth of the Polish Republic: A Study in the Diplomatic History of Europe, 1914-1920*, London, 1957.

Korostowitz, W. K. *Lenin im Hause der Väter*, Berlin, 1928.

Koschnitzke, R., "Die Innenpolitik des Reichskanzlers Bethmann Hollweg im Weltkrieg," University of Kiel PhD dissertation, 1951.

Koszyk, Kurt, *Zwischen Kaiserreich und Diktatur: Dis Sozialdemokratische Presse von 1914 bis 1933*, Heidelberg, 1958.

————, *Deutsche Pressepolitik im Ersten Weltkrieg*, Düsseldorf.

Kotowski, Georg, *Friedrich Ebert: Ein politische Biographie*, Wiesbaden, 1963, Volume I.

Kraft, H., "Das Problem Falkenhayn. Eine Würdigung der Kriegsführung des Generalstabschefs," WG, 1962, pp. 49-68.

Kühlmann, Richard, *Erinnerungen*, Heidelberg, 1948.

————, *Gedanken über Deutschland*, Leipzig, 1931.

Kurtz, Harold, *The Second Reich: Kaiser Wilhelm II and his Germany*, London, 1970.

Küsten, Heinz, "Die Kriegsziele des deutschen Imperialismus zu Beginn des ersten Weltkrieges (1914-1916)," University of Berlin PhD dissertation, 1961.

Lama, Friedrich Ritter von, *Der vereitelte Friede. Meine Anklage gegen Michaelis und den Evangelischen Bund*, Augsburg, 1926.

————, *Die Friedensvermittlung Papst Benedikt XV. und ihre Vereitlung durch den deutschen Reichskanzler Michaelis (August-September 1917)*, Munich, 1932.

Lancken-Wakenitz, O., *Meine 30 Dienstjahre 1888-1918*, Potsdam, Paris, Brussels, Berlin, 1931.

Landwehr, Ottocar, *Hunger. Die Erschöpfungsjahre der Mittelmächte 1917/18*, Vienna, 1931.

Landsdowne, Marquess, "The 'Peace Letter' of 1917," NCA, March, 1934, pp. 370-84.

Lansing, Robert, *War Memoirs*, New York, 1935.

Lasswell, Harold D., *Propaganda Technique in the World War*, New York, 1927.

Leberke, Botho, *Die wirtschaftlichen Ursachen des amerikanischen Eintritts 1917*, Berlin, 1940.

Lehman, Hartmut, "Österreich-Ungarns Belgienpolitik im ersten Weltkrieg. Ein Beitrag zum deutsch-österreichischen Bündnis," HZ, 192, pp. 60-93.

Leiber, Robert, S. J., "Die Friedenstätigkeit Benedikts XV, " SZ, 1921-22, pp. 267-80.

Lemke, Heinz, "Georg Cleinow und die deutsche Polenpolitik 1914-1916," in *Politik im Krieg*, Berlin, 1964, pp. 134-55.

————, "Konferenz über den ersten Weltkrieg," ZfG, 1964, pp. 1428-32.

————, "Polen und die Mittelmächte im Ersten Weltkrieg," Unpublished Habilitationsschrift, Berlin, 1966.

Lewerenz, Lilli, "Die deutsche Politik im Baltikum," University of Hamburg PhD dissertation, 1958.

Liddell Hart, B. H., *The Real War 1914-1918*, Boston/Toronto, 1930.

Liebig, Hans, *Die Politik von Bethmann Hollwegs: Eine Studie*, Munich, 1919.

Linde, G., *Die deutsche Politik in Litauen im Ersten Weltkrieg*, Wiesbaden, 1965.

Link, Arthur S., *Wilson*, Oxford/Princeton, 1960, Volume III.

————, *Wilson the Diplomatist: A Look at his Major Foreign Policies*, Baltimore, 1957.

Livermore, Seward W., *Politics is Adjourned: Woodrow Wilson and the War Congress, 1916-1918*, Baltimore, 1972.

Lloyd George, David, *War Memoirs*, London, 1938, Volumes I-II.

Lorenz, Reinhold, *Kaiser Karl und der Untergang der Donaumonarchie*, Graz/Vienna, Cologne, 1959.

Louis, W. R., *Great Britain and Germany's Lost Colonies 1914-1919*, Oxford, 1967.

Lowe, C. J., "The Failure of British Diplomacy in the Balkans 1914-1916," CJH, March, 1969, pp. 73-100.

Lowe, C. J. and Dockrill, M. L., *The Mirage of Power. British Foreign Policy, 1914-1922*, Volume II, and *Documents, 1902-1922*, Volume III, London, 1972.

Ludendorff, Erich, *Meine Kriegserinnerungen, 1914-1918*, Berlin, 1919.

————, *Kriegsführung und Politik*, Berlin, 1922.

————, "Der Zwang im Kriege," MWB, 26 February 1922.

Lupu, Nicholas, *Rumania and the War*, Boston, 1919.

Lynar, Ernst W. Graf (ed.), *Deutsche Kriegsziele, 1914-1918*, Frankfurt/Berlin, 1964.

Mach, Richard, *Aus bewegter Balkanzeit, 1879-1918*, Berlin, 1928.

Magnes, J. L., *Russia and Germany at Brest-Litovsk. A Documentary History of the Peace Negotiations*, 1919.

Magnus, Philip, *Kitchener*, New York, 1959.

Mamatey, Victor S., *The United States and East Central Europe, 1914-18. A Study in Wilsonian Diplomacy and Propaganda*, Princeton, 1957.

Mann, B., *Die baltischen Länder in der deutschen Kriegszielpublizistik 1914-1918*, Tübingen, 1965.

Mann, Golo, "Der Griff nach der Weltmacht," NZZ, 28 April 1962.

————, "1914-1939: Der zweite Weltkrieg war die Widerholung des ersten," *Zeit*, 21 August 1964.

Margutti, Albert, *La Tragédie des Habsbourg*, Vienna, 1919.

Martin, Lawrence W., *Peace Without Victory: Woodrow Wilson and the British Liberals*, New Haven, 1958.

Marwick, Arthur, "The Impact of the First World War on British Society," JCH, January, 1968, pp. 52-64.

Matthias, Erich, *Die deutsche Sozialdemokratie und der Osten 1914-45*, Tübingen, 1954.

Max von Baden, *Erinnerungen und Dokumente*, Berlin, 1927.

May, Arthur J. *The Habsburg Monarchy, 1867-1914*, New York, 1968.

————, *The Passing of the Habsburg Monarchy, 1914-1918*, Philadelphia, 1966, Volumes I-II.

————, "Woodrow Wilson and Austria-Hungary to the End of 1917," in Festschrift for H. Benedikt, Vienna, 1957, pp. 213-42.

May, Ernest R., *The World War and American Isolation, 1914-1917*, Cambridge (Mass.), 1959.

Mayer, Arno J., *Political Origins of the New Diplomacy, 1917-1918*, New Haven, 1959.

Meenzen, Johann, "Aussenpolitik und Weltfriedensordnung der deutschen Sozialdemokratie 1914-19," University of Hamburg PhD dissertation, 1951.

Mehlen, Arno, "Das deutsch-bulgarische Weltkriegsbündnis," HV, 1935, pp. 771-805.

Mehnert, Gottfried, *Evangelische Kirche und Politik 1917-1919. Die politischen Strömungen im deutschen Protestantismus von der Julikrise 1917 bis zum Herbst 1919*, Düsseldorf, 1959.

Meier-Welcker, Hans, "Die deutsche Führung an der Westfront im Frühsommer 1918. Zum Problem der militärischen Lagebeurteilung," WG, March, 1961.

————, *Die militärischen Planungen und ihre Ergebnisse 1917/18. Weltwende 1917*, Göttingen, 1965.

Meine, Arnold, *Wilsons Diplomatie in der Friedensfrage 1914-1917*, Stuttgart, 1938.

Meinecke, Friedrich, *Strassburg, Freiburg, Berlin, 1901-1919: Erinnerungen*, Stuttgart, 1949.

————, *Politische Schriften und Reden*, Darmstadt, 1958.

————, "Kühlmann und die päpstliche Friedensaktion von 1917," PAW, 1928, pp. 250-69.

Mermeix, (G. Terrail), *Les Négotiations secretes et les quatres armistices*, Paris, 1919.

Meyer, Henry Cord, *Mitteleuropa in German Thought and Action, 1815-1945*, Hague, 1955.

————, "Germans in the Ukraine, 1918," ASEER, April 1950, pp. 21-40.

Michaelis, Georg, *Für Staat und Volk*, Berlin, 1922.

Michaelis, Wilhelm, "Der Reichskanzler Michaelis und die päpstliche Friedensaktion von 1917," GWU, 1956, pp. 14-24, 128.

————, "Der Reichskanzler Michaelis und die päpstliche Friedensaktion 1917. Neue Dokumente," GWU, 1961, pp. 418-34.

————, "Stellungnahme zu dem Aufsatz von Ernst Schütte," GWU, 1956, pp. 197-307.

Michon, Georges, *The Franco-Russian Alliance, 1891-1917*, London, 1929.

Minesco, Constantin, *L'Action diplomatique de la Roumanie pendant la guerre*, Paris, 1922.

Mitatz, Alfred, "Der Friede von Best-Litowsk und die deutschen Parteien," Unpublished PhD dissertation, University of Hamburg, 1949.

Moltke, Helmut, *Erinnerungen, Briefe, Dokuments, 1877-1916*, ed. E. Moltke, Stuttgart, 1922.

Mommsen, Wolfgang J., *Das Zeitalter des Imperialismus*, Frankfurt, 1969.

————, "The Debate on German War Aims," JCH, July, 1966, pp. 47-72.

Mommsen, Wolfgang J., "Die italienische Frage in der Politik des Reichkanzlers von Bethmann Hollweg, 1914-1915,"QFAB, 1968.

————, "Die Regierung Bethmann Hollweg und die öffentliche Meinung, 1914-1917," VfZ, 1969, pp. 117-59.

————, "L'Opinion allemande et la chute du gouvernement Bethmann Hollweg en juillet 1917," Rhmc, 1969, pp. 39-53.

Montgelas, Max, "War in Sommer 1917 ein Verständigungsfrieden möglich?" BMH, July, 1932, pp. 626-60.

Monts, Anton Graf, Erinnerungen und Gedanken des Botschafters, Berlin, 1932.

Moses, John A., (ed.), The War Aims of Imperial Germany: Professor Fritz Fischer and His Critics, St. Lucia (Queensland, Australia), 1968.

Mühlmann, Carl, Das deutsch-türkische Waffenbündnis im Weltkriege, Leipzig, 1940.

————, Oberste Heeresleitung und Balkan im Weltkrieg 1914 1918, Berlin, 1942.

Müller, Alfred, Die Kriegsrohstoffbewirtschaftung 1914-1918 im Dienst des deutschen Imperialismus, Berlin, 1955.

Müller, Georg Alexander, Regierte der Kaiser? Kriegstagebücher, Aufzeichnungen und Briefe des Chefs des Marine-Kabinetts Admiral G. A. von Müller 1914-1918, ed. Walther Görlitz, Göttingen, 1951.

Müller, K. A. Mars und Venus, Stuttgart, 1954.

Nabokoff, C. The Ordeals of a Diplomat, London, 1948.

Namier, Lewis B., Avenues of History, London, 1948.

Naumann, Victor, Profile, Munich, 1925.

————, Dokumente und Argumente, Berlin, 1928.

Neck, Rudolf, "Kriegszielpolitik im ersten Weltkrieg," MOS, XV.

————, "Das 'Wiener Dokument' vom 27 März 1917," MOS, 1954, pp. 294ff.

Nekludoff, Anatole, Diplomatic Reminiscences Before and During the World War, 1911-1917, New York, 1920.

Nelson, Harold I., Land and Power: British and Allied Policy on Germany's Frontiers, 1916-1919, London, 1963.

Nicolai, W., Nachrichtendienst, Presse und Volkstimmung im Weltkrieg, 1922.

Niemann, Alfred, Revolution von oben. Umsturz von unten. Entwicklung und Verlauf der Staatsumwalzungen in Deutschland 1914-1918, Berlin, 1927.

Novotny, F., "La Propagande austro-allemande sur le front russe en 1917," RHGM, 1925, pp. 49-77.

Ostfeld, Hermann, Die Haltung der Reichstagsfraktion der Fortschritt Volkspartei zu den Annexions- und Friedensfrage in den Jahren 1914-1918, Kallmünz, 1934.

Page, Walter H., *The Life and Letters of Walter H. Page.*, ed. B. J. Hendricks, New York, 1925, Volumes I and III.

Paleologue, Maurice, *Journal intime de Nicolas II*, Paris, 1934.

————, *La Russie des tsars pendant la grande guerre*, Paris, 1921, Volume I.

Pares, B., *The Fall of the Russian Monarchy*, London, 1939.

Patemann, R., *Der Kampf um die preussische Wahlreform im Ersten Weltkrieg*, Düsseldorf, 1964.

Patin, W., *Beiträge zur Geschichte der deutsch-vatikanischen Beziehungen in den letzten Jahrzehnten*, Berlin, 1942.

Paulus, Günther, "Der Bankrott der Militärdiktatur 1918," in *Politik im Krieg*, pp. 230-52.

Payer, Friedrich, *Von Bethmann Hollweg bis Ebert. Erinnerungen und Bilder*, Frankfurt am Main, 1923.

Petzold, Joachim, "Zu den Kriegszielen der deutschen Monopolkapitalisten in dem ersten Weltkriege," ZfG, 1960, pp. 1396-1415.

Pidhaini, Oleg S., *The Ukrainian-Polish Problem in the Dissolution of the Russian Empire, 1914-1917*, Toronto/New York, 1962.

Pingaud, Albert, *Histoire diplomatique de la France pendant la grande guerre*, Paris, 1940, Volumes I-III.

Pohl, Hugo, *Aus Aufzeichnungen und Briefen während der Kriegszeit*, Berlin, 1920.

Poincaré, Raymond, *Au Service de la France: Neuf années de souvenirs*, Paris, 1928, Volumes IV-X.

Polovinov, A., *Memoiren*, Merkur, 1924.

Polzer-Hoditz, Graf A., *Kaiser Karl. Aus der Geheimmappe seines Kabinettschefs*, Zürich/Leipzig/Vienna, 1919.

Potiemkine, Vladimir, *Histoire de la diplomatie*, Paris, 1947, Volume III.

Rathmann, Lothar, *Stossrichtung Nahost 1914-1918*, Berlin, 1963.

Raumer, K., *Zwischen Brest-Litowsk und Compiègne: die deutsche Ostpolitik vom Sommer 1918*, Berlin, 1939.

Redlich, Joseph, *Das politische Tagebuch Joseph Redlichs: Schicksalsjahre Osterreichs 1880-1919*, ed. Fritz Fellner, Graz/Cologne, Volumes, I-II.

Reiners, Ludwig, *In Europa gehen die Lichter aus. Der Untergang des wilhelminischen Reiches*, Munich, 1955.

Renouvin, Pierre, *La Crise européenne et la première guerre mondiale*, Paris, 1952.

————, "Les Buts de guerre du gouvernement français (1914-1918)," Rh, January-March, 1966, pp. 1-38.

Renzi, William A., "Italy's Neutrality and Entrance into the Great War: A Re-examination," AHR, June, 1968, pp. 1414-33.

Reshetar, John S., *The Ukrainian Revolution, 1917-1920. A Study in Nationalism*, Princeton, 1952.

Revertera, Nikolaus Graf, "Nochmals das Buch des Prinzen Sixtus von Parma," HPBKD, 1922, I, pp. 129-30.

————, "Kaiser Karls Bundestreue," HPBKD, 1922, I, pp. 513-9.

Rheinbaben, Werner, *Kaiser-Kanzler-Präsidenten: Erinnerungen*, Mainz, 1968.

Ribot, Alexandre, *Journal et correspondence inedité*, Paris, 1936.

Richter, Werner, *Gewerkschaften, Monopolkapitalisten und Staat im ersten Weltkrieg und in der Novemberrevolution, 1914-1919*, Berlin, 1959.

Riddell, Lord, *Lord Riddell's War Diary, 1914-1918*, London, 1933.

Ritter, Gerhard, *The Schlieffen Plan,* London, 1958.

————, *Staatskunst und Kriegshandwerk. Das Problem des "Militarismus" in Deutschland*, Munich, 1960, Volume II, 1964, Volume III,

————, "Bethmann Hollweg im Schlaglicht des deutschen Geschichts-Revisionismus," SMH, May, 1962, pp. 799-808.

————, "Bethmann Hollweg und die Machtträume deutscher Patrioten im ersten Jahr des Weltkrieges," *Festschrift für Percy Schramm*, Wiesbaden, 1964.

————, "Eine neue Kriegsschuldthese? Zu Fritz Fischers Buch 'Griff nach der Weltmacht,' " HZ, 191, pp. 646-668.

————, "Die politiische Rolle Bethmann Hollwegs während des ersten Weltkrieges, " in *Comité International des Sciences Historiques*, XII Congrès International des Sciences Historiques, Vienna, 1965, IV, Rapports, pp. 271-78.

————, *Der erste Weltkrieg. Studien zum deutschen Geschichtsbild*, Schriftenreihe der Bundeszentrale für Politische Bildung, Bonn, 1964, Heft 65.

Rohlfes, Joachim, "Französische und deutsche Historiker über die Kriegsziele," in GWU, 1966, pp. 168-80.

Rohrbough, Philip E., "Brockdorff-Rantzau and the Politics of World War I," University of Washington MA dissertation, 1969.

Rosen, Edgar R., "Italiens Kriegeintritt im Jahre 1915 als innenpolitisches Problem der Giolitti-Ära," HZ, 1959, 187, pp. 289-300.

Rosenberg, Arthur, *The Birth of the German Republic, 1871-1918*, New York, 1931.

Rosenfeld, G., *Sowjetrussland und Deutschland 1917-1922*, 1960.

Rothwell, V. H., *British War Aims and Peace Diplomacy 1914-1918*, Oxford, 1971.

Rudzianko, M. V., *The Reign of Rasputin: An Empire's Collapse*, London, 1927.

Rupprecht, Crown Prince of Bavaria, *Mein Kriegstagebuch*, Berlin, 1928, Volumes I-II.

Salandra, Antonio, *Italy and the Great War: From Neutrality to Intervention*, London, 1932.

Sazonov, Serge, *The Fateful Years, 1909-1916*, London, 1928.

Schädlich, Karl-Heinz, "Der 'Unabhängige Ausschuss für einen Deutschen Frieden' als ein Zentrum der Annexionspropaganda des deutschen Imperialismus im ersten Weltkrieg," in *Politk im Krieg*, Berlin, pp. 50-65.

Schäfer, Theobald, "Das militärische Zusammenwirken der Mittelmächte in Herbst 1914," WW, 1926, pp. 213-34.

Scheel, Heinrich, "Der Aprilstreik 1917 in Berlin," in *Revolutionäre Ereignisse und Probleme in Duetschland während der Periode der Grossen Sozialistischen Oktoberrevolution 1917/18*, Berlin, 1957, pp. 3-88.

Scheidemann, Philipp, *Zusammenbruch*, Berlin, 1921.

————, *Papst, Kaiser und die Sozialdemokratie in ihren Friedenbemühungen im Sommer, 1917*, Berlin, 1921.

————, *Memorien eines Sozialdemokraten*, Dresden, 1928, Volumes I-II.

Schellenberg, Johanna, "Die Herausbildung der Militärdiktatur in den ersten Jahren des Krieges," in *Politik im Krieg*, Berlin, 1964, pp. 22-49.

Schorske, Carl E., *German Social Democracy, 1905-1917. The Development of the Great Schism*, Cambridge, 1955.

Schröter, Alfred, *Krieg-Staat-Monopol 1914 bis 1918*, Berlin, 1965.

Schüddekopf, Otto-Ernst, "Politik und Kriegsführung. Die Kriegszielpolitik der Mittelmächte während des Ersten Weltkrieges," NPL, 1965, pp. 247-61.

Schütte, Ernst, "Noch einmal: Der Reichskanzler Michaelis und die päpstliche Friedensaktion von 1917, GWU, 1956, pp. 293-97.

Schwabe, Klaus, " Zur politischen Haltung der deutschen Professoren im ersten Weltkrieg," HZ, 193, pp. 601-34.

————, "Ursprung und Verbreitung des alldeutschen Annexionismus in der deutschen Professorenschaft im ersten Weltkrieg. Zur Entstehung der Intellektuelleneingaben vom Sommer 1915," VfZ, April, 1966, pp. 105-38.

————, *Wissenschaft und Kriegsmoral: Die deutschen Hochschullehrer und die politischen Grundfragen des Ersten Weltkrieges*, Göttingen, 1969.

Schwarte, Max (ed.), *Der grosse Krieg 1914-1918. Die Organisation-en der Kriegsführung*, Leipzig, 1921.

Schwepke, Hans-Jürgen, "U-Bootkrieg und Friedenspolitik. Ein Bei-trag zum Thema 'Politik und Kriegführung' der Jahre 1914-1917 unter Benutzung in- und ausländischen Pressematerials," Unpub-lished PhD dissertation, University of Heidelberg, 1952.

Seymour, Charles, *American Diplomacy during the World War*, Balti-more, 1942.

Shukman, Harold, *Lenin and the Russian Revolution*, New York, 1967.

Silberstein, Gerard E., "The Central Powers and the Second Turkish Alliance, 1915," SR, March, 1965, pp. 77-89.

————, "The Serbian Campaign of 1915: Its Military Implica-tions," IRHPS, December 1966, pp. 115-32.

————, "The Serbian Campaign of 1915: Its Diplomatic Back-ground," AHR, October, 1967, pp. 51-69.

————, *The Troubled Alliance: German-Austrian Relations, 1914-1917*, Lexington, Ky., 1970.

Siney, Marion C., *The Allied Blockade of Germany, 1914-1916*, Ann Arbor, 1955.

Singer, L., *Ottocar Graf Czernin. Staatsmann einer Zeitwende*, Graz, 1965.

Sixte de Bourbon Parma, *L'offre de paix séparée de l'Autriche*, Paris, 1919.

————, *"Quinze ans après,"* RdP, 1932, I, pp. 5-29.

Smith, C. Jay, *The Russian Struggle for Power, 1914-1917: A Study of Russian Foreign Policy during the First World War*, New York, 1956.

————, *Finland and the Russian Revolution, 1917-22*, Athens (Georgia), 1958.

————, "Great Britain and the 1914-1915 Straits Agreement with Russia: The British Promise of November, 1914," AHR, July, 1965, pp. 1015-34.

Smith, Daniel M., *Robert Lansing and American Neutrality 1914-1917*, Berkeley/Los Angeles, 1958.

Snell, John L., "Socialist Unions and Socialist Patriotism in Ger-many, 1914-1918," AHR, October, 1953, pp. 66-76.

————, "Benedict XV, Wilson, Michaelis and German Socialism," CHR, July, 1951, pp. 151-78.

————, "Wilson on Germany and the Fourteen Points," JMH, December, 1954, pp. 364-69.

————, "The Russian Revolution and the German Social Demo-cratic Party in 1917," ASEER, 1956, pp. 339-50.

Snell, John L., "Des Reiches verlorenes Jahrzehnt: Die ausgeblie-
bene Wahlrechtsreform in Preussen, 1904-1914," PAPZ, 1966,
8, pp. 14-23.

Spahn, Martin, *Die Päpstliche Friedensvermittlung*, Berlin, 1919.

Spender, J. A., and Asquith, Cyril, *Life of Herbert Henry Asquith,
Lord Oxford and Asquith*, London, 1932, Volumes I-II.

Spindler, Arno, *Der Handelskrieg mit U-Booten*, Berlin, 1932,
Volumes I-II.

Spring-Rice, C., *Letters and Friendships of Sir Cecil Spring-Rice*,
London, 1929, Volume II.

Squires, J. D., *British Propaganda at Home and in the United States
from 1914 to 1917*, Cambridge (Mass.), 1935.

Stadelmann, Rudolf, "Friedensversuche in den ersten Jahren des
Weltkriege," HZ, 156, pp. 220-41.

Steglich, Wolfgang, "Bündnissicherung oder Verständigungsfrieden,"
Göttingen, 1958.

————, *Die Friedenspolitik der Mittelmächte 1917/18*, Wiesbaden, 1964, Volume I.

Stegmann, Dirk, *Sammlungspolitik 1897-1918. Parteien und Ver-
bände in der Spätphase des Wilhelminischen Deutschland*, Cologne,
1970.

Stenkewitz, Kurt, *Gegen Bajonett und Dividende*, Berlin, 1960.

Stern, Leo, *Der Einfluss der grossen sozialistischen Oktoberrevolution
auf Deutschland und die deutsche Arbeiterbewegung*, Berlin, 1958.

Straus, Oscar, *Under Four Administrations*, Boston, 1922.

Stürgkh, J., *Im deutschen Grossen Hauptquartier*, Leipzig, 1921.

Suarez, Georges, *Briand, Sa Vie, son oeuvre avec son journal*, Paris,
1940, Volumes I-IV.

Suchomlinov, W. A., *Erinnerungen*, Berlin, 1924.

Swartz, Marvin, *The Union of Democratic Control in British Politics
During the First World War*, Oxford, 1971.

Sweet, Paul R., "Leaders and Policies: Germany in the Winter of
1914," JCEA, October, 1956, pp. 229-53.

————, "Germany, Austria-Hungary and Mitteleuropa, August,
1915-April 1916," in *Festschrift für Heinrich Benedikt*, Vienna,
1957, pp. 180-212.

Swing, R. G., "First World War Peace Offers," *Esquire*, April, 1939.

Szemere, Paul, and Czech, Erich (ed.), *Die Memoiren des Grafen
Tamás von Erdödy. Habsburgs Weg von Wilhelm zu Briand. Vom
Kurier der Sixtus-Briefe zum Königsputschisten*, Zurich/Leipzig/
Vienna, 1931.

Tabouis, Geneviève R., *The Life of Jules Cambon*, London, 1938.

Taylor, A. J. P., *A History of the First World War*, New York, 1938.
————, "The War Aims of the Allies in the First World War," *Essays Presented to Sir Lewis Namier*, London, 1956, pp. 475-50.
Terraine, John, *Impacts of War 1914-1918*, London, 1970.
Thieme, H., *National Liberalismus in der Krise: Die nationalliberale Fraktion des preussischen Abgeordnetenhauses, 1914-1918*, Schriften des Bundesarchives, Hamburg, 1963, Volume XI.
Thoumain, Richard (ed.), *The First World War*, New York, 1964.
Tirpitz, Alfred, *Erinnerungen*, Leipzig, 1919.
Tisza, Stephan, *Briefe, 1914-1918*, Berlin, 1928.
Torrey, Glenn E., "German Policy toward Bulgaria, 1914-1915," Unpublished MA thesis, University of Oregon, 1957.
————, "Rumania and the Belligerents, 1914-1916," JCH, 1966, III, pp. 171-91.
Trask, David F., *The United States in the Supreme War Council: American War Aims and Inter-Allied Strategy, 1917-1918*, Baltimore, 1960.
Trevelyan, G. M., *Grey of Falloden*, London, 1940.
Trumpener, Ulrich, *Germany and the Ottoman Empire, 1914-1918*, Princeton, 1968.
————, "Turkey's Entry into World War I: An Assessment of Responsibilities," JMH, December, 1962, pp. 369-80.
————, "German Military Aid to Turkey in 1914: An Historical Re-evaluation," JMH, June, 1960, pp. 145-49.
Ullman, Richard H., *Intervention and the War. Anglo-Soviet Relations*, Princeton, 1961.
Valentin, Viet, *Deutschlands Aussenpolitik von Bismarcks Abgang bis zum Ende des Weltkrieges*, Berlin, 1921.
Valentini, Rudolf, *Kaiser und Kabinettschef. Nach eigenen Aufzeichnungen und dem Briefwechsel des Wirklichen Geheimen Rats R. von Valentini*, ed. B. Schwertfeger, Oldenburg, 1931.
Valiani, Leo, "Italian-Austro-Hungarian Negotiations 1914/15," JCH, 1966, 3, pp. 113-36.
Vietsch, Eberhard, *Wilhelm Solf: Botschafter zwischen den Zeiten*, Tübingen, 1961.
————, *Arnold Rechberg und das Problem der politischen West-Orientierung Deutschlands nach dem 1. Weltkrieg*, Coblence, 1958.
————, *Bethmann Hollweg. Staatsmann zwischen Macht und Ethos*, Boppard, 1969.
Vigezzi, Brunello, "Die Politik der 'Pfänder'", in Wolfgang Schieder (ed.), *Erstern Weltkrieg...*, Cologne/Berlin, 1969, pp. 373-407.
Volkmann, Erich O., *Der grosse Krieg, 1914-1918*, Berlin, 1938.

Volkmann, Erich O., *Der Marxismus und das deutsche Heer im Welt-kriege*, Berlin, 1925.

Wacker, Frida, *Die Haltung der deutschen Zentrumspartei zur Frage der Kriegsziele im Weltkriege, 1914-1918*, Lohr am Main, 1937.

Wade, Rex A , *The Russian Search for Peace, February-October 1917*, Stanford, 1969.

Wahnschaffe, Arnold, "Der Reichskanzler von Bethmann Hollweg und die preussischen Wahlreform," DR, June, 1922, pp. 193-203.

Walz, Erhard, *Reichsleitung und Heeresleitung in der Periode des Friedens von Brest-Litovsk. Der Konflikt über die Ostannexionen*, Düsseldorf, 1936.

Warth, Robert D., *The Allies and the Russian Revolution. From the Fall of the Monarchy to the Peace of Brest-Litovsk*, Durham (North Carolina), 1954.

Watt, Richard M., *Dare to Call it Treason*, New York, 1963.

Weber, Frank G., *Eagles on the Crescent: Germany, Austria and the Diplomacy of the Turkish Alliance, 1914-1918*, London, 1971.

Weber, Hellmuth, *Militärdiktatur in Aktion. Ein Beitrag zur deutsch-en Kriegspolitik der Jahren 1916-1918*, Berlin, 1966.

———, *Ludendorff und die Monopole: Deutsche Kriegspolitik 1916-1918*, Berlin, 1966.

Werkmann, K., *Deutschland als Verbündeter. Kaiser Karls Kampf um den Frieden*, Berlin, 1931.

Werner, Lothar, *Der Alldeutsche Verband, 1890-1918: Ein Beitrag zur Geschichte der offentlichen Meinung in Deutschland*, Berlin, 1935.

Westarp, Kuno, *Konservative Politik im letzten Jahrzehnt des Kaiser-reiches*, Berlin, 1936, Volume II.

Wetzell, G., *Der Bündniskrieg. Eine militärpolitisch operative Studie des Weltkrieges*, Berlin, 1937.

Wheeler-Bennett, J. W., *Brest-Litovsk: The Forgotten Peace*, London, 1938.

———, *The Wooden Titan*, London, 1936.

Wohlgemuth, Heinz, *Burgkrieg, nicht Burgfrieden. Der Kampf K. Liebknechts, R. Luxemburgs und ihrer Anhänger um die Rettung der deutschen Nation in den Jahren 1914-1916*, Berlin, 1963.

Wolff, Theodor, *Der Marsch durch zwei Jahrzehnte*, Amsterdam, 1936.

Woodward, E. L., *Great Britain and the War of 1914-1918*, London/ New York, 1967.

Wormser, Georges, "Les Sondages de l'Allemagne en 1915 et 1916 en vue d'une paix separée avec la France," RTASMP, 116th Year, 4th Series, 1963, pp. 255-72.

Wortmann, K., "Ottokar Czernin und die Westmächte im Weltkriege,"
HV, 1929, pp. 199-252.

Wrisberg, Ernst, *Erinnerungen an die Kriegsjahre im Königlich Preussischen Kriegsministerium*, Leipzig, 1920-22, Volumes I-III.

Zarnow, Gottfried, *Verbündet.—Verraten! Habsburgs Weg von Berlin
nach Paris*, Zürich, 1936.

————, *Gekrönt. . . Entehrt! Europas Schicksal — Habsburgs
Schuld. Das Problem des XX. Jahrhunderts*, Bern, 1937.

Zechlin, Egmont, "Friedensbestrebungen und Revolutionierungsversuche: Deutsch Bemühungen zur Ausschaltung Russlands im
ersten Weltkrieg," Beilagen zu *Das Parlament, Aus Politik und
Zeitgeschichte*, 17 May 1961, 14 June 1961, 21 June 1961, 15
May 1963.

————, "Das 'schlesische Angebot' und die italienische Kriegs-
gefahr 1915," GWU, September, 1963, pp. 533-56.

————, "Deutschland zwischen Kabinettskrieg und Wirtschaftskrieg," HZ, 199, pp. 347-458.

————, "Probleme des Kriegskalküls und der Kriegsbeendigung
im Ersten Weltkrieg," GWU, February, 1965, pp. 69-88.

————, "Die Illusion vom begrenzten Krieg: Berlins Fehlkalkula-
tion im Sommer 1914," *Die Zeit*, 17 September 1965.

Zeman, Z. A. B., *The Breakup of the Habsburg Empire 1914-1918:
A Study in National and Social Revolution*, Oxford, 1961.

————, *A Diplomatic History of the First World War*, London,
1971.

————, and Scharlau, W. B., *The Merchant of Revolution: The
Life of Alexander I. Helphand (Parvus)*, Oxford, 1965.

Zessner-Spitzenberg, Hans Karl, *Kaiser Karl. Aus dem Nachlass*, Salz-
burg, 1953.

Zwehl, Hans, *Erich von Falkenhayn, General der Infanterie: eine
biographische Studie*, Berlin, 1926.

EAST EUROPEAN MONOGRAPHS

1. *Political Ideas and the Enlightenment in the Romanian Principalities, 1750-1831*. By Vlad Georgescu. 1971.
2. *America, Italy and the Birth of Yugoslavia, 1917-1919*. By Dragan R. Zivojinovic. 1972.
3. *Jewish Nobles and Geniuses in Modern Hungary*. By William O. McCagg, Jr. 1972.
4. *Mixail Soloxov in Yugoslavia: Reception and Literary Impact*. By Robert F. Price. 1973.
5. *The Historical and Nationalist Thought of Nicolae Iorga*. By William O. Oldson. 1973.
6. *Guide to Polish Libraries and Archives*. By Richard C. Lewandski. 1974.
7. *Vienna Broadcasts to Slovakia, 1938-1939: A Case Study in Subversion*. By Henry Delfiner. 1974.
8. *The 1917 Revolution in Latvia*. By Andrew Ezergailis. 1974.
9. *The Ukraine in the United Nations Organization: A Study in Soviet Foreign Policy, 1944-1950*. By Konstantin Sawczuk. 1975.
10. *The Bosnian Church: A New Interpretation*. By John V.A. Fine, Jr. 1975.
11. *Intellectual and Social Developments in the Habsburg Empire from Maria Theresa to World War I*. Edited by Stanley B. Winters and Joseph Held. 1975.
12. *Ljudevit Gaj and the Illyrian Movement*. By Elinor Murray Despalatovic. 1975.
13. *Tolerance and Movements of Religious Dissent in Eastern Europe*. Edited by Bela K. Kiraly. 1975.
14. *The Parish Republic: Hlinka's Slovak People's Party, 1939-1945*. By Yeshayahu Jelinek. 1976.
15. *The Russian Annexation of Bessarabia, 1774-1828*. By George F. Jewsbury. 1976.
16. *Modern Hungarian Historiography*. By Steven Bela Vardy. 1976.
17. *Values and Community in Multi-National Yugoslavia*. By Gary K. Bertsch. 1976.
18. *The Greek Socialist Movement and the First World War: The Road to Unity*. By George B. Leon. 1976.
19. *The Radical Left in the Hungarian Revolution of 1848*. By Laszlo Deme. 1976.
20. *Hungary between Wilson and Lenin: The Hungarian Revolution of 1918-1919 and the Big Three*. By Peter Pastor. 1976.
21. *The Crises of France's East Central European Diplomacy, 1933-1938*. By Anthony J. Komjathy. 1976.
22. *Polish Politics and National Reform, 1775-1788*. By Daniel Stone. 1976.
23. *The Habsburg Empire in World War I*. Robert A. Kann, Bela K. Kiraly, and Paula S. Fichtner, eds. 1977.
24. *The Slovenes and Yugoslavism, 1890-1914*. By Carole Rogel. 1977.
25. *German-Hungarian Relations and the Swabian Problem*. By Thomas Spira. 1977.
26. *The Metamorphosis of a Social Class in Hungary During the Reign of Young Franz Joseph*. By Peter I. Hidas. 1977.
27. *Tax Reform in Eighteenth Century Lombardy*. By Daniel M. Klang. 1977.
28. *Tradition versus Revolution: Russia and the Balkans in 1917*. By Robert H. Johnston. 1977.
29. *Winter Into Spring: The Czechoslovak Press and the Reform Movement 1963-1968*. By Frank L. Kaplan. 1977.
30. *The Catholic Church and the Soviet Government, 1939-1949*. By Denis J. Dunn, 1977.
31. *The Hungarian Labor Service System, 1939-1945*. By Randolph L. Braham. 1977.
32. *Consciousness and History: Nationalist Critics of Greek Society 1897-1914*. By Gerasimos Augustinos. 1977.
33. *Emigration in Polish Social and Political Thought, 1870-1914*. By Benjamin P. Murdzek. 1977.
34. *Serbian Poetry and Milutin Bojic*. By Mihailo Dordevic. 1977.
35. *The Baranya Dispute: Diplomacy in the Vortex of Ideologies, 1919-1921*. By Leslie C. Tihany. 1978.
36. *The United States in Prague, 1945-1948*. By Walter Ullmann. 1978.
37. *Rush to the Alps: The Evolution of Vacationing in Switzerland*. By Paul P. Bernard. 1978.
38. *Transportation in Eastern Europe: Empirical Findings*. By Bogdan Mieczkowski. 1978.
39. *The Polish Underground State: A Guide to the Underground, 1939-1945*. By Stefan Korbonski. 1978.
40. *The Hungarian Revolution of 1956 in Retrospect*. Edited by Bela K. Kiraly and Paul Jonas. 1978.